# the Vanlife Companion

**by Ed Bartlett and Becky Ohlsen**

# Contents

*Right: Coastline on Highway 1 near Big Sur*

# Welcome to vanlife

Welcome to *The Vanlife Companion*. This book has been created as a helpful – and hopefully inspiring – guide to assist you in navigating the increasing array of options for buying, converting, kitting out and using a van for a range of recreational purposes.

From enabling a sport or hobby, to taking the family on a weekend camping trip or even living full-time 'off-grid', the humble van is more popular than ever, meaning more choice, better value and an increasingly diverse range of owners. With internet forums and online social platforms acting like a virtual campsite, this global network of like-minded people has been able to unify as one community under the 'vanlife' moniker. Travel has long been synonymous with freedom and discovery, and this is especially true of the road trip. For millions of owners around the world, the campervan is the ultimate road trip companion, but it's also a symbol of freedom. More than just a vehicle, it's a way of life and a personalised gateway to the open road – be it for a night, a weekend, several months or even years.

## Using the book

Section 1 of the book focuses on practical information and advice, from deciding what kind of van suits your needs, through the myriad conversion options, to tips for storage, trip planning and getting the most out of the camping experience.

Section 2 profiles 10 trailblazing vanlifers and their vehicles, exploring their motivations and experiences as well as examining their conversions in detail.

Section 3 showcases a selection of inspiring route ideas from around the world.

Whatever your situation – from vanlife veteran to someone still dreaming up their future slice of van-shaped freedom – this book will share new ideas and provide inspiration for your journey.

## What is vanlife?

It's a fair question to kick things off. After all, the campervan is hardly a new invention: VW first launched its iconic splitscreen in 1950. So, why has a new generation felt the need to reinvent it under a catchy, marketable moniker? Is there real substance behind the hashtag?

The current rise of vanlife is arguably a result of contemporary global social, economic and cultural trends in much the same way as the events that made the original movement so successful. In the 1960's and 1970's, it was first the hippie movement, and then the surfers – both of whom gravitated to the VW campervan, which had a near-total monopoly on the market at that stage – that thrust both the vehicle itself and romantic notions of the accompanying lifestyle into mainstream consciousness.

Fast-forward to today, with a younger generation increasingly eschewing home ownership and delaying parenthood, and large chunks of the middle-aged wanting to break free from the shackles of mortgages and the nine-to-five. The internet has given people the ability to create earning potential without the necessity of a fixed office space, while Facebook and Instagram let vanlifers connect, tell stories, share tips and even arrange to physically meet up – not so far removed from the hippie campfires of old. Amidst this sea change the vanlife scene has coalesced and developed its own momentum, spurred on by artfully posed photos of sunsets, campfires, and interesting van conversions in a variety of exotic locations, far from any campsites or crowds.

At the current time of writing, the #vanlife hashtag has had over three million uses, with various close derivatives all well into six-figures. And despite the occasionally saccharine filters and stock image poses, it's almost impossible not to scroll through and come away feeling inspired. Of course, it's important to remember that with social media the images are filtered in more ways than one: what you see is more than likely to be the edited highlights of the real thing. The true reality of vanlife is summed up perfectly by Mirte van Dijk, owner of the wonderful vintage Citroën Type H featured on page 42: 'Don't expect rainbows and unicorns all of the time, because vanlife can be tough.'

Living in a van can be cramped, too hot, too cold, dirty, noisy, frustrating, and occasionally even dangerous. If you value a lifestyle where things are generally easy and go according to plan, it's more than likely not for you! But you don't need to quit your job, sell your house and belongings and learn how to wire solar panels onto the roof of your new four-wheeled abode to come along. Vanlife is a state of mind, and all are welcome.

## Choosing a van

Whether you crave five-star hotels or a bivvy bag under the stars, campervans offer something for everyone. From a converted ex-work panel van to a fully fitted motorhome, something suits every budget and purpose. But when buying any vehicle, the first step is to think about exactly what your requirements are. Start a checklist like the one below as you mull over the options. For a daily driver used for the occasional weekend trip you don't want a fully featured 5-berth motorhome, in the same way that it's not ideal to buy a two-seat convertible sports car if you have a family of five. A campervan has a lot of additional considerations to make above and beyond a standard car, so it's worth putting pen to paper and listing what features are essential, desirable and merely nice-to-have. You'll need to prioritize these according to your situation and budget as you select a van model for purchase or conversion. Some important checklist questions follow.

## Checklist

**Will it be my daily driver?**
- Reliability/economy
- Size/manoeuvrability
- Will I regularly encounter height restrictions or narrow/steep roads?

**Will I be going off-road?**
- 2WD vs 4WD
- Tyre choice

**How many people does it need to carry?**
- Legal seating requirements
- Sleeping arrangements

**Will I be staying mainly on formal sites or wild camping?**
- Power options - hook–up/split-charge/solar
- Toilet and shower access

**Will I cook regularly or mainly eat out?**
- Fitted kitchen vs portable/modular options
- Water/fresh food storage

**Will I be carrying bulky equipment outside of the vehicle?**
- Options for towbar/roof rack etc.
- Loading/unloading/storage considerations

### The 'c' word

A word you will become very familiar with throughout your vanlife journey is the 'c' word: Compromise. Every aspect of vanlife demands give and take. Want more interior space? A bigger vehicle will struggle on those narrow roads you'll need to traverse to find your perfect wild camping spot. Want to wild camp regularly? You'll need to think about off-grid essentials like solar power, a large water tank and food storage. Every decision you make will likely have an impact elsewhere, so think carefully about what really is most important to you, and learn to accept and work around any pitfalls. Use your checklist to track your essentials and identify what's merely optional.

### Budget

The key advice is to decide in advance if you want to buy a 'finished' van ready for adventure, or a blank-slate project vehicle that you can gradually convert as time and budget allows. If you have the time and patience, the latter certainly offers a fulfilling experience.

   The biggest deciding factor for your choice of van will most likely be your budget. If you are planning to buy a brand new factory-fitted camper, you can relax and focus your energy and money on trips for the first three years. However, the majority of people are more likely to be either buying a pre-owned conversion, or looking for a base vehicle to convert. It's here that things get a little more complicated.

   Budgeting for vanlife is a very personal undertaking, and it's impossible to suggest a one-size-fits-all recommendation. In general it's

*Left: On the road in Alberta, Canada*

sensible to budget generously for the best possible base van, since getting to and from places reliably is the main goal of any vehicle. Cutting corners on spending upfront might cost later. Of course, you may be mechanically minded and happy to get hands-on, in which case you might focus more on the quality or completeness of any conversion work, safe in the knowledge that you can deal with breakdowns, repairs and rust later.

### Try before you buy

It goes without saying that research is the key not only to finding the right van, but also on getting the most of it on the road. Be prepared to spend a significant amount of time not only on retrofitting the vehicle, but on reviewing the vast range of build options and camping gear that will transform your vanlife from good to great. Online forums and in-person meets are great resources for delving deeper into available options than your first forays into the glossy shots on Instagram may surface. But one of the best tips before committing to any major purchase is to try before you buy, and this is especially true of a van, particularly if you plan to live in your vehicle. There are now many places that specialise in hiring vans, giving you invaluable real-world experience that will help to inform your decisions and answer some of the checklist questions in a much more confident fashion. There's even an Airbnb-style app that connects van owners directly with potential hirers.

Try to find something in a size and style as close to your intended requirements as possible, and take the longest trip you can afford. Time – and money – spent now might save you a fortune in the long run, and hopefully the enjoyment you have during the trip will help to justify the outlay as well as giving you valuable insight into your vehicular needs.

## What makes a good van?

Regardless of the brand or model, there are certain common elements of any vehicle to be aware of. Once you've decided on the size and type of van, it's worth bearing in mind some of these points before making your final purchase.

### Drivetrain

A strong, reliable drivetrain is essential, so make sure that servicing has been adequate and well documented. Note that mileage is not necessarily a reliable indicator – low-stress modern diesel engines can comfortably do hundreds of thousands of miles with little more than routine servicing, and many ex-work vans will have been maintained meticulously.

You'll also need to carefully consider the kind of routes you'll be taking, and plan accordingly:

● Regular use of rough, muddy, off-road terrain will ideally require 4WD, which will limit your vehicle choice. 4WD also generally uses more fuel on normal roads and adds to both weight and servicing costs.
● Automatic gearboxes can be more relaxing, but manual gears give much more control in steep mountainous terrain.
● Cruise control is an easily overlooked but

very worthwhile feature if your routes will include long periods of time on major roads.
● Rare and vintage vehicles have added cool factor, but might leave you stranded waiting for parts when things inevitably go wrong.
● A larger, more powerful engine makes cruising and longer journeys easier but will use more fuel and possibly cost more to insure.

## Suspension

Depending upon your conversion, a significant amount of additional weight is going to be added to your vehicle. This will adversely affect the handling and ride quality, and in extreme cases might push some parts beyond the window in which they were designed to safely – and legally – operate.

Popular vehicles for conversion often start life as working vans, meaning they already feature suspension designed to carry significant weights. If you want something more suited for passenger comfort, try looking at multi-purpose vehicles (MPVs) or minivans instead.

*If in any doubt about safety matters for areas such as tyres, brakes and suspension, always consult a qualified expert.*

## Insulation

Insulation is not something you'd think about when buying a normal car, but for vanlife it's essential. This is especially true when converting an ex-work van, which typically has no rear cab insulation, leaving large areas of exposed metal that will amplify every bit of noise and resonate horribly on faster roads. Insulation will also help

with temperature regulation.

Thankfully, insulating a van is one of the easier DIY tasks, and can be completed with environmentally friendly materials. As with suspension, an MPV or minivan will typically have the added benefit of factory-fitted insulation.

## Roof height

Internal standing space is at or near the top of most people's desirability lists when it comes to their vehicle, and is especially important if you are intending on more than just occasional weekends away. If you've never used a van for camping trips before, roof height is perhaps the most important element for you to try out before you commit to a vehicle.

Most commercial vans are available in at least a couple of different wheelbase dimensions and roof heights, so your decision shouldn't drastically affect your model plans. But getting it wrong could cause you a lot of pain – physically and financially – later on.

The obvious solution is simply to buy one of the many hi-top vehicles available. However, if you live or regularly travel somewhere that has a lot of height restrictions in place, or your van is your sole vehicle, you might find it's more trouble than it's worth. Additionally, in some parts of the world, landowners have begun erecting height restrictions on parking specifically to limit overnight parking and wild camping by vans and motorhomes.

# Converting a van

You could just throw a camping mat in the back

of an empty work van, but part of the experience of vanlife is finding and converting a vehicle to your exact specification.

The great outdoors is generally the reason people buy and convert vans for camping, but what's inside is just as important for your overall enjoyment. Don't let the artfully posed Instagram images fool you; vanlife can be cramped, noisy and frustrating. Time spent researching and planning your setup, as well as thinking about things like storage, packing and loading, will pay dividends later on.

One thing to check carefully when preparing to convert a van is the local law governing changes to a vehicle. For example, in the UK it is possible to re-register a commercial panel van as a motor caravan once a certain number of conversion steps have been completed. This can result in cheaper insurance and even allow you to travel at higher speeds on certain roads. Either way, you should always make sure your insurance company is fully updated with any changes you make.

## Buy or build?

The first question to ask yourself is whether you want to complete any of the conversion work yourself, or pay to have it done by a professional fitter.

In many cases you will find that you pay a premium on a van with conversion work that has already been completed, and so you might find that it is more cost effective for you to buy a base vehicle and do it yourself. This route obviously takes more time and hassle, but the advantage is knowing exactly what work has been done, plus you have the opportunity to create exactly what you want. Be sure when budgeting that you get accurate quotes for materials (and labour, if you are using a third-party) and that you have thought of absolutely everything that needs doing.

In the same way as when undertaking major home improvements, it's also a good idea to include at least a 10% contingency fund, and most seasoned vanlifers will tell you to at least double your initial time estimates when doing any job yourself, even if it seems straightforward.

## Seating

Whatever the purpose of your van, you're going to need somewhere to sit when you're not driving. Depending how many people you intend to carry, flexible seating is crucial.

Given that seats are also one of the most space-consuming items in any vehicle, it's important to carefully consider their placement, as well as if they can be easily moved or removed via sliders, bolts or quick-release hinges. Having seats with flexible configurations and a dual purpose – whether hiding storage areas or folding into a bed – can make a huge difference to your vanlife experience.

Your eventual rear cab layout will depend upon the size of your vehicle as well as your priorities. Even if you have a large enough van to include side-facing bench seats and dining table, what you gain in Instagram-friendly photos of your semi-al fresco dining views you might lose in usable storage space. Put pen to

*Right: Campervan on the road in New Zealand's Tongariro National Park*

paper, and mock up your ideas before committing. You can even experiment by marking out the footprint of the usable area in your house, garage or driveway.

In the front cab, for those without a bulkhead one of the most popular and affordable options that can be added to most seats is a rotating swivel base, which allows them to rotate 180° when parked. This simple modification means they can be utilised in the rear cab area of the van when parked, adding to both the usability and sense of space in the vehicle.

One thing to note is that there are strict laws governing the use of passenger seats in transit, so when buying or converting a vehicle with a custom seating setup that differs from the original manufacturer specification, be sure to check that it complies 100% with the requirements, otherwise you might find that your insurance will be invalidated in the event of an accident.

## Sleeping

After seating options, sleeping arrangements are the next biggest consideration. Popular options include the below:

**>> Convertible bed:** The average vanlife van – if such a thing exists – will most likely feature a convertible bed of some sorts. Regardless of vehicle size, there will be a solution for quickly transforming seats and/or dining areas into a flat area for sleeping. Common convertible bed options include the simple but effective folding 'rock n' roll' bench seat, which comes in both three-quarter width and full width sizes.

The obvious advantage of a convertible bed

is that you maximise the use of internal space, however it does also mean that at least twice a day you need to literally make and unmake the bed, as well as storing bedding when not in use. Rock n' roll beds can also vary dramatically in quality, so always check the reputation and safety certification before you buy, and ensure they are fitted correctly.

**>> Fixed bed:** Where space allows, a dedicated sleeping space is the ultimate setup for most people. Having a bed permanently made up saves a lot of time over the course of a trip, meaning that you can focus on enjoying your adventures. You may also find yourself enjoying the occasional daytime nap!

Fitting a permanent bed into a car-sized van such as the VW Transporter series can be too compromising to other aspects of the vehicle, depending upon your priorities. However, hi-top vans such as the increasingly popular Mercedes Sprinter can easily be configured with a raised sleeping area above a dedicated garage/storage space (see page 98.)

Arguably the most important factor of sleeping, however, is not the location, but what you are lying on. Inflatable camping mattresses are perfect for convertible beds thanks to their space-saving potential when not in use, however they are also time consuming to inflate/deflate and sensitive to damage. For permanent beds it's well worth considering options like memory foam, which is relatively lightweight, available in a range of different densities and can be easily cut to size.

**>> Pop-up roof:** One of the best – and most

popular – solutions for smaller vans is the pop-up (or pop-top) roof, where all or part of the roof is replaced with an elevating section to create additional sleeping space. Given the structural role of the roof of a vehicle, this is typically a professional conversion job, although many official manufacturer campervan models come with a pop-up roof as standard.

Since pop-tops are typically fitted to vehicles with limited internal height, the added headroom also means no more crouching when inside. Many manufacturers include additional zipped vents and windows in their designs, the combination of which contributes significantly to making a smaller van feel much more airy and comfortable when camping.

Once you get the hang of operating it, using the roof extension becomes a quick and easy enough process that you will find yourself using it even when simply parked up for a while, and sports enthusiasts in particular will appreciate the ability to get changed in privacy and comfort.

**Cooking**

More than perhaps any other aspect of vanlife, your cooking solutions will depend upon your usage case. A couple living full- or part-time in their vehicle are going to have dramatically different requirements to a single person using their van at weekends.

The extent of your cooking setup will also depend on your general relationship with food. If you're a passionate foodie, you're more likely to look at vanlife meals as a creative opportunity rather than a chore to be avoided.

If you're only planning occasional overnight trips, it is possible to get away without any cooking at all, but for longer trips, consider some of these options:

**>> BBQ:** The perennial camping favourite, the BBQ is also a vanlife staple. With the extra space available inside a van, many owners will permanently carry their grill, and for space-constrained vehicles there are a number of folding designs that pack almost totally flat. For more casual users there are also disposable options, but please recycle where possible.

BBQs are designed for outdoor use, so this can be an issue when the weather is inclement. However, an awning can quickly and easily create an outdoor kitchen. For those wishing to light a fire when camping, there are also a number of combination grills that double up as both BBQ and fire pit.

**>> Portable gas stove:** The portable stove is one of the most flexible items in the vanlife cooking armoury, and ranges from a single standalone unit to multi-hob setups, typically built into a handy folding carry case/stand.

The smaller stoves are extremely handy for a variety of situations, however they are susceptible to wind and low temperatures, burn relatively inefficiently and the small, single-use Butane gas canisters run out fairly quickly, meaning you will need to keep spares on hand.

One of the most versatile portable gas stoves is the Cadac Safari grill, which looks a lot like a gas-powered BBQ, and can run from larger refillable Propane gas bottles. The Safari Chef

includes several different cooking options, meaning it can manage everything from a fry-up to a casserole, and folds into a relatively light and compact bag for storage.

For boiling water quickly and efficiently, it's also worth considering an integrated canister stove. These clever Butane units essentially turbocharge the standard gas stove by using an insulated pot with an inbuilt heat exchanger in the base, multiplying the effectiveness of the flame.

**>> Fitted gas stove:** For those with plans for a fitted kitchen, there are a huge variety of drop-in and slide-in units available, some of which even include a sink for additional space saving. You can permanently install a grill and oven if your cooking plans extend beyond casual weekend use.

There is also a growing trend for modular fitted solutions built into other areas of the van, such as a pull-out drawer in the tailgate area. This neat design keeps more space available in the main cab area, and those with a rising rear tailgate have the added benefit of shelter above their heads while cooking, as well as excellent venting.

**>> Electric:** Although gas is the most popular option for campervan use, it is possible to find suitable electric options, including a compact microwave. If the vast majority of your van use is likely to be on sites where you can utilise shore power, there are significant advantages to using electric, not least the potential space saving. It also stops ongoing worries about running out of gas. The significant power draw of electric setups, however, means that it's not really possible to run them independently of shore power.

*Gas is a highly combustible substance and there are numerous safety considerations when choosing, installing and using gas-powered utilities in a campervan. If in doubt, always consult a trained expert.*

## Hygiene

Like cooking, hygiene can just about be a secondary concern if you're taking short trips and are willing to put up with a little discomfort. For anything more than a weekend though, you're going to need to think about solutions for keeping yourself, your clothes and your van clean. The latter is surprisingly important, and you'll want to carefully consider your floor covering material if you plan to regularly carry wet or muddy equipment, people and pets inside.

Most things are amplified in a campervan, due to the small space, and that includes unpleasant odours! Thankfully there are numerous different options for keeping clean – or at the very least disguising smells – when you're camping:

**>> Nature:** For the more adventurous vanlifer, the ultimate option for keeping clean is a wild swim. From rivers and lakes, to the sea, it's a great way to combine hygiene with a little recreational exercise. Just remember to use eco-friendly products, and consider your safety at all times.

**>> Shower:** For those with the space, a fitted shower is a luxury well worth having; there is little more transformative than a hot shower

*Left: Vanlife camping in Cochise Stronghold, Arizona*

when spending time on the road. Of course, beyond the space considerations you will also need to think about water storage and supply, and particularly what to do with grey water. Even when using eco-friendly products, it's best to only dump grey water at official service points or into drains that you are certain feed into the main sewer.

For those without the space for a proper fitted solution, portable solar showers can provide just enough warmth and flow rate to wash with, and you can easily fashion an enclosure to protect your modesty. There are even pop-up enclosures available, which can double up as a toilet cubicle. The solar shower is also handy for rinsing dirty dishes, pets or even just your feet after a day on the beach or trails.

>> **Sports facilities and services:** It might not be an obvious choice, but almost every town and even some villages will have a public pool happy to take your money in return for a swim or even just use of their shower. What's more, an increasing number of service stations now feature shower facilities.

>> **Dry wash:** More of a temporary fix than a bona fide hygiene solution, dry shampoo products can be a good back-up in between washes, especially for those with long hair.

>> **Wipes:** As with dry wash, wipes are best employed sparingly. Many campers end up with a 'day on, day off' strategy when it comes to washing, and baby wipes and dry wash can help make this more palatable. As with all aspects of vanlife, be sure to consider the environment, especially when disposing of single-use items like wipes.

>> **Dishes:** Dishes are best dealt with as soon as possible after cooking, since dried-on food can be extremely tricky to deal with when camping. As with cleaning at home, try to soak pans and heavily soiled dishes, and wash cups and glasses first, followed by plates and, finally, pans and grills.

For those without a fitted kitchen, most sites have a communal area for dishes, and it's worth having a bucket for transporting them to and fro. This can also be used as a washbowl, although for the space-constrained you can even buy folding and collapsible bowls. As with a fitted shower, it's important to consider how to deal with grey water from washing dishes, as well as the eco-friendliness of your detergent.

>> **Clothes:** For shorter trips – even up to a week or two – it's easily possible to pack enough not to have to worry about washing, just like going on a regular holiday. However, for those engaging in muddy sports, rinsing clothing and equipment immediately will help significantly, and it's very easy to fashion a line to air-dry your washing when parked.

Sites will at the least have facilities for hand washing, and many will even have a laundry, so it can be worthwhile staying on a site for a night or two now and again in order to wash and dry your clothes. Of course, most towns will also have laundry facilities that you can pay to use.

>> **Toilet:** Undoubtedly the least savoury topic in the book, how to deal with the call of nature is an unavoidable part of vanlife.

In an ideal world, public toilets would be

available everywhere you go, and in fact there are many who only stay on dedicated sites entirely for this reason.

**>> Cassette toilet:** For those with a permanent fitted toilet, it is possible to connect the incoming water feed to the same tank used for showering and washing dishes. The black water is then collected in a removable tank or 'cassette', which can be independently removed from the vehicle and emptied in a suitable place.

**>> Porta Potty:** The most common solution for vans without space for a fitted cassette toilet, the porta potty works in a similar way, just on a smaller scale. The self-contained portable unit includes a small reservoir for flushing – typically using chemicals to help with odours and the breakdown of waste – and a removable section containing the resulting black water. The porta potty is small enough that it can be easily stowed, and can be used both inside and outside the van as well as in conjunction with a pop-up shower/toilet cubicle.

### Power

Regardless of your camping plans, you will need to carefully consider your power requirements and usage. Most hardened vanlifers will, at some point or other, experience the dreaded moment when the key turns and nothing happens due to a dead battery.

Generally speaking there are three things that are always worth having more of than might be necessary when planning a trip: Water, fuel and electrical power. Running out of any one of these three can be extremely frustrating at the least, and even potentially dangerous in extreme cases.

With power-hungry on-board items such as a refrigerator, and an increasing number of electronic devices such as mobile phones, tablets, cameras and sporting equipment all requiring regular recharging, even a short weekend trip can quickly drain a vehicle's battery.

There are a number of robust systems for supplementing and monitoring a vehicle's charge, and it's worth speaking with a range of people – from other van users to qualified expert fitters – as well as thinking carefully about your current and future requirements, since adding or upgrading elements such as wiring and sockets at a later stage will almost certainly create significant extra costs and disruption. Solutions to consider include the following:

**>> Leisure battery/split charge:** The standard solution for most light to medium duty use, this setup involves adding a second high-capacity battery to the vehicle. Typically this conversion will see ancillary powered items such as rear cab lighting and 12v sockets rewired to the secondary battery, plus the addition of a 'split charge' system, which diverts some of the power from the vehicle's alternator to recharge the leisure battery when the vehicle is on the move.

A split charge will limit or even prevent the chances of being unable to start the vehicle due to a flat main battery, but the obvious disadvantage of this system is that if you don't have the engine running, there is no excess charge to keep the leisure battery topped up. As such, if most or all of your vanlife plans consist of multiple days on the same site without moving, you might need to think about different or additional power options.

**>> Shore power hook-up:** For those who are planning to stay regularly on formal sites – or who perhaps leave their van parked for long durations between trips and want to be able to keep it charged – a shore power conversion allows the vehicle to be connected directly to mains power via an extension lead. Most modern sites will have at least some pitches that include a shore power connection, although they typically cost extra and will likely require booking in advance. For those who plan to spend most or all of their time wild camping, however, this addition is less important.

For regular shore power users, conversions can include the installation of a permanent external connection point for convenience, although this does typically involve cutting the vehicle bodywork.

**>> Solar:** As solar panels continue to fall in price and the technology advances, it is becoming an increasingly desirable and affordable option for vehicles. In many ways, solar power is the perfect option for vanlife: most vans have a large, flat roof area, vehicles are almost exclusively used outside where the sun can reach the panels, and it's a source of limitless and completely green energy.

Of course, this might apply somewhere like California, where the sun always seems to shine. However, the suitability of solar might need to be considered a little more carefully if you are spending the majority of your time in Scotland or Scandinavia.

Solar is certainly not a solution for everyone – many vanlifers regularly carry items such as sporting equipment or additional storage on the roof of their vehicle, for example – however it is also possible to buy smaller folding panels, which can be deployed quickly and easily to supplement power temporarily when parked. These won't provide the same levels of charge as a dedicated install, but can certainly help to keep a secondary leisure battery topped up.

**>> Power banks:** As batteries become smaller, more powerful and affordable, the market for portable power banks is growing at an astonishing rate, with the global market forecast to be worth over US$25bn by 2022.

Currently of little use for larger, more power-hungry items, portable power banks can be a versatile solution for keeping smaller devices like mobile phones fully charged. Many vanlifers also use their mobile phones for navigation and information when exploring new areas, so having a reliable portable power source to take with you is essential.

As technology continues to advance, expect to see an increasing number of hybrid solar power banks, as well as larger-capacity units that could end up supplementing or even replacing the leisure battery.

**>> Other considerations:** Aside from deciding which kind of power is right for you, those

*Right: Campervan on road with sheep dotting the rolling hills of New Zealand's North Island.*

undertaking a conversion will also need to consider important factors such as how many sockets to include and where to locate them, which can be tricky until you've actually used the van. It's a chicken and egg scenario, which can be mitigated slightly by hiring or borrowing a similar vehicle.

For vans without fitted sockets but requiring plug-in capability for items such as laptop computers, it's also possible to buy a power inverter, which will convert the 12v power produced by the vehicle into the voltage required by your appliance. It should be noted that this can put a very high strain on your vehicle's battery, however, and so should ideally only be used when there is a significant excess of charge, eg when driving or using shore power.

Finally, a range of different power management systems and controllers can do everything from protecting and monitoring circuits, through to complete automated control of charge maintenance, and can be an important addition for power-hungry users or people wishing to spend a lot of time off-grid.

## Storage

If you're already used to traditional camping, you'll be familiar with the need to pack light. However, with a campervan, part of the benefit for many people is the ability to bring more equipment and include some home comforts. This is especially true for those on longer journeys and 'full-timers' living in their vans. As such, storage could easily be argued as the most important feature of your van, since

almost everything you bring has to be stored and carried somehow. You will quickly learn the adage of 'a place for everything', but first you need to plan and create those spaces.

When using a campervan of any size or style, the key to a simple and enjoyable experience is to minimise everyday frustrations, which means having your most used items to hand quickly and easily. On the one hand, this relates to the obvious essentials like clothing, water and cutlery, but it's also important to consider the other reasons you use your van. For example if you are a passionate cyclist, you probably don't want to have to build up and break down your bike each time you ride, and so thinking about an external rack or dedicating more internal space to bike storage might be worthwhile.

You will also find that you can never have too many cubbyholes – something that accessory manufacturers have quickly realised. As such there is a huge variety of add-on storage and organisers available, which can clip, stick and screw to every possible interior surface. In particular, think about easy to access but out of the way locations such as seat backs, or strategically staple some elasticated netting to walls or ceiling. The main van areas to focus on when creating extra storage space are listed here:

>> **Roof:** Many vanlife vehicles will start out as a working van, and as such there's a high probability of some fairly substantial racking solutions being available for the roof. This can range from standard bars to affixed items like a roof box or bike racks, through to robust half-

cage structures that cover the entire upper surface of the roof. Both of these solutions can provide a lot of extra storage space, however it's important to also consider aspects such as height restrictions, access to the roof area for loading, and any restrictions it might put on solar or pop-top conversions. You are also adding weight in the worst possible place for the vehicle handling, so extra care should be taken both when fastening items as well as when driving.

>> **Towbar:** Part of the joy of a campervan is the purity and simplicity of travelling in a single vehicle. As such, it's rare to see a fellow vanlifer towing a trailer, but the towbar can still be a handy addition, since it is able to bear a very significant load and is quick and easy to attach things to. Many modern towbars even allow the hitch itself to be folded or disconnected when not in use.

There are a number of useful items designed to be towbar mounted, ranging from luggage racks and BBQs to steps and even a toilet. However, probably the most common use for the towbar mount is to carry sporting equipment, and particularly bicycles.

Thanks to the sheer load-bearing capability of a towbar, modern bike carriers can easily accommodate four full-size bikes, though it should be kept in mind that anything mounted in this part of the vehicle might restrict opening of the rear tailgate. Designers of carriers such as the Atera Strada DL have taken this into consideration, allowing the carrier to both slide and tilt backwards even when loaded. Note that some racks that only tilt may still block the tailgate, so try to check before you buy.

>> **Tailgate rack:** For those not wanting to fit a towbar, the rear tailgate is still a good option for extra storage, since it keeps objects in the slipstream of the vehicle, which helps with both wind noise and fuel economy. Bear in mind though that depending on your vehicle, parts of the rack might be designed to rest on your bodywork, which even with protective pads can eventually cause marks and discoloration. They are also much slower to attach than towbar-mounted accessories, and most will totally restrict any opening of the tailgate.

>> **Belly pan:** Many vans will already feature the capability to mount items underneath the vehicle, and this is particularly useful for vans featuring bathroom or kitchen conversions since it's the ideal location for fresh and grey water tanks. The belly pan is a good location too for bulky, heavy, weatherproof items that rarely need to be accessed, such as spare wheels or tools. As with anything fixed outside of the vehicle, be sure to pay extra attention to how securely it is attached, and check it regularly.

## Packing

As for what you're storing? The three primary categories to consider dedicated storage for are food and drink, clothing, and equipment.

>> **Food and drink:** If you have or are planning a full conversion including a functional kitchen area, it's likely that food and drink storage will be taken care of already. As in a residential dwelling, your fresh goods will probably live in a powered fridge, with other foodstuffs, plates, cutlery and

related items housed in cupboards. Just remember that your kitchen on wheels will need to turn corners and possibly navigate bumpy roads. You will need to consider how everything stays where you put it when on the move.

A slightly more complex scenario exists for those who eschew the fitted kitchen in favour of more internal space. Assuming that you still want to be able to prepare food on trips, you'll need to find room for most of the same things as with a permanent conversion. However, you gain the flexibility of how and where things are stored, which in turn allows you a much greater range of interior layout options.

The trade-off is the extra hassle around meal times, as you unpack and repack everything, and find hygienic surfaces for preparation. This is fine for most people if trips are fairly short and infrequent – many vanlifers exist perfectly happily with a small barbecue and a single gas burner – but if you are on longer trips or catering for a larger family, it might ultimately prove a challenge.

For part-time users, the single box solution packs the essentials together into an easily portable, stowable and accessible way, covered in more detail on page 31.

>> **Clothing:** Storage of clothing is typically straightforward, since most people will have sturdy bags that will be packed and transported to and from the house. These can continue to be used for storage once in the van, either in a dedicated location (beneath bench seats is a popular location) or simply moved around as needed.

Regular site campers will sometimes utilise covered outside space such as awnings or a pup tent to store bulky clothing bags once camp is set up, keeping the van interior as uncluttered as possible.

Those on longer trips or with larger vans will benefit from being able to unpack at least some of their regularly used clothes, in which case fitted drawers and cupboards can easily be incorporated into many layouts.

>> **Equipment:** Many owners start out their vanlife in order to facilitate a sport or hobby, since a van offers much more space and flexibility than the average car. Whether your passion is cycling, skiing or photography, it's likely that you'll want to keep valuable (and bulky) equipment inside the vehicle where possible.

If a hobby is your primary reason for owning a van, it makes sense to prioritise how and where you store your equipment. Hobbies should be fun, so the last thing you want is to associate it with stress and hassle. Try to find a setup where everything you need is immediately to hand, and the steps for loading and unloading are kept to a minimum. Think also about how to deal with adverse weather conditions: How will you store muddy kit and equipment? Can you stand up inside the vehicle to get changed easily?

Given the number of people using their vans for sport, there's a smart answer out there for most gear storage issues. Spend some time looking at specialist online forums, as it's highly likely other owners will have had similar questions and found suitable solutions.

*Right: Ed Bartlett's Volkswagen Transporter T4 utilises its awning to get extra outdoor space*

## Windows

The vanlife experience is ultimately about getting into nature, but when you do inevitably find yourself stuck in the vehicle, it's great to bring the outside in. Most ex-work vans will likely have few or even no windows in the rear, which can actually be a positive if you are planning to fit cabinets and storage. However, you may want to budget in the cost of having at least some windows fitted to enhance the indoor experience when parked or camping.

## Outside space

The space inside your van is not the limit of your possibilities when it comes to actual usable footprint, and there are numerous different ways of deploying your immediate surroundings as an extension of the interior.

**>> Awning:** About as close to an essential piece of kit as any, most regular vanlifers will have some form of awning to extend the all-weather protection of the van interior into the immediately surrounding area, whether fixed or not (see below).

**>> Fixed:** A fixed awning is typically adhered to the structure of the vehicle, and extends using a wind-out action exactly like you might find above a shop or home window.

The main advantage of a fixed awning is that it is 'fit and forget'. You don't need to remember to pack it, it doesn't take up valuable space inside the vehicle, and it can be rolled out literally in seconds, meaning it can be used extremely spontaneously. The downsides are that it can add slightly to wind noise and reduce fuel economy

when cruising, and needs to be bolted and glued to the chassis, which might put off those with rare or vintage campers.

**>> Non-fixed:** Non-fixed awnings come in a wide variety of shapes, sizes and styles, ranging from open-sided tents to pop-up gazebo-style enclosures. The most popular type of non-fixed awning is known as a 'drive-away' awning; so-called because the van can physically be driven away from the structure once it has been erected. This type of awning is ideal for those regularly using official sites for multi-day stays, since it allows you to easily use the vehicle for local exploration without having to deal with the awning twice for each round trip. It's also a good test of your driving skills as you attempt to perfectly line up the awning with the vehicle upon your return.

Unsurprisingly, a huge market exists for awning add-ons; from side panels, to smart lighting, and the ever-handy clothes drying line.

**>> Tents:** Bringing a tent with you in a campervan might seem a little like missing the point, but there are a number of scenarios where in fact it makes perfect sense:

- When you have guests camping with you
- When the weather is very hot and sleeping outside might be preferable
- When you are wild camping and want to sleep somewhere interesting that isn't vehicle accessible
- When you want to increase your storage space whilst parked
- When you want to create a shaded area for a pet

Much of this can also be achieved with a tent-style awning, however many vanlifers will still carry a small pop-up tent (known as a pup tent) that can be erected and packed away extremely quickly. The pup tent will often be the first thing set up once parked, so that bulky interior items like clothes bags can be quickly unloaded and stored, making most subsequent tasks quicker and easier.

## Drivetrain

Assuming you've researched your vehicle carefully, it's unlikely that you will want or need to make significant changes to the drivetrain, although there are plenty of van owners who think nothing of fitting 19in alloy wheels and air suspension.

Wheels and tyres are certainly an important consideration, and with many vans being taken onto rough, muddy terrain for camping, it's worth looking at the suitability of your setup. Note that vans typically require load-rated wheels, so be careful when changing for a new or different design.

Any conversion that adds substantial weight to the original vehicle also potentially changes the centre of gravity, so it's worth checking with a qualified expert to ensure that items like brakes and suspension do not need upgrading or adjusting. Likewise it's essential to ensure you do not exceed the Maximum Technically Permissible Laden Mass, or MTPLM, rating for the vehicle. In particular, adding mass behind the rear axle can cause unexpected handling issues.

One other drivetrain conversion worth considering is having the engine converted to LPG/Autogas. Although the initial outlay is expensive, some countries have incentivised the switch by reduced taxes, plus it typically offers a saving on both insurance and of course fuel. With the average mileage of a passionate vanlifer, an LPG conversion can pay for itself surprisingly quickly. The added advantage is that it's kinder to the environment, which is part of what most of us love vanlife for in the first place.

On the downside, the tanks are fairly large, the range is not as big as with petrol or diesel, and not every filling station sells it, so you need to be fastidious in your route planning and fuelling strategy. However, it is also possible to get a dual fuel conversion to cover both bases.

# Using a van

So you've done the research, bought the van and poured your time and money into your conversion. Now comes the really fun part: using it. Be it for daily, weekly or monthly use, you'll want to maximise the enjoyment of your time on the road.

## Trip Planning

Knowing how much to plan ahead and what to pack depends a lot on the kind of trip you're undertaking. Every vanlifer should – at least once – just grab a bag and go with little or no plan, other than perhaps a rough area on a map to head towards. It's easy to manage a night or two away with little or no concerns for cooking or personal hygiene, and even if it ends up not being the perfect setup, you can invariably find somewhere suitable to stop overnight. At the very least you will learn something about both yourself and your van, and you might even discover a fantastic new location.

For longer or more specific trips you will want to consider some or all of the following.

## Route planning

Part of the joy of a road trip is in the driving itself. If you see the route as a chore, or something to be tolerated simply to get you to and from your destination, you aren't maximising the potential of vanlife.

A significant amount of your trip is going to be spent driving, so while it's tempting to stick to freeways and motorways to cut down on travel time, ask yourself on each trip if it wouldn't be better to take the road less travelled? Although minor roads will be slower, longer and use more fuel, it will also almost certainly be more scenic and interesting, and you are more likely to discover possible new stopover locations – the Holy Grail for many vanlifers. In countries that operate toll systems on their highways, you will likely find that it's cheaper to travel this way too.

If possible you should try to factor in at least a rough idea of where you plan to overnight, or at least allow time in your itinerary to find somewhere. It can become very stressful trying to find a place to sleep after dark, in an unfamiliar location. If you are planning extended trips or semi-permanent van dwelling, you'll want to get comfortable with this aspect of vanlife very quickly; it's commonly cited as one of its most stressful aspects.

When it comes to planning your route in more detail, there are a number of tools and resources that can help.

>> **Google Maps:** Without doubt the ultimate do-it-all route-planning resource, Google Maps covers every base, with most roads able to be viewed from both satellite and first-person – an absolute boon for scoping out road conditions as well as potential overnight stopover points. You can see your route's approximate drive time, as well as businesses and points of interest along the way.

For more advanced users, there is the ability to create your own custom maps – for example your favourite wild camping locations – as well as being able to share them either publicly or with select friends. A huge number of community-created maps already exist, so many that they can sometimes be slightly overwhelming; many people will end up creating their own edited highlights for personal use.

>> **Printed maps and guides:** Although Google Maps is an amazing resource it does have limitations, mainly for the less tech-savvy, those with smaller screens or tablets, and for people without readily-available internet access. The internet is also yet to invent something to rival the tactility of simply drawing on a paper map.

Many guidebooks to an area will include specific recommendations, and despite the increasing range of information now available online, these fixed listings add huge value. This is especially true if you are already on the road, where web access and screen size is most likely to be an issue.

*Right: Don't discount a paper map for times when you may be out of service range for satellite navigation*

>> **Satellite navigation:** Once you have your basic route and itinerary, you'll need to translate that into the real thing. Here, GPS and Satnav can play an important role in quite literally keeping you on track.

With many campervans converted from older vehicles and work vans, it's likely that the inbuilt Satnav will be an older model or even completely non-existent. However, with the screen quality and inbuilt GPS capabilities of even the average contemporary smartphone, most owners will simply install a dash-level charging dock and use a specialist app such as Waze. The advantage of apps is that most of them are interconnected, meaning that they can monitor traffic flow and hazards in real-time, potentially warning you of issues before you encounter them. Some will even help to re-route you to the cheapest fuel stop when you're running low.

Of course, the issue with relying on technology is that it can leave you hamstrung if it breaks or fails, so it's always recommended that you keep either a printed map handy or a print-out of your planned route as a backup.

>> **Online communities:** Personal recommendations are a big part of vanlife, and it's almost certain that someone will have already attempted what you are planning. The same is true with routes and locations; if you want to know if a particular site or area is good (or safe) or just want general recommendations for a region, try asking online in one of the many dedicated forums or Facebook groups. Some people can be very

protective over the best wild camping spots, but the more involved you are in a given community, the more likely someone is to give up their secrets!

>> **Weather apps:** The weather also plays a large part when it comes to vanlife, and with forecasting getting more accurate all the time it pays to check both the expected seasonal climate as well as the 10-day forecast for your intended route and destination. The joy of a van is that it's mobile, so if the weather is really bad you always have the option of moving. Indeed, many long-term van dwellers will spend their time following the seasons.

## Formal sites vs wild camping

One of the biggest discussion points between vanlifers are the pros and cons of overnighting in dedicated, paid sites or using 'wild' spots. The issue is a complex one, and while the situation itself is not a new one, the balance has undoubtedly been tipped due to the growth of social media, which is full of inspiring images of vans parked up in incredible locations with nary a camp site to be seen. This has undoubtedly been a big driver for at least some of the current influx of new vanlifers who are more interested in searching for elusive wild spots.

The inevitable result of this is the added impact of increased vehicular and human traffic in otherwise un-spoilt locations, with some of the more popular areas occasionally becoming almost as cluttered as a formal site. Likewise, the narrow roads – which so often go hand-in-hand with the very best wild locations – are becoming increasingly snarled up in peak season.

In many places around the world, wild camping is technically illegal, and although you're unlikely to get more than a knock on the window to move you on, it's less than ideal if it's getting late and you have to pack up and try to find another spot. Ultimately, it is your decision. There are places that have more relaxed wild camping laws such as Scotland, although even there new bylaws have been introduced in some locations due to the deemed overuse.

The number one rule with wild camping is to be respectful of the environment and other people, and leave it how you found it. Like it or not you are representing the entire vanlife community when using your van, and your perceived actions can have negative impacts for everyone.

If you really want to feel like you are wild camping but don't want the risk or hassle, there are many sites – both formal and informal – that offer less sanitised locations for camping. Often it might be a farm or a producer that has space in a field, plus a simple toilet block. These locations are typically cheaper, less busy and feel much more like wild camping, although in return you might need to put up with some interesting noises and smells!

### Foreign trips

Most vanlifers will take themselves and their vehicle across a border or four at some point, and in many respects this is no different to planning any other trip. The primary consideration is typically a legal one; different countries will have different laws governing use of their highways, which can range from the safety gear you need to carry on-board, to specific modifications such as headlight adjusters. However, none of this is typically specific to campervans, and is easy to look up ahead of time. Pay special attention to size and weight restrictions when booking trains and ferry crossings.

Some countries are deemed to be 'friendlier' to campervan drivers than others, and a little research in advance can pay dividends. France, for example, has a huge network of mostly free overnight/service points (known as 'Aires de service'), as well as the ingenious 'France Passion' scheme. The latter involves a very modest joining fee, which allows you to stay overnight at thousands of sites in the country owned and run by 'producers' – typically farms and vineyards. It's an amazing way to traverse a country, sampling fantastic local produce and brushing up on your language skills along the way. Other countries have similar schemes – in the UK many pubs will let you stay in their car park overnight if you buy a meal or some drinks – so check before you travel.

### Loading and unloading

Loading and unloading the van is never a highlight, but the effort can be minimised by packing smart.

First and foremost, try to keep as much as

### Top planning apps

**1. Google Maps/Earth:** Unrivalled all-round global mapping, POI's, route planning, street-level view and satellite images.

**2. Maps.me:** Extremely detailed community-sourced mapping with full offline functionality, including navigation.

**3. Waze:** Turn-by-turn navigation and re-routing with live traffic and hazard information.

**4. Freecampsites. net:** Community-driven database of free camping locations.

**5. Park4night:** Similar to Freecampsites.net but in app form and with more of a European bias.

**6. iOverlander:** Similar to Park4night but focusing off the beaten track for 4WD vans.

**7. Wifi Map:** This neat app helps you find and log on to free Wi-Fi.

**8. Meetup.com:** A way to meet like-minded individuals on the road.

**9. Google Translate:** Essential for travelling in countries where you don't speak the language.

**10. Instagram:** To post your inspiring #thevanlifecompanion photos.

possible stored permanently in your vehicle. Secondly, when loading and unloading, make the most of each trip to and from the van by combining smaller items together into larger bags or a folding box. Finally, try to pack everything strategically so that the things most likely to be needed first are immediately available to hand.

Once you're on-site, developing a simple routine to find a place for everything as quickly as possible will save time and stress later.

### Clothing

Planning your clothing for vanlife is generally focused on controlling two things: temperature and body odour. Fortunately there's one product that excels in both areas.

Merino wool is a completely natural fabric used in technical sportswear thanks to its temperature regulating properties and ability to resist the build up of odour-causing bacteria. It also dries extremely quickly, meaning it can be washed and reused.

Although Merino-based products were initially very expensive, prices have tumbled in recent years, and the range of available items has expanded to include more casual items, meaning you can wear it without looking like you're permanently about to climb a mountain. A decent Merino base layer and leggings can also make for perfect sleepwear.

The other area of clothing to consider is wet weather protection. It's worthwhile keeping at the very least a good waterproof jacket and shoes or boots in the van at all times, as well

as a pair of technical sandals or flip-flops. They come in handy more often than you'd imagine.

### Cooking

As with every aspect of vanlife, you'll want to consider your dining options and personal food and nutritional preferences in your advance planning. Food storage, preparation and cooking is a subject that varies from palate to palate, but there are a number of universal tips that can make mealtimes easier.

### The One-box solution

For the majority of owners who do not have a fully fitted kitchen in their van, the one-box solution is a handy option.

The goal of the one-box solution is to create a semi-portable store of 'essential' foodstuffs, typically long-life dried foods such as pasta, quick-cook rice and oats as well as tinned foods like beans, vegetables and fruit. Add sauces like pesto and some ready-meals like soup or ramen, and you ensure that you always have a quick, nutritious meal available even if you're on a fairly unplanned trip.

Ideally you want to find a well-vented box with carry handles, that's deep enough to store larger tins and bottles, but small enough to store somewhere out of the way, such as under a seat. A wine box can make a perfect single-box food store; just remember to restock between trips.

The one-box approach can also work well for kitchen items in lieu of fitted units, bringing together the less bulky cooking accessories into a single location. This usually

### 10 of the best one-box foods

1. Pasta
2. Quick-cook rice
3. Porridge oats
4. Canned soup
5. Trail mix
6. Tinned fish
7. Mac and cheese
8. Baked Beans
9. Ramen packs
10. Rice cakes

*Left: Campervan parked at Lake Taupo, North Island, New Zealand*

works better in a longer, flatter box such as an under-bed storage unit, preferably with wheels so that it can slide easily in and out of place.

## Water

For those without a fitted running water solution, instead of buying expensive bottled water that typically comes in plastic bottles, it's well worth investing in portable water tanks. They are reusable, easily cleaned or sterilised between uses, and will last forever if treated well. They can also be stored in a variety of locations depending on size, and even moved out of the van when on-site to help with space. Most also come fitted with a simple tap attachment, meaning you won't need to worry about spillage in regular use.

Water is obviously very heavy, and anything larger than 10 litres/2 gallons will become difficult to move, although for basic drinking and cooking duties this will just about last 2 people a weekend away, based upon the guideline of adults drinking 2 litres of water per day. If you're engaging in strenuous sports on your trip, or in a hot climate, you might need to double that if you are unsure about being able to access more water on-site. Always fill your hydration packs or other reusable sports bottles separately before your trip as well. Better safe than sorry is a good maxim when it comes to water storage.

Cleaning dishes and showering are activities that require significantly more water, but even here it's possible to get by with fairly simple solutions. Solar showers hold up to 20 litres of water, and utilise heat-attracting materials to warm the contents throughout the day to make

them ready for use in the evening. These are typically gravity-fed, but it's also possible to buy products that use a hand or foot pump to generate pressure, which is handy for rinsing dishes. The more DIY-minded can easily find instructions online to build a functioning electric shower that runs from the 12v connector.

## Cooling

If you're going to buy and store fresh foods, you'll need a way to keep them cool.

>> **Coolbox:** Installing a dedicated fridge/freezer is a relatively major undertaking, both from a financial as well as space and power standpoint. If the majority of your vanlife is made up of shorter trips and primarily on dedicated sites, however, it's perfectly possible to get by with just a good coolbox/cooler.

Larger, modern coolboxes with thick insulation such as the Coleman Xtreme can keep things cool for several days provided they are packed well, so a weekend away is no problem. Many formal sites will have a communal freezer where you can refreeze ice boards and blocks, allowing you to use them for longer trip durations. Powered coolboxes are also available, although they will not get as cold as a dedicated fridge.

Strategic packing can also help to keep things cooler for longer. Try keeping the most frequently-needed things easily to hand to minimise the amount of the time the lid is open, and place foods that most need to be kept cold nearer the bottom. People who regularly use their vans for shorter trips will often pack a

**An average kitchen box might include:**

- Cutlery/knives
- Thin plastic cutting boards
- Lighter/matches/firelighters
- Bottle opener/sealer
- Tin can opener
- Tea towels and dish scourer/sponge
- Eco-friendly dish soap and clothes wash
- Pegs and washing line
- Lightweight enamel plates, bowls and mugs
- Plastic reusable glasses
- Spare butane gas canisters
- Collapsible colander
- Nested pan set
- Small folding BBQ
- Folding wind shield
- Aeropress/compact coffee grinder
- Nested airtight Tupperware in various sizes
- Hand sanitiser
- Flask

*Right: One-box storage solutions make cooking on the go easier*

© Courtesy of Ed Bartlett

pre-prepared frozen meal that will gradually defrost ready to be eaten on day 2 or 3, acting as an extra ice block in the meantime. Of course, investing in the right size and quality of freezer blocks will also pay dividends; the optimal solution tends to be a mix of large, thin 'boards' around the edges with a couple of blocks in the middle. Finally, think also about where to keep your box at different times of day, as it may well be much cooler outside the van, especially overnight.

>> **Fridge/freezer:** For extreme climates, longer trips or van dwelling, a more robust fridge or fridge/freezer combo will likely be necessary. The benefits are obvious, but the power consumption is significant, so it is something that needs to be carefully planned.

The two main options for vanlife are the standard compressor fridge, which is a smaller version of a standard residential unit, and the 3-way fridge, so-called as it can be powered by 12-volt, mains/grid electricity or gas.

Each unit has pros and cons, but it's hard to beat a compressor fridge allied with a solar setup, although it's certainly not a budget option. A gas fridge has the advantage of near silent running, as well as being perfect for off-grid use, but they are bulky and require the cutting of ventilation holes in your van. They also generally require more servicing and care than the simple and proven compressor option.

## Buy local

Given that most vans have fairly limited storage for fresh food and drink, you'll likely need to buy things while you're away. Rather than heading for the nearest supermarket, think instead about using it as an opportunity to buy from smaller local independent stores. Better still, if the chance arises, buy direct from a producer. Look for farm shops, village stores and roadside stands.

## Eat out

Lastly, cooking (and washing up) three meals a day in a van can become very stressful and time consuming, especially if your rig doesn't have a dedicated kitchen area with running water. Eating out for one meal a day doesn't have to be a huge expense. It's also a great way to support the local economy, meet new people, explore new areas, and to eat food that you perhaps wouldn't prepare in the van.

## Sleeping

Getting a good night's sleep can – sometimes literally – take a back seat for shorter trips. For anything longer, especially if you're a light sleeper or really need your 8 hours a night, you'll want to pay close attention to your sleeping arrangements:

>> **Van positioning:** Given that external factors have a huge influence on your ability to sleep well, it goes without saying that where and how you position your van is important. Don't just pull up to the first available spot; take a moment to consider your surroundings and think about anything that might prove to be an overnight irritation. You'll also want to try to park on as close to level ground as possible; a

set of leveling chocks is one of the first pieces of kit most van owners will buy, along with a mini spirit level.

>> **Light:** Unless you have proper blackout blinds or curtains, most vans are very susceptible to light ingress, meaning you'll likely be awake at dawn. This can be a benefit if you want to make the most of your trips away, but simply angling your van so that your head is in the darkest part of the interior can make a big difference. Think about where the sun will rise, and how it will enter the van first thing in the morning. Or just invest in those blinds!

>> **Noise:** If you're staying on an organised site, you'll possibly have your spot dictated to you. If not, try to find the quietest area, and don't be afraid to take a quick look at your neighbours. Rest assured they'll be sizing you up too as you encroach on 'their' space. Remember that children, animals and party animals all run the risk of keeping you up at night. A good set of earplugs is highly advisable, although if you're wild camping you might want to keep at least one ear open for security.

>> **Temperature:** Temperature is extremely important for sleep, and something that can fluctuate wildly in a van. This is especially true for those using a pop-top roof bed, which is the first thing to get cold at night and the first thing to get hot in the morning.

Assuming you've insulated the rest of your van sufficiently, the other main areas of heat transfer are the windows. It's possible to buy padded foil panels to fit most if not all models of van, and they help significantly when dealing with both direct sunlight and cold night temperatures. Most will come with pre-installed suction cups, meaning they can be added and removed very quickly. For pop-top owners, it's also possible to buy a cover that completely encapsulates the raised roof area.

Note that caution should always be exercised when leaving windows or doors open for venting overnight, or if using an internal heater: the former for security reasons and the latter due to risk of fire and dangerous fumes.

>> **Bedding:** Choice of bedding comes down to not just the climate, but also personal preference, budget and your co-habiting status; a romantic weekend getaway isn't going to be as much fun if you're both in individual sleeping bags!

Like clothing, bedding is all about layering, since two trips in the same season – and even two days in the same trip – can be totally different when it comes to night temperatures. As with Merino clothing, natural down is arguably the best solution for temperature management, be it for a technical sleeping bag or a duvet. This can be coupled with extra blankets, and extra clothing layers when the mercury drops.

Unless you are lucky enough to have a permanent bed and mattress in your rig, what you sleep on is at least as important as what you sleep beneath, and advances in memory foam have led to it gradually replacing noisy and cold inflatable mattresses as the default choice for vanlife.

It's possible to buy memory foam in a variety of thickness and densities, and have it cut to specific sizes and shapes to fit your vehicle. It also rolls easily into a fairly compact size for storage, and it's even possible to buy sleeping bags with inbuilt memory foam, such as the award-winning Duvalay. These are also great for nights that you want to sleep outside, or in a tent.

**>> Condensation:** Campervans present almost perfect conditions for condensation, and it can present all sorts of unwanted problems, including mold and rust. The best way to limit condensation is ventilation, and this can be achieved in many different ways, from leaving windows slightly ajar to a dedicated ceiling vent or fan. Most pop-top roofs will include zipped vents, which can help significantly throughout the day and night. It's also good practice to let bedding air as much as possible, especially if you need to pack it away during the day.

**>> Insects:** A surefire way to stay awake all night is a van full of flying and buzzing critters, especially those that like to bite or sting. Midges and mosquitoes tend to go hand-in-hand with camping, so it makes sense to do what you can to limit their ability to set up home in your vehicle.

Unless you are camping in winter conditions, you won't want to keep the van hermetically sealed, so the first defence is as simple as some mosquito netting for your main openings. This becomes especially important after dark. If you have lights on inside the van during the evening, do all you can to limit the potential entry points as the light will attract them.

Other solutions include repellent skin lotions and sprays, as well as citronella sticks and candles. Be prepared to spend 10 minutes before bed doing what you can to rid the interior of any unwanted guests. A single light source can be used here in your favour to attract and concentrate insects, in order to be dealt with as efficiently as possible.

## Entertainment

Although digital entertainment such as phones, tablets, laptops and handheld consoles mean you can essentially bring your entire music, game and movie collection with you, a well-sorted campervan also has plenty of cubbyholes for trusty analog joys, which don't require constant recharging

## Safety and security

Lastly, although a big part of the joy of vanlife is the feeling of getting away from the seemingly endless constraints omnipresent in modern life, as with any kind of camping or vehicle use, safety is something that needs consideration.

Most thieves will know that a campervan is likely to be full of interesting and potentially valuable equipment, so try not to leave it anywhere that might be deemed 'high risk' and never leave valuables on show. It's a good idea to keep curtains or blinds closed when leaving the van, since it limits the view inside.

Secondary locks, visible deterrents such as steering and pedal locks, as well as audible alarms are all helpful tools to combat opportunists.

**10 best compact recreational items**
- Cards
- Scrabble
- Chess
- Kite
- Frisbee
- Fishing rod
- Football
- Bocce/boules
- Slackline
- Badminton

*Left: Mirte van Dijk's cosy Citroën HY bedroom features a permanent mattress*

Breakdowns are almost inevitable, making some form of roadside breakdown assistance is essential. Some insurance policies now include breakdown assistance, but in many cases there are special restrictions for larger vehicles like campervans and motorhomes, so always double check ahead of a trip. International breakdown is also regularly excluded, and must be purchased separately.

One of the biggest causes of camping injuries relates to campfires. If staying on a formal site always check the rules before building a fire, as many sites have restrictions or specific conditions governing their use.

Lighting a fire when wild camping adds significant extra environmental risks, and it's essential that you take every precaution around woodlands, grasslands or any potentially combustible land or substances. This includes your van, tents, gas canisters for camping stoves and basically anything other than the wood you are burning. It's incredibly easy for a small fire to quickly get out of control and ignite a wildfire, with devastating consequences. You could easily end up with a large fine, and maybe even a lot worse.

Some van owners carry a dedicated fire pit which keeps fire contained and off the ground, and also doubles as another cooking method. Yet even these can cause sparks, so never leave any fire unattended and always ensure it's completely extinguished before sleeping or leaving the site.

>> **Pets:** Bringing pets along is something that needs careful consideration. Adding an animal that needs both space and regular exercise, not to mention things like food and toilet breaks, is an additional challenge. If you already have a pet, this is something to test before committing to a van purchase and build. Some sites will not allow pets, and even 'wild' locations and National Parks may have restrictions,. Meanwhile, leaving an animal inside a vehicle for any length of time is generally unwise; it can be extremely dangerous in warm weather.

However, assuming you are sensible and always put your pets' needs first, their companionship can add greatly to your enjoyment of vanlife.

## The open road awaits

Vanlife brings unlimited opportunities for exploration and adventure, with some character-building challenges thrown in for good measure. You'll expand your know-how, get off the beaten path, make new friends, and experience the joys of self-sufficiency and exploration.

Now that you're prepared for a build, see the next two sections for inspiration from ten vanlifers who've done their own drool-worthy conversions and to get ideas for your next epic vanlife road trips. Buckle up, enjoy, and send on your tips and pictures along the way.

@edbartlett
Ed Bartlett
#TheVanlifeCompanion

**10 important safety items to keep in the van**

**1.** First aid kit
**2.** Fire extinguisher/ blanket
**3.** Torch/head torch
**4.** Carbon Monoxide detector
**5.** Steering wheel/ pedal lock
**6.** Warning triangle/ hi-vis jacket
**7.** Tyre foam/pump
**8.** Locks for bikes/ sports gear
**9.** Mini-safe
**10.** Multitool

# Glossary

**3-way fridge** – a flexible fridge that can run off gas, 240v mains or a 12v car battery

**Aire** – short for 'Aires De Service'; a French network free municipal stopover locations

**Awning** – an external cover typically attached to the vehicle to provide outdoor shelter

**Black water** – wastewater from the toilet

**Boondocking** – (also dry or wild camping) camping for free, typically in a picturesque, secluded location

**Buddy seat** – a compact extra seat that may be removable, folding or have inbuilt storage space

**Bulkhead** – a solid divider between the cab and rear cab typically found in ex-work vans

**Cassette toilet** – a toilet with a removable waste-holding tank

**Chemical toilet** – a toilet that uses chemicals to minimise odours

**Class A** – large, cab-less motorhomes typically built onto a bare bus or truck chassis

**Class B** – medium-sized motorhome, typically built from a converted commercial van

**Class C** – a motorhome built onto a chassis that includes a separate cab, typically with a sleeping area above

**Day van** – (also leisure van) a van designed for day trips and sports, not longer camping trips

**Digital nomad** – someone whose work only requires a laptop and WiFi, not a fixed office

**Dinette** – an informal dining area by the kitchen

**Full-timer** – a person living full-time on the road

**Glamping** – 'glamorous camping', which typically involves additional luxury items

**Grey water** – sink wastewater from washing (everything except for the toilet wastewater)

**Hardstanding** – campsite area with a hard, flat, often reinforced surface for parking vehicles on

**Hi-top** – a van with a fixed, DIY elevated roof

**Hook-up** – (also shore power) an external power point that recharges batteries and power appliances while on-site

**Inverter** – changes 12-volt direct current to 110-volt alternating current

**Kombi** – a van designed for people and goods with easily removable/convertible rear seats

**Leave no trace** – to leave every location how you found it, with no litter or unnecessary mess

**Leisure battery** – (also split-charge) a secondary battery designed to power the 12v appliances in a van

**Off-grid** – time spent living away from formal campsites or hook-ups

**Passion site** – a French network of stopover locations on land owned by farmers

**Pop-top/pop-up** – an elevating roof to temporarily increase internal height

**Potable water** – water deemed fit for human consumption

**Preheater** – a secondary heater that can operate when the engine isn't running

**Pup tent** – a small tent erected next to the vehicle, giving greater living space in the van

**Rig** – another word for a van

**Rock 'n' roll bed** – a rear bench seat which converts quickly into a bed

**RV** – a recreational vehicle

**Service point** – dedicated spot to refill fresh water and dispose of grey and black water

**Splittie** – the common term for the classic VW 'split-screen' models

**Surf bus** – a day van built primarily for surf trips

**Top-box** – removable roof storage

**Twin slider** – van with sliding doors on each side

# Meet the Vanlifers

Get up close and personal with these vanlife trailblazers as they show off their vehicles of choice, which run the gamut from sleek and modern to hulking and utilitarian. Each van is just as unique as its owner. What will yours be like?

Citroën HY

Ram ProMaster

Unimog

Airstream

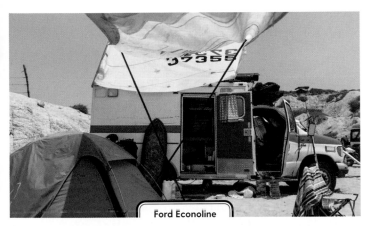
Ford Econoline

Sprinter

Chevy 3500

Land Cruiser

International

Volkswagen T4

# Citroën HY

**Digital nomad Mirte van Dijk was almost literally born into vanlife, the child of parents who roamed Europe in a van she still drives today. Decades later, 'Mister H' is still going strong and transporting Mirte on an eclectic mix of adventures.**

Growing up in a small village in the south of the Netherlands, Mirte van Dijk spent school holidays criss-crossing Europe with her parents and siblings in their Citroën HY van, purchased new by her father in 1977. Mirte learnt from a young age not only about the challenges of unexpected breakdowns but also the excitement of adventure and the kindness of strangers.

Fast-forward to today and those experiences have helped shape her career as a copywriter and journalist in the outdoor and travel industry. Her dad's old van, 'Mister H', is still providing thrills – and the occasional breakdown bill.

## Type of van

Though the idea of owning a vintage van – be it a mirror-finish Airstream or a classic split-screen VW – is a romantic one, the reality can be very different. For many vanlifers, reliability is one of the most important factors in their choice of vehicle. To Mirte, the unpredictability of her vintage ride is simply part of the charm.

Mister H is a 1976 Citroën HY van with a 4-cylinder 1911cc engine, boasting 48 horsepower, a three-speed gearbox, drum brakes and no power steering. First manufactured in 1947 as a simple commercial van, production continued until 1981, with almost half a million units manufactured in total.

The low floor gives the van a 6ft standing height despite the compact exterior dimensions, but it's the corrugated bodywork that sets it apart from its peers and places it alongside other iconic Citroën designs such as the DS and 2CV. Although mechanically fairly basic, its independent suspension was rare even on period passenger vehicles, making relatively swift progress possible on the rural roads it was designed for. Swift progress is, of course, relative, and with a top cruising speed of 80km/h (50mph) and ineffective brakes, journeys are best completed at a leisurely pace.

Having originally bought the van with a small inheritance, Mirte's father set about adding some basic features to allow the family to camp more efficiently. 'When my father bought it, it was just a square box inside,' says Mirte. 'He built a simple kitchen, bench seat and table out of wood, but there wasn't enough room for the whole family to sleep inside so my parents would sleep outside in a tent.'

On taking ownership of the van, Mirte set about refreshing and upgrading parts of it, including installing a stainless-steel exhaust system and devising a modular solution for two adults to sleep inside. With a solar panel, environmentally friendly products and one extra jerry can of fuel, it's possible for Mirte and Mister H to live off-grid for a week or more.

**Vehicle model:** Citroën HY (aka 'Mister H')
**Seats:** 6-8
**Sleeps:** 2 inside, 2 on the roof in the open air
**Engine/mpg:** 1911cc, 48hp/23mpg
**Cost of van:** €5000 in 1977
**Cost of conversion:** Unknown
**Longest trip:** The Netherlands to northern Sweden via Germany, Poland, the Baltic states and Finland, crossing Norway and Denmark back to the Netherlands
**Favourite trip:** The forest roads of Finland
**Dream trip:** Exploring Eastern Europe
**Instagram:** @meetmisterh

*Left: Mirte van Dijk's Citroën HY, Mister H*

# How she did it...

## The conversion

Mirte van Dijk wanted to be able to live off-grid in the wild for at least a week, without the need for trips back to civilisation.

Key aspects for Mister H included:

● The ability to use the roof as a solid platform
● Fully opening rear doors
● Flexible living and working space, both inside and outside
● Being able to stand upright when inside
● Sleeping space for two adults inside

## Roof space

Thanks to the 6ft internal height, the HY doesn't require an extending roof. Instead, Mirte decided to utilise the top of the van as a platform. 'I always wanted to be able to sit and sleep on the roof, close to the stars, curled up in a sleeping bag and waking with the sunrise.'

The HY has a very strong rooftop, which Mirte has further reinforced with wood to provide the perfect base for people and equipment, all accessed via a ladder. 'There is just one thing that needs to be taken into consideration, and that is it should not get too heavy,' she says. 'Building with wood is already creating extra load on the old frame of the vehicle and having it mounted so high can cause some stability issues with the centre of gravity. We are still searching for the perfect piece of wood.'

## Outside space

Another interesting feature of the Citroën HY is the way the entire rear of the van can be opened up. The upper portion opens vertically like a traditional tailgate, forming a handy extension to the roof, which can provide shelter from the elements.

Beneath the tailgate, a pair of 'barn door' panels open outwards from the centre, giving full access to the interior of the vehicle. Mirte was quick to spot the opportunity for this inside/outside area. 'We built a tabletop that fits exactly on the lower doors, which creates a kind of bar space that we can use for everything from working to preparing and eating food,' she says.

'Living outside is way more comfortable when you have an extension of your van. During hot summer days you can sleep with the back door open and enjoy the view right from your bed. And when it's raining it's possible to sit in the van and still enjoy the outdoors.'

## Living space

As any seasoned vanlifer will tell you, no matter how much time you plan to spend outdoors it's important for your vehicle to feel like home when you are actually inside. Despite its compact dimensions, the interior of Mister H could easily pass for a tiny rustic French

apartment, complete with pastel-painted cabinets, reed screens and fabric curtains.

'The original layout of the interior was designed and built by my father 40 years ago and he clearly thought it through very well,' says Mirte. 'There are storage options everywhere you look; from a space and practicality standpoint almost everything has more than one use or function. I'm still surprised about how much stuff actually fits inside.'

In the lounge area there is a choice of two tables, seating on both the left and right sides, and the bed can be left partially made up for daytime lounging.

## Cooking, cleaning and hygiene

When owning and operating a vintage vehicle such as Mister H, part of the charm is in its simplicity. What it lacks in a fancy kitchen, wet room and toilet it more than makes up for in sheer character.

Of course, you still need a vanlife vehicle to be practical and so Mister H features a mini fridge, a 10-litre water tank and a pump that operates from the main battery, as well as a large gas canister for cooking, which is stored underneath the vehicle.

Hot water is typically provided via a solar shower on the roof, or simply by boiling water on demand on cooler, overcast days. There are more ways than one to keep clean, however. 'Instead of showering we generally try to just

jump in a lake or swim in the sea,' says Mirte. 'You can often find us running around naked to dry off in the last sunlight of the day.'

## Electrical

A vintage van does not have to mean a total rejection of modernity, and with so much of contemporary living – especially off-grid – relying on electric power, this is one area of any build that needs careful consideration. For Mister H, Mirte installed a removable Goal Zero solar panel, which in turn charges the main 400Wh, 33Ah (12v) battery.

'As a digital nomad I do a lot of work on the road,' says Mirte. 'With one phone, two laptops, two small Goal Zero lights, a wi-fi receiver and two DSLR cameras to charge, the solar panels plus battery have been sufficient for our trips so far.'

More power-hungry equipment, such as the mini fridge, runs while driving via a 12v plug connected to the battery. 'I dry my hair in the wind and only wash clothes when really necessary. We wear an extra sweater when it's cold, build campfires for barbecuing and eat fresh food,' she says.

*Previous spread: Mirte's Citroën HY includes a handy table extension; Left: The interior of Mister H features a kitchen, a workspace, and a roomy front; Right: Being a digital nomad makes a work desk setup imperative; the reinforced roof and back table provide an extra open-air living space*

# Q&A

**Has the van worked out as expected?**
Yes, but only by being realistic about what to expect. An old-timer is slow, smelly and breaks down typically at least once per trip. You have to be prepared for a long journey and to still be able to see the charm of vanlife while standing at the side of the road with a smoking engine, not knowing what to do next.

**With hindsight, is there anything you'd have done differently?**
There are always things that need improvement, like the quality of a mattress, the way you store things or the amount of water you bring. Almost all of these things can be solved by time, money and ingenuity, and if it can't be solved that way, you need to consider that you might not be cut out for vanlife.

**Do you have further plans for the van?**
A new adventure! Wherever that may lead us.

**What is it about vanlife that has most surprised you?**
It's amazing how much of a magnet an old van like Mister H is for interaction. Whatever the situation, the amount of people who wave or beep or knock on your door for a chat is tremendous.

**What would be your three top tips for vanlife?**
**1.** Don't expect rainbows and unicorns all of the time, because vanlife can be tough. If you like an easy holiday that always goes as planned, it really might not be the best option for you.
**2.** Make the most of summer trips. You can practically live outside.
**3.** Enjoy the ride and keep smiling. Make light of the bad situations and don't be upset when it's too cold, too warm or too broken down.

---

*Right: Mirte van Dijk and her Citroën HY visiting the seashore*

© Courtesy of Mirte van Dijk

# Ram ProMaster

**Environmental policy graduate Caroline Winslow decided to add a practical angle to her studies, spending her senior year living full-time in a self-converted van in order to better understand – and hopefully reduce – her carbon footprint.**

Growing up in the small mountain town of Telluride, Colorado, Caroline Winslow developed a strong passion for exploration from a young age. Her first taste of vanlife came in the summer of 2014 when she purchased a Ram ProMaster van with her boyfriend in order to explore the US. After two summers in the van, Caroline realised that she could combine her love of vanlife with a desire to live off-grid. To reduce her carbon footprint, she set out to spend her senior year in a self-converted, solar-powered Ram ProMaster built from the funds of her off-campus living stipend.

## Type of van

Launched in North America in 2013, the Ram ProMaster is in fact a rebranded Fiat Ducato – the most common motorhome in Europe. The result of a joint production venture between Fiat and Groupe PSA (Peugeot, Citroën, Opel/Vauxhall), the van is essentially the same vehicle as a Citroën Jumper or Peugeot Boxer.

Having previously marketed the Dodge Ram van and a version of the Mercedes Sprinter, Chrysler and Fiat unveiled the Ram ProMaster as its first commercial van in North America since its bankruptcy in 2009. The van came with three different wheelbases, four body lengths and two available heights. The North American market also featured a 3.6-litre V6

Chrysler petrol engine and 6-speed automatic transmission as standard.

Caroline had already owned a Dodge Ram van, and decided to purchase a ProMaster for a number of reasons. 'First and foremost, I knew that I wanted a high-top van, which would enable me to stand fully upright and move comfortably throughout the vehicle,' she says. 'My plan was to live in the van year-round, including through the cold Maine weather, so I wanted the internal living space to be maximised. For that reason, I decided to buy the 136in wheelbase because it would allow me ample space for a build-out, while still enabling me to park in a traditional parking space.'

To meet her goal of living full-time in the van, Caroline intended to create a space that would be a comfortable and cosy home while also incorporating environmental sustainability into its design and operation.

'I purchased the vehicle as an empty cargo van with the intention of building out the interior myself using repurposed, natural, non-toxic materials,' she says. 'After months of planning and researching construction materials, I began the conversion in June 2017. Three months later I had completed my new home, "Roxi". Every time I look in the rearview mirror, or wake up and look around, I am deeply proud of what I have accomplished.'

**Vehicle model:** Ram ProMaster (136in wheelbase high-top model)
**Seats:** 2
**Sleeps:** 2
**Engine/mpg:** 2500cc/17-18mpg
**Cost of van:** $25,000
**Cost of conversion:** $7000
**Longest trip:** Maine to Utah
**Favourite trip:** West coast of the United States, from California to Washington
**Dream trip:** New Zealand
**Instagram:** @RePoweredRam

*Left: Caroline Winslow with her Ram ProMaster in Colorado; Next page: Roxi was customised to store two pairs of skis and poles in a fitted compartment*

# How she did it...

## The conversion

Environmental policy graduate Caroline Winslow wanted to spend her final year in college living full-time in a van in order to experience off-grid living and learn more about her own energy use.

Goals for her build included:

● Enough space for the interior to feel and function like a home
● An area to store her ski equipment and climbing gear
● A high roof that would enable her to stand up and move comfortably throughout the van
● A fully functional kitchen with a stove, oven and sink
● Rooftop space and internal storage for solar array and battery bank

## Electrical

As sustainability and power usage was at the forefront of the project, the solar-electrical setup was one of the most essential aspects of the whole build. 'The first step was to determine what size panels and battery bank I would need to run my fridge, outlets and lights,' says Caroline. 'After much research and testing, I installed two 300w solar panels onto the roof of the vehicle, which in turn connected to a 60-amp solar controller, a 2000w inverter/charger, and finally to a 480Ah battery bank. I also installed a shore power connection, which has been housed under the rear bumper for ease of access.'

When self-building, there's always a risk of making mistakes, and this is especially the case with electrical systems, as Caroline duly discovered two days prior to leaving for college. 'I realised that when wiring the solar array, some of the positive wires had been attached to the grounding bar instead of the fuse box,' she says. 'Overall, these moments were frustrating but fairly inevitable and I learnt an immense amount about both the technology and myself through the struggles and failures.'

## Cooking, cleaning and hygiene

With cooking and baking being high on the list of priorities for Caroline, she didn't want to sacrifice her ability to undertake these tasks by moving into her van. The well-equipped kitchen area takes up approximately half of the main space, and features at its heart a two-burner stove that runs on methylated spirits. 'The kitchen build takes up a lot of room in the van but having the comforts of a home along with me was well worth it,' she says.

A stainless-steel kitchen sink with a foot pump deals with dishes and general water requirements, and a solar shower handles personal hygiene and laundry during the warmer months. 'When I am in school full-time, I often utilise my friends' showers and laundry,' says Caroline. 'When I'm on the road, however, I will typically visit laundromats, gas stations and gyms or other recreation centres in order to use their facilities.'

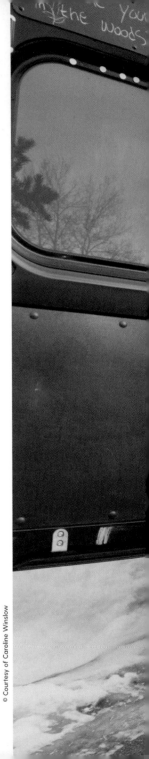

© Courtesy of Caroline Winslow

## Living space

One of the benefits of converting a van yourself is the ability to plan exactly how you want to arrange the space for functional living, while also optimising the all-important storage space.

Many converted cargo vans are designed with a permanent raised sleeping area, which gives storage space underneath for equipment such as bikes, as well as fitted drawers and organisers. However, Caroline knew that she wanted the ability to have friends over and to entertain in a more apartment-style seating area. 'I designed the back of the van to be convertible, with two benches that face one another and a table that can be mounted in the centre,' she says. 'At night-time, a leaf folds from one side of the bench and rests on the frame of the other bench.'

Clothing and kitchen equipment are stored in overhead cabinets on both sides of the van, meaning most items can be reached without even having to bend down.

## Conscious construction

In order to align the build with her sustainability goals, Caroline aimed to utilise building materials that, where possible, were natural, repurposed and non-toxic. 'Due to the lack of transparency in many construction-material supply chains, this required a lot of research. However, I was able to find some amazing products. My entire van was insulated with sheep's wool, which is a natural, regenerative material that has great thermal properties.

Additionally, I was able to find old fence panels, as well as plywood destined for the dumpster, to create my cabinet doors and end-grain countertops.

'As I was going to be living in such a small, contained space, I strived to use VOC-free sealants and paints on the interior surfaces, and natural latex cushions that would not give off potentially harmful gases. These products were not only better for myself and the environment but also incorporated unique attributes and stories into the various components of Roxi.'

## Recreation

Growing up as an enthusiastic ski racer, Caroline knew she would need to create space to securely store her equipment inside, where it would be able to dry. Consequently, the first cabinet box she built was designed to fit two pairs of skis and poles, situated under a bench seat directly accessible from the back doors.

Perhaps the most interesting and fun feature of the van, however, is a functional swing. 'I had never seen a van equipped with a swing before and I decided that I needed to find a way to incorporate one into Roxi,' says Caroline.

Prior to insulating the van, she worked out a way to secure some old climbing rope and carabiners to the struts in the van's metal frame. 'Once I knew it would securely take my weight,' she says, 'I simply took a piece of scrap wood, cut it to size and attached it to the supports. I never tire of swinging out of the back doors, taking in the views around me.'

© Courtesy of Caroline Winshaw

© Jesse James Hoffman

# Q&A

**Has the van worked out as expected?**

Vanlife in Roxi thus far has been an amazing journey and learning experience. From living in a van for two summers prior to owning her, I had already experienced life on the road and living in a small space, but taking on the project to construct my full-time home has been incredible. Though there are additional tasks such as ensuring adequate solar charging or manually filling and emptying my water tanks, vanlife has worked out as I had expected, if not better.

**With hindsight, is there anything you would have done differently?**

Very little. I'm glad I took multiple months to plan out the build in advance, as I was able to include all of the elements that were important to me. If there was one thing I did perhaps overlook, and that could have been better, it was storage for dirty clothes. When building your own home on wheels it is important to think of the tiny things that you might otherwise overlook, such as where the trash will be kept. Although I seem to have remembered most things, the dirty clothes were definitely an oversight.

**What is it about vanlife that has most surprised you?**

I have definitely been taken aback by the amount of interest shown in and support for my full-time vanlife, both from friends and family but also the broader vanlife community. It has been a wonderful experience getting to learn about other people's lives on the road and seeking out tips and help from them when running into difficulties.

**What further plans do you have for the van?**

I will be graduating from college with a degree in environmental policy, and I'll be moving to start a new job. As such, I am in the process of deciding if I will continue living in Roxi while I work. What I do know, though, is that I will be taking a few more epic trips in the meantime. Whatever happens, vanlife will definitely not end there for me.

**What are your three top tips for vanlife?**

**1.** Think about every little thing that is important in your life and find ways to incorporate them in the van.

**2.** Don't take things too seriously: laughing at the countless mistakes, breakdowns and challenges is a really important part of vanlife.

**3.** Make the most of the opportunities that the lifestyle gives you to meet new people and to engage with new communities.

*Previous page, left:*
*1. The sheepswool insulation is all-natural;*
*2. Cutting plywood to fit;*
*3. Roxi includes a table that can mount in the centre; Right: 1. The two-burner kitchen uses half Roxi's interior space;*
*2. Opposing benches prioritise socializing;*
*3. The sleeping area rests on an extendable leaf;*
*Opposite: Roxi's swing in action*

# Unimog

**LA-based filmmaker David Roth has always loved vans. His first vehicle was a '91 Chevy Astro – a compromise with his parents who wouldn't let him buy an ex-school bus. Fast-forward to adulthood and he owns perhaps the ultimate vehicle for tackling both the urban and actual jungle.**

B orn and raised in Cincinnati, Ohio, David Roth moved west to California to study film, and never left. 'Mark Twain once said, "When the end of the world comes I want to be in Cincinnati, because it's always 20 years behind the times." I share his sentiment.'

Having spent some time pondering a 'fun' project vehicle of various kinds, a late-night chat with a friend about seizing the day led to a fateful few hours on Craigslist. After exhausting an assortment of jeeps and convertibles, David's attention honed in on a 1964 Mercedes-Benz Unimog.

## Type of van

The Unimog is definitely not for shrinking violets. Launched in the shadow of World War II, Mercedes Benz designed the Mog (as it's affectionately known among enthusiasts) as a working vehicle, with the aim of injecting new life into desperately needed German agricultural production. It's highly unlikely that its designer Albert Friedrich would have imagined selling over 400,000 units worldwide to date. Among a wealth of unusual features was the huge flexibility for attaching both static and powered implements. Indeed, by 1954 there were almost 70 different agricultural appliances designed specifically for use with the Unimog platform.

A torque-rich engine, innovative drivetrain layout – still used on the vehicle over 70 years later – and very high ground clearance of 15.8in means the Mog can tackle everything from 45-degree inclines to large boulder fields, and the flexible ladder chassis and torque tube suspension allow it to traverse terrain that would leave many otherwise-capable off-road vehicles floundering. YouTube reveals an assortment of configurations making light work of every extreme terrain condition imaginable.

David's own vehicle is an ex-factory ambulance, but the base model has been utilised in dozens of different configurations around the world, from agricultural and military use to fire-fighting and exploration, and even as a successful race vehicle, winning its category in the infamous Paris-Dakar rally. A traditional covered front cab is a nod to practicality, but as David points out; 'Living in Los Angeles, there is no real practical reason to own a Unimog.'

With a kerb weight of around 8,500lbs, 20-inch off-road tyres and brick-like aerodynamics the Mog will only return around 8-10mpg, however a fuel capacity of 2 x 15.9 gallons gives a relatively large cruising range of around 350 miles.

'I love the truck – it's an extension of me – but it also has no power-assisted brakes, power steering, air conditioning or any concessions to comforts, which means that driving it is an adventure in and of itself, particularly in the city.'

**Vehicle model:** Unimog U110 404.1
**Seats:** 2 in the cab, 6 in the rear
**Sleeps:** 3-4
**Engine/mpg:** 2.2L Mercedes-Benz M180 with Zenith 32 NDIX off-road carburettor/ 8-10 mpg
**Cost of van:** $10,000
**Cost of conversion:** $6000
**Longest trip:** California coastline
**Favourite trip:** Old Mojave Road
**Dream trip:** Pan-American Highway (Alaska to Chile)
**Instagram:** @theUniblog

*Left: David Roth with his Unimog*

# How he did it...

## The conversion

Before settling on his Unimog, filmmaker David Roth was searching for a fun vehicle for recreational use in and around LA.
His wish list included:
- Mechanically sound
- Easy to work on/repair in the field
- Ability to remove the roof and/or doors
- Interesting, fun or unusual (or, in the case of the Mog, all three!)
- Something original with upgrade potential

## Living space

While the shell of the ex-ambulance rear box is factory-fitted and original, David gutted the entire interior and built out a comfortable camper. 'Part of my Unimog's charm is in keeping most of the major mechanics original, while finding ways to upgrade practicality and comforts,' he says.

The sizeable rear space is a perfect blank page for conversion, and David constructed bespoke cabinets and a combined dinette/ bed out of birch plywood, and fashioned a propane stove on top of a caeserstone counter. 'The last time I worked with wood was in my seventh-grade class,' he says. 'But I taught myself how to build cabinets, door frames and doors just for this project, which was extremely fulfilling. A local stonemason cut the countertop from remnant black caesarstone quartz and a local upholstery shop in Los Angeles helped me sew cushions for the rear dinette/bed.'

Each dinette bench features significant inbuilt storage, accessible both from above when inside the vehicle as well as from behind via the rear doors, with food and cooking equipment stored in dedicated units around the stove.

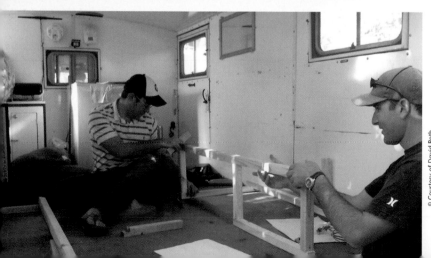

## Electrical and A/V

The cab is a traditional military 24-volt with a 19-amp, 300-watt generator, but David has upgraded the rear box to a 12-volt, 125-watt rack-mounted solar panel powering dual Odyssey PC31-2150 deep-cycle batteries.

Aside from an assortment of power sockets, the abundant Californian solar energy powers an Engel 45qt fridge/freezer to keep food fresh on long, hot journeys, as well as a Pioneer stereo powering four 6x9 three-way speakers.

The front cab forgoes any kind of tradition stereo system. 'The cab is incredibly loud on the move, and even with insulation and soundproofing, speaking with my co-pilot or friends in the rear box is incredibly challenging.' To combat this, the Unimog has been fitted with a system typically found in small aircraft or helicopters, with Sigtronics SPA-400 and RES-400 units powering the onboard intercom, accompanied by three matching headsets.

In addition, David has added a reversing camera using the Rear View Safety 3-camera setup. If you need to ask why, you've obviously never attempted to reverse-park a Unimog.

## External Space

The Unimog is renowned for its numerous options for external attachments, and this flexibility extends increasingly to leisure use.

Arguably the most essential add-on for any

adventure vehicle, David has added a pair of FrontRunner roof racks, which house both the solar panel and 2×5-gallon drinking water tanks, as well as providing a platform to secure items such as surfboards and ski gear. Under-slung jockey boxes house tools and items such as snow chains, plus the option for up to three additional 5-gallon jerry cans of fuel. 'I prefer to carry spare fuel whenever I'm on a trip, since once we leave the pavement we might not come across a gas station for days,' says David.

With the kinds of terrain the Unimog encourages you to traverse, a hitch-mounted winch – which can easily be switched between the front and rear of the vehicle – has also been fitted. A swing-out propane grill also connects to the rear hitch point, making outdoor barbecues an extremely straightforward affair.

Finally – and arguably the vehicle's party trick – the entire roof and doors of the front cab can be removed in a matter of minutes, transforming it into a convertible truck. 'It takes a lot to make people look twice in LA,' says David. 'But a topless Unimog cruising the Pacific Coast Highway usually does it!'

*Previous page: The front cab; Left: 1. the shell of the Unimog; 2. Installing the Engel fridge/freezer; 3. Building out the interior; Right: 1. The combined dinette/bed; 2. Taking the Unimog out into the desert; 3. David enjoying the view out of the back doors*

# Q&A

**Has the van worked out as expected?**
I never expected to be so into it, actually. I lived in Los Angeles for 7-8 years before meeting the Unimog and never once did I make a camping trip outside the city.

Now, I've gone through something of a camping renaissance, and try to get out of LA and off the beaten path at least once a month. Some of my favourite camping spots are within 200 miles of the city, which makes for great long-weekend styles of trips.

I wish I could say I had a lofty purpose when I bought my Unimog. But sometimes the best adventures are those that we didn't intend to take in the first place.

**With hindsight, is there anything you'd have done differently?**
I should have added indoor plumbing earlier! I have a great time heading onto the dirt trails and getting lost, but I do miss the luxury of running water on dry camping trips.

**What is it about vanlife that has most surprised you?**
The people I've met as a direct result. I never thought it would be such a big influence on my life.

**Do you have further plans for the van?**
The Unimog has some limiting factors. It was never meant to be a long-distance high-speed cruiser, and at sustained highway speeds the transmission will eventually overheat. Every two hours or so, I have to pull off and rest for 30-45 minutes just to let the transmission cool, so I'd love to add a transmission radiator to take away that limitation.

I'd also love to add indoor plumbing – at least a sink and shower that mounts to the rear. I don't have enough room for an in-cab toilet, but truck-mounted running water would be a nice luxury. My ultimate dream would be to integrate my Unimog into my work somehow!

**What are your three top tips for vanlife?**
**1.** Firstly, stay under 45mph. I like to say that my Unimog will go over anything; it just won't do it very quickly. But in actual fact, it's the Zen-like pace of my adventures I've come to like the most.
**2.** Secondly, find a good co-pilot. Adventures are even better shared.
**3.** Thirdly and finally – get off the pavement. Hopefully this one is self-explanatory!

*Opposite: Top-mounted surfboards come along for the ride thanks to a custom rack*

© Courtesy of David Roth

# Airstream Argosy Motorhome

**Canadian couple Eric McCutcheon and Fanny Rice set out to create a comfy home away from home on wheels, allowing them to get off the beaten path and explore in stylish simplicity. Having already restored many Airstream trailers, their obvious choice was a motorhome version.**

Former Canadian athletes Eric McCutcheon and Fanny Rice took very different paths towards entrepreneurship: Eric went into marketing, design and technology, while Fanny is a contemporary artist.

Growing up in Mont-Tremblant, Québec, Fanny learned about vanlife from an early age thanks to nomadic parents who still spend six months each year travelling the US and Mexico in their tiny Karmann van. Montreal native Eric, meanwhile, has a passion for the classic Airstream, something which he extended to his business, sourcing and converting them for corporate marketing tours.

Not wishing to travel with a trailer in tow, the couple set out to find a self-contained solution and Eric eventually sourced a vintage Airstream motorhome that was ripe for restoration and conversion.

## Type of van

Eric and Fanny's vehicle is a 1975 Airstream Argosy Motorhome, featuring the torque-rich Chevy 'big block' 454 engine made famous by classic Chevrolets such as the Corvette and El Camino. Airstream began producing a line of motorhomes under the Argosy brand in 1974, with the basic design lasting through to 1992. Early versions, such as Eric and Fanny's,

are known as 'painted Airstreams' due to their colourful exteriors, with the iconic mirror finish not introduced until 1979.

Despite Eric's experience converting Airstream trailers, the couple wanted a traditional vanlife experience. 'We wanted something that allowed us to get up and go on a whim,' says Eric. 'We planned not to stay more than a couple of days in any given location so we settled on a motorhome model as it would demand less work than a trailer. We liked the advantage of having everything under one roof.'

Upon purchase, the vehicle was original to its 1975 spec, which suited the couple's desire for a shell-up restoration and conversion. When designing his units, Eric aims to reinvent vanlifing with open, airy interiors. 'We wanted a quality residential feel that allowed us to move around without feeling cramped,' he says.

The size of their Airstream is the shortest available that still allows for a rear queen-size bed floorplan, further enhancing the potential for a homey feel without compromising the manoeuvrability of the vehicle. 'Having the ability to sleep in our favourite hiking, surfing, kiting and cycling spots was also a primary objective,' says Eric. 'So we had to strike a balance between something technically able to get us there versus the levels of comfort we'd have once we did.'

**Vehicle model:** 1975 Airstream Argosy Motorhome
**Seats:** 6
**Sleeps:** 4
**Engine/mpg:** Chevrolet 454mpg
**Cost of van:** 95000CAD
**Cost of conversion:** $50,000CAD + labour
**Longest trip:** Montreal (Québec) to Florida
**Favourite trip:** Florida Keys
**Dream trip:** Montreal to California via Colorado, Utah and Arizona
**Instagram:** @wanderlustairstream

*Left: The 1974 Airstream Argosy Motorhome pre-dates the days of the mirror finish*

# How they did it...

## The conversion

Eric and Fanny have always loved design, Airstreams and road trips, but didn't want to sacrifice home comforts or be confined to campsites when travelling. Their vehicle wish list included:

● Something small enough to get almost everywhere but large enough to feel residential
● A tailgate that would allow the towing of a Vespa or bicycles, as well as plenty of storage for sports gear
● Enough space to be able to make up a bed for guests
● A complete kitchen installation
● A proper bathroom with a large shower

## Living space

With the vehicle stripped back to its shell for restoration, the original interior was entirely replaced. The new floor plan now closely resembles that of the original except for the addition of a queen-size bed to replace the standard twins.

The main living area originally had a picnic-style dinette, which the couple found too restrictive. They have replaced it with a four-seat, queen-sized sofa bed with extra storage space underneath. The seating area also includes an optional integrated work/dining table for maximum flexibility. 'We rarely eat indoors as we try to take advantage of our surroundings as much as possible when on the road,' says Eric. 'As such we only install the table when we really need it, which allows us to maximise the interior space.'

## Exterior

The original vehicle came with an awning, which had seen better days. The torn and weather-bleached fabric was replaced with one that gave the couple an extra 180 sq feet of outdoor living space.

The tailgate storage area had been modified several times over the years, but the couple decided to return it to its former glory, adding a custom mount for their Vespa scooter at the same time. 'It works like a charm and gives us a ton of extra freedom for longer and more urban trips,' says Eric.

They also added bicycle mounts and an assortment of anchor points, allowing them to swap the Vespa for other sports gear depending on their itinerary.

'The next project for the exterior is to add a custom grill mount so that we no longer need to cook at floor level when stopping in random spots,' says Eric. 'We also plan to add an exterior wall-mounted paddleboard rack.'

*Right, from top left clockwise: 1. The rear queen size sofa bed features storage below; 2. Vintage dashboard gauges are a throwback to 1974; 3. Subway tile completes the bathroom with a classic touch; 4. The tailgate Vespa storage also can allow for bicycles and other active gear*

© Courtesy of Eric McCutcheon and Fanny Rice

## Cooking, cleaning and hygiene

Continuing the minimalist, high-quality residential feel of the interior, the kitchen area features luxurious, tactile materials including copper and marble, with bulky items such as the microwave and a dual energy propane/electric refrigerator hidden from sight. A new twin-burner propane stove-top handles cooking, with a portable barbecue for external use when conditions allow. Kitchen storage consists of two full-depth drawers for dry food, a 5 cubic ft fridge/freezer for fresh food, plus five other drawers for dishes, utensils, pots and pans.

Water is always a critical factor for a comfortable vanlife experience and it is provided for here by a 50-gallon tank, allowing the couple to take full advantage of their stunning wet room-style shower while remaining off-grid for as long as possible.

## Electrical

As with the rest of the Airstream, all of the van's electrics were reconfigured while it was stripped back to the shell. Luckily for the couple, Fanny's father is an electrician. 'We really wanted to bring the unit up to date,' says Eric. 'So we added a Nest smoke detector, iPad navigation, more than a dozen recessed ceiling lights across four zones, a Bluetooth portable sound system and a 32" smart TV.'

The couple also installed a new power inverter as well as a power isolator, which allows them to charge the auxiliary battery while driving. Unsurprisingly, this wasn't a standard feature back in 1975.

Continuing the modernisation will include adding solar panels and a wi-fi signal booster, as well as a Bluetooth-controlled door lock.

## Mechanical

Keeping reliability at the front of their minds, the couple replaced or rebuilt almost all of the drivetrain, including the engine, transmission, brakes, suspension, tyres, radiator and electrical wiring. Of course, even new or reconditioned kit can fail, as they would discover.

'Two weeks prior to leaving for our first road trip we had the transmission replaced, as it had suddenly started showing signs of age and wear,' says Eric. 'The new transmission worked beautifully, so after four months of hard work, endless days and a few arguments we were finally set for our 3000km [1865 mile] trip to Florida. Midway through the Adirondacks, on a steep climb, the van started puffing thick white smoke out of the exhaust. We were stranded only 120km [75 miles] into our trip.'

It turned out that the new transmission had a faulty part that would take five minutes to change. However, finding a big enough recovery truck in the middle of rural Vermont took the couple an entire day and cost them $900 in the process. Proof that with vanlife, even the best-laid plans can sometimes go awry.

© Courtesy of Eric McCutcheon and Fanny Rice

# Q&A

**Has the van worked out as expected?**
Yes, and we've been having an absolute blast driving and exploring in it!

Rebuilding most of the mechanical side of things was a good decision as it gives us peace of mind, and aside from the initial glitch with the transmission it has been super reliable thus far.

**With hindsight, is there anything you would have done differently?**
This is something that we wanted to do for quite some time, so we put a lot of thought into the ideal setup. If we were to build another van, we can honestly say that it would be identical in terms of the features and the layout.

**What is it about vanlife that has most surprised you?**
That it's not only possible but also easy and indeed liberating to live with the strict minimum of things, even for extended periods of time. This way of living has taught us that it's only the experiences and moments shared that are key to our happiness. It's also taught us that there's no need to wait for retirement to hit the open road.

**Do you have further plans for the van?**
Only to make more trips! We'd love to make it to the West Coast of America and drive the California coastline, ideally via Colorado, Utah and Arizona. Fanny mostly finds inspiration for her art in waterfronts, so seeing how travelling through the mountains and desert affects her work would be interesting.

**What are your three top tips for vanlife?**
**1.** Let go of your regular daily routine by focusing on the present moment.
**2.** Be adventurous! It's OK to stray from your GPS. Maybe you'll find the ideal hidden spot.
**3.** You can't plan for every eventuality.

*Previous page: Left, top to bottom: 1. A combo work/dining table adds flexibility; 2. Focusing on a modern interior design meant emphasizing space and airiness; Right, top to bottom: 1. High-end kitchen finishes give a luxe feel; 2. Clever storage solutions maximise space without adding visual clutter; Opposite: Fanny and Eric in the sidedoor of their Argosy Motorhome*

# Ford Econoline ambulance

**Self-confessed California beach rat Ian Dow spent his formative years surfing, skating and snowboarding before leaving to travel the world in 2008, visiting 68 countries. On returning to the US he acquired a dog, a motorcycle and an old ambulance, and set off to explore Central America.**

Perhaps unsurprisingly for someone growing up in the 1980s and 1990s on the golden shores of Southern California, Ian Dow was exposed to vanlife culture from a very early age.

'As a child my family had a Westy that we would take on camping trips, but I would also regularly use it in the driveway for sleepovers with friends,' he says.

Fast-forward to adulthood, and on returning to the US after 10 years abroad, with little money and even fewer plans, a speculative bid on an eBay listing led to the unlikely purchase of a used ambulance and the start of a new adventure.

## Type of van

Few vehicle models live to see their golden anniversary but the Ford Econoline is an exception. Debuting in 1961 it sold for 56 consecutive years, and was America's best-selling van from 1980. Originally launched as a modified Ford Falcon passenger car, it wasn't until the third generation in 1975 that the van gained its trademark long nose, by which point the engine options had expanded to include both 'big block' petrol and diesel V8s. The third generation Econoline introduced a longer sub-frame, allowing for a wider variety of configurations, including box vans and ambulances. Its fourth and final iteration (1992 until 2014) saw further refinements, and it's this generation ex-ambulance Econoline that is Ian Dow's home on wheels.

'An ambulance spoke to me because of its size and the quality of construction,' he says. 'As something of a carpenter, I know that building in a square box is easier than dealing with the curved walls of most vans. The E350 ambulance is big enough for a large living space without impairing driveability, and it's strong enough to carry my tools, toys and motorcycle.'

Another key point in Ian's consideration was the maintenance history. Lives depend on the reliability of ambulances: they are driven hard but the servicing is typically immaculate and well documented. As his planned journey was likely to take him into some remote terrain, a strong engine and reliability were both essential.

Other benefits include inbuilt storage compartments and benches; advanced electrical systems, such as the upgraded air-con and high-output alternator; exterior storage space; extra insulation; and standard ambulance extras like the siren and spotlights.

Thanks to having so much equipment and a workable internal layout as standard, Ian was able to complete the conversion work in the front yard of his parents' house over the course of four months.

**Vehicle model:** 1994 Ford E350 Dually Type III ambulance
**Seats:** 2 up front. Rear bench seating for 5 more
**Sleeps:** 7 including rooftop tent
**Engine/mpg:** 7.3L powerstroke diesel/12mpg
**Cost of van:** $2,800
**Cost of conversion:** $5,200
**Longest trip:** California to Costa Rica and back via Mexico, Guatemala, El Salvador, Honduras, Nicaragua and Belize
**Favourite trip:** Jalisco to Oaxaca (Mexico)
**Dream trip:** One year circling Africa by car or motorcycle
**Instagram:** @vanlife_ian_dow_travels
**Dino the Dog's Instagram:** @dinodogtravels

# How he did it...

## The conversion

After returning to the US hungry for more travel, Ian Dow set his sights on converting a vehicle to explore Central America. With very little cash to spare and rugged terrain on the horizon, he discovered that the Ford E350 ambulance ticked all of the key boxes for the trip. These included:

- Reliability
- Large interior living space
- Strong diesel motor
- Affordability
- Room to load a motorcycle

## Sleeping

As anyone who has designed and built their own van conversion will tell you, one of the greatest feelings is creating neat engineering solutions within a compact space. One area where this is particularly useful is with sleeping arrangements, and here Ian has excelled by providing not one but six different options.

'The ambulance came pre-equipped with a fitted bench seat, so I built removable beams from it to the storage space opposite to form an L-shaped couch used for lounging and eating at the table,' says Ian. 'With the beams in place, plywood stored under the rear cushion slides out, the cushions are rearranged and topped with memory foam, and you have a very comfortable queen-size bed.'

Additional options include a flat reclining passenger seat, an internal hammock and the sturdy roof platform that also provides the ideal base for a tent. 'Since being on the road I prefer an easier setup, with my cushions arranged on the floor,' says Ian, 'leaving space on the bench seat for a guest.'

## The roof

One of the benefits of commercial vans and larger vehicles such as buses is that many have a flat, reinforced roof. 'The rooftop is my favourite outside space,' says Ian. 'It's perfect for providing a better vantage point, camping tents off the ground, morning coffee and extra storage. I've even had a DJ play a set up there in Nicaragua.'

For access, Ian has attached a salvaged teak boat ladder to the rear door, and the roof space includes a 30-gallon water tank, an 8ft boat and even a roll of turf lawn and an umbrella that mounts inside the spare tyres on a rack above the cab. The umbrella is fixed to an arm that reaches across the entire rooftop and can be adjusted to supply shade wherever it's needed.

'When the ground is good enough I have a 27ft boat sail that hooks to the roof and ratchets to a tree or a stake in the ground,' says Ian. 'It provides ample shade while also looking a bit ridiculous!'

*Previous page, clockwise from top left: 1. The Econoline has extensive roof storage; 2. Inbuilt storage benches came standard; 3. Ian brings a tent for sleeping out; Opposite: The 27ft boat sail*

© Courtesy of Ian Dow

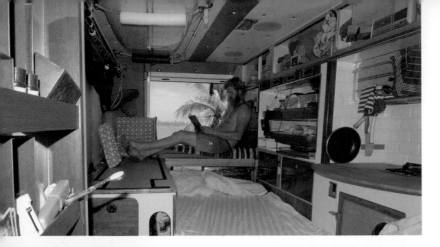

## Cooking

The kitchen area was the main focus of the conversion work for Ian as he has a real passion for food and cooking and much of the interior layout was already set.

'I added a subway tile as a splashback for easy clean-up and a bamboo cutting board surface as the countertop and sink cover,' he says. 'My faucet hangs above the sink to save surface space and I've also built a wine rack and some drawers out of Purpleheart wood – I'm a bit of an exotic hardwood fan, despite the weight penalty.'

For cooking duties, Ian chose a two-burner propane stove meant for a house rather than using an RV-specific model, which he felt lacked both functionality and visual appeal. He also built a closing porthole to the rubbish bin, which is accessed from an exterior door. 'Having hot trash in my bedroom didn't sound like much fun!'

## Cleaning

Ambulances are designed to be kept sterile inside, and Ian has used easy-clean materials throughout. 'Continuing my passion for hardwood, I used finished teak flooring, which sweeps out with ease,' he says. 'And the tile, glass, stainless, laminate and bamboo in the kitchen needs little more than a paper towel.'

Of course, having a pet along for the ride adds to the cleaning requirements. 'I have a few sets of sheets for the bed and serapes on the cushions,' says Ian. 'These are the hardest things to keep clean because of Dino – his love of water and eternally dirty feet definitely keep me busy.'

For showering, there's a 30-gallon system

pressurised by air and heated by the sun, plus hot water on demand, if required, via a propane heater.

'The key to cleanliness for me is storage,' says Ian. 'With enough places to pack things away, the dirt of the day is easily cleaned out with my daily sweep and I can go from complete mess to spotless in less than an hour.'

## Electrical

Another advantage of utilising an ambulance as a base vehicle conversion is the upgraded electrical systems, including a high output alternator and external shore power connector.

'I run the van entirely off my starter batteries, although as a backup I have a 1000w generator,' says Ian. 'The shore power connection charges the batteries while also giving me two sockets for my other electrical needs, such as powering my projector for movie nights (another advantage of a large, flat-sided van). I also have an inverter attached to two sockets that are live when the engine is on.'

One thing Ian didn't take advantage of with the original build was solar power, although he does use a small foldable 28w panel to charge both his phone and a small external battery pack during the day.

*Left, top to bottom: 1. Customised wall storage helps maintain order; 2. Creating a usable kitchen was a high priority and resulted in this two-burner and sink prep area; 3. The Econoline hauls Ian's motorcycle on its tailgate; Right, top to bottom: 1. Dino the Dog always rides along; 2. Lights are powered by the starter batteries; Next page: Dino the Dog ranges in view of the rooftop umbrella and tent*

# Q&A

**Has the van worked out as expected?**

I knew the ambulance would make a great home but once I started thinking about travelling in it I had some worries about weight. I was also worried people might actually think I'm a real ambulance. I would feel horrible if someone approached me for help and found me instead.

I worked hard to build this rig tough and to craft it beautifully so that it would give me a sense of home no matter where I am. It's proven to be very capable of hauling my toys and myself on any adventure and down any road, while truly feeling like my home.

**What is it about vanlife that has most surprised you?**

The interest in this type of lifestyle from the masses. When I bought my van I did so primarily because I needed an affordable place to live. I certainly wasn't aware that it was in any way fashionable.

I guess a lot of people have found themselves with similar needs, because the community is huge, and has some serious characters! Platforms like Instagram have made it much easier to come together and share tips and ideas, and most people seem happy to help.

**With hindsight, is there anything you'd have done differently?**

I would have loved to add solar as part of the original build, but I just didn't have the money. With solar power I would have installed a permanent fridge rather than have my freezer-cooler between the front seats. I would also have put my water tanks underneath the rig instead of on top, freeing up more roof space and lowering my height and centre of gravity. A water filtration system would also mean that I could drink tap water without worry. Oh, and I'd probably have brought a smaller motorcycle with me!

**Do you have further plans for the van?**

I have huge plans full stop! Next year I intend to give the ambulance away in a raffle to raise money alongside a crowd-funding campaign for my 'hostelbus' project. The idea is to convert a large bus and drive it through the Pacific Northwest of America filled with a bunch of fellow travellers. It will essentially be a hostel on wheels for 20 people to live and travel together in a very economic way.

I've enjoyed this lifestyle so much that I want to share it with as many people as possible, and this is the best idea I've come up with to do just that while keeping Dino and myself on the road as well.

**What are your top three tips for vanlife?**

**1.** Have a travel companion. I have my pup Dino who keeps me busy and smiling all day every day, but a significant other or good friend is also a great way to share the experience.

**2.** It's important to understand what you're getting into. Vans are small and can be very hot or very cold. They get dirty and need maintenance. Not everywhere is free or easy to park in and sleep, and sometimes it just plain seems like nobody wants you around. You may have neighbours but typically only for a few days, and then you or they will move, so lasting friendships are hard to find.

**3.** Last but not least, I think building a small home that happens to be on wheels should be the goal, not building a van that you can live in. This way you will build a comfortable van and be at home whenever you're parked.

When I'm driving my home on wheels down a bumpy road or beautiful highway I know that wherever I end up, I'll be home. And that keeps me smiling from ear to ear.

# Chevy Express 3500

**Filmmaker Zach Both chose his van via a gut feeling rather than a spec list. Starting out with a basic cargo van, he has created a conversion that wouldn't look out of place in a boutique hotel brochure, belying the vehicle's less than glamorous past life.**

Born into a small hippie enclave in remote Minnesota, filmmaker Zach Both grew up surrounded by the free-spirited nature that goes hand in hand with vanlife.

However, it wasn't until later in life, while working at a children's publishing company, that Zach considered the idea of living in something typically reserved for transportation. And so, unable to splash out on the latest all-singing, all-dancing Sprinter, he began weeks of trawling Craigslist for something inspiring and affordable.

## Type of van

In vanlife, as elsewhere, people often have a tribal leaning towards particular brands. Volkswagen is the marquee example, with decades of evocative stories and imagery weaving a highly desirable narrative around the lifestyle. That wasn't a factor for Zach.

'Unlike many others I've met, I don't carry an allegiance to any particular car brand,' he says. 'I can't even tell you why I chose a Chevrolet Express van over the Ford Econoline, for example. Frankly, if I had the cash at the time, I probably would've bought a high-top Sprinter or Transit. I base most of my decisions in life on a gut feeling.' That gut feeling hit home when Zach first laid eyes on his 2003 Chevy Express.

The Chevrolet Express originally launched in 1995, and along with its mechanically identical twin sister, the GMC Savana, it makes up nearly half of the full-sized van market in the US. This means that there are plenty of them available for conversion.

Sitting in the same basic category as Ford's market-leading Econoline, both models offer similar capabilities for someone seeking a basic camper conversion. It's not until you drill down into the finer details that small differences become important. For example, the Ford has better aftermarket support, more powerful engines and a more rugged chassis.

For Zach, the distinguishing quality of his Chevy Express was the three gull-wing windows that encased the cargo space on the 2003 model he found online, and within an hour of spotting the post on Craigslist he was shaking hands with the seller. 'What I imagined as an opportunity to enjoy the surroundings from within the vehicle, I quickly learnt was more useful in airing out the nefarious stenches that were clinging to the interior,' he says.

The online listing did not understate the condition of the van, with its mouse droppings, missing seatbelts and leaking fluids aplenty. 'Despite the small obstacles this van presented, I knew immediately that the vehicle had potential to be a blank canvas for any ideas that could fit within its 50 square ft confines,' says Zach. 'It would just require lots of blood, sweat and tears.'

**Vehicle model:** 2003 Chevy Express 3500
**Seats:** 2
**Sleeps:** 2
**Engine/mpg:** 5.3L v8/12mpg
**Cost of van:** $4500
**Cost of conversion:** $12,000
**Longest trip:** Boston to Los Angeles
**Favourite trip:** Baja California Peninsula
**Dream trip:** Fairy Meadows Road, Pakistan
**Instagram:** @zachboth
**Website:** thevanual.com

*Left: Three gull-wing windows add extra access to the outdoors as well as providing welcome ventilation*

# How he did it...

## The conversion

'The most important consideration I had when buying a van was that it had to have four wheels,' jokes Zach. 'Vans are notoriously difficult to drive with three wheels and even more so with two or one.'

With this in mind, Zach's requirements were:

● A steering wheel. 'Despite an early idea of only driving in straight lines, I ultimately decided to buy a van with a steering wheel for use in extreme cases or an emergency.'

● A working engine. 'This was an important factor in distinguishing my van from the less efficient Little Tikes push cars I drove as a much younger man.'

● Brakes. 'Not the most essential, but certainly helpful.'

● An AM radio. 'This one should be self-explanatory.'

## The ceiling

For many owners, a van is an expression of individuality. And whereas some are happy just to spec a standard conversion at their nearest garage, Zach wanted more than merely functional. 'I had some very specific plans from day one,' he says. 'And one design decision that I thought would differentiate this conversion was a simple wood-patterned ceiling.'

Zach's plan was to attach reclaimed plaster lath to the ceiling, running parallel to the length of the van, thus creating the illusion of the space feeling bigger and longer. The plaster lath came from a 19th-century Cleveland church, which was being renovated by a new owner. The wood was sanded, stained and methodically affixed to the van interior.

'Its inclusion is the one element people seem to be immediately drawn to when seeing the van for the first time,' says Zach. 'And it's always great to be able to repurpose materials.'

## Solar power and lighting

Due to advances in solar technology, this is an increasingly desirable option for even relatively straightforward van conversions, especially for those living in sunnier climes.

The roof of Zach's Chevy features two 90w solar panels secured to an aluminium rack repurposed from a Hummer truck. The power from the solar panels is fed to a solar generator, which in turn powers almost every electronic device inside the van – from the fan and refrigerator to the lights and laptop charger. The lights in the van are simple LED strips connected to a dimmer, neatly hidden from view.

Overcast conditions do obviously present problems with a solar setup, since less sun means less power. 'When that time comes it's important to have one's priorities straight,' says Zach. 'Do I want to keep my deli meat from spoiling or would I rather glue my eyeballs to my laptop screen for several hours? I usually find myself eating trail mix for dinner.'

© Courtesy of Zach Both

## Living space

The entire living space was designed and custom built with precise dimensions and uses in mind. 'I found the key to using limited space efficiently was to have multiple uses for everything,' says Zach.

The bed converts to a futon (which can be opened in either direction) and beneath it is enough storage space to house clothes, tools and a small library of books and magazines.

The kitchen area is dominated by a large countertop that can be used both for food prep and as a workspace. Hidden beneath the counter lies a two-burner alcohol stove more commonly found on boats (see page 13 for more details about stoves and cooking options).

Within the kitchen cabinet are a 5-gallon water jug, a small pantry for dry foods, storage space for cooking utensils and a 50-quart refrigerator. Everything has been built to fit each particular object perfectly.

## Windows

The gull-wing windows on Zach's van are a rare factory option and they heavily influenced his original purchase decision. 'The pop-up windows are my favourite quality of this van,' he says. 'While they're normally intended as a method for contractors to grab tools from the van without climbing inside, my use is quite different. The panels are opaque, so when closed I retain a sense of privacy. But when they are open, I'm able to feel the fresh air and enjoy a panoramic view of wherever I'm parked.'

On the interior, the window panels have been covered with riveted aluminium and then

spray-painted with chalkboard paint, perfect for scribbling everything from shopping lists and Instagram-friendly motivational quotes to more serious work-related notes.

An additional benefit is that when the panels are fully closed the van simply reverts to appearing to be just a standard work van, facilitating more stealthy parking options.

## Home cinema

As a filmmaker and movie buff, it was important for Zach to find a way to incorporate his work and passion into the design of the van.

Whereas many vans would feature a solid bulkhead, a white light-blocking curtain instead divides the living and driving spaces. After some intense research, Zach found the perfect projector with a compact form factor that could be adhered to the ceiling of the van and projected onto the curtain. 'With the couch up, the windows open and a bowl of popcorn in hand, I have the perfect mobile movie watching setup,' he says. 'There's something surreal and epic experiencing a great piece of cinema surrounded by the best that nature has to offer.'

When not in use, the projector and wireless speakers can be easily stowed away, with films stored and played digitally to save space.

---

*Previous page: The van's rooftop aluminum rack secures solar panels; Left, top to bottom: 1. The gull-wing window view; 2. A plaster lathe ceiling creates a sense of space; Right, top to bottom: 1. The kitchen counter hides a two-burner alcohol stove; 2. A projector mount hides on the ceiling*

---

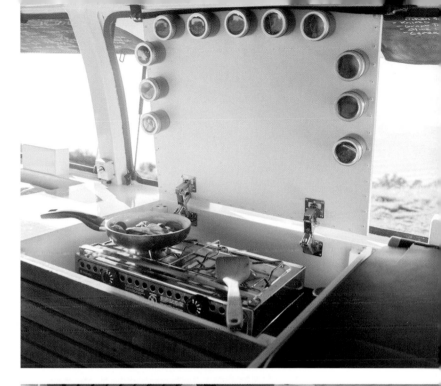

© Courtesy of Zach Both

# Q&A

**Has the van worked out as expected?**
I set out with a very specific idea of what I wanted this van to be and I think the final product has exceeded that. It looks good, functions well and has taken me to places I probably would have never seen otherwise. I'm convinced a converted van is the best way to travel and I see myself embracing vanlife forever.

**With hindsight, is there anything you'd have done differently?**
I would have liked to buy a van I could comfortably stand up in, such as a Sprinter or Transit. With that being said, there are also some advantages of a lower roof and there's always the option of a further roof conversion later.

**What is it about vanlife that has most surprised you?**
The days when things go really wrong – getting stuck in the Mexican desert, breaking down in a snowstorm, hitchhiking for gas, driving sketchy cliff roads – those are the days I remember the most fondly. Those are the days that build character and make for the best stories.

**Do you have further plans for the van?**
When the van finally calls it quits after a fruitful life on the road, I'm going to convert it into a chicken coop and it will spend the rest of its days sheltering free range, egg-laying hens.

**What are your three top tips for vanlife?**
**1.** Before embarking on the vanlife journey, rent a van or car and go on a decent-sized road trip – a minimum of one week. You'll quickly find out whether vanlife is for you.
**2.** Shoot for buying a van that has low mileage and no rust. Whatever extra money you spend on a newer van initially, you will most likely save on less frequent or significant repairs.
**3.** Convert an empty, opaque laundry detergent bottle into a pee bottle. Empty and wash it frequently, for the love of all things holy...

*Right: Zach and his Chevy Express camp out under the stars*

# International 3800 school bus

**Adventure-seeking couple Ben and Mande Tucker wanted to break from routine and embrace the freedom and spontaneity of their youth. They managed to do so in more ways than one, converting a retired school bus into a beautiful and practical home on wheels.**

Michigan natives Ben and Mande Tucker both grew up in adventurous, outdoor-loving families, with countless road trips and camping excursions during their formative years.

After completing college, Mande moved to Utah to teach and Ben dived headfirst into vanlife, renovating an old school bus with friends for a project they dubbed 'The LOST Bus' (LOST is an acronym for Lending Our Services Traveling) and volunteering across the country.

In 2011, Ben and Mande were introduced by mutual friends and immediately bonded over a love of travel, adventure, and the humble bus.

## Type of Van

Fern the Bus is a converted 1992 International 3800 ex-school bus with a reliable but thirsty 7.3L IDI engine.

Though a bus-sized conversion is arguably pushing the concept of vanlife to the limit, the underlying ideas and ideals are the same, just grown to supersized proportions. Buses are typically extremely robust and reliable, readily available in assorted shapes and sizes, and surprisingly affordable, but best of all they offer an even broader blank canvas upon which to work. After several years browsing the retired school bus market, Ben and Mande eventually struck gold.

'When we saw Fern listed for sale, we knew she would be the perfect blank slate to build our dream rig. In a 25-year career, she'd only operated during the summer months and never endured the brutally corrosive effects of salty winter roads, so although her paint was faded and peeling, she was nearly rust-free.'

At 24ft, Fern is big enough to comfortably live in while remaining compact and manoeuvrable, and the relatively rare manual transmission also gives more control in mountainous terrain. 'After a little negotiating we drove her home, excited to give the old girl new life!'

With a school bus, there's no option other than a fully custom build, and so the process began, with the vehicle stripped back to its bare shell. Given Ben's previous experience converting a bus, the couple knew the project would be time consuming and labour-intensive, but even with this prior knowledge they still underestimated the effort required to build Fern.

'Now, when talking about time, we differentiate between "bus time" and "real time". "Bus time" typically turns out to be roughly three times longer than "real time", so when planning for each part of the project, we'd guess how much time it would require and then multiply it by three.'

Unfortunately for Ben and Mande, this formula proved to be extremely reliable.

**Vehicle model:** 1992 International 3800 school bus
**Seats:** 7
**Sleeps:** 3
**Engine/mpg:** International 7.3L IDI/10 mpg
**Cost of van:** $5000
**Cost of conversion:** $10,000
**Longest trip:** Banff, Alberta to Holland, Michigan
**Favourite trip:** Canadian Rockies: Waterton Lakes-Banff-Jasper
**Dream trip:** Alaska to the Baja Peninsula
**Instagram:** @fernthebus

*Left: The ample dimensions of Fern the Bus mean there's plenty of room for gear; Next page: Rear bike storage lets the Tuckers enjoy exploring by pedal power*

# How they did it...

## The conversion

Ben and Mande's aim was to have adequate space for day-to-day living during a long trip, but without losing manoeuvrability on tighter roads and passes.

Goals for Fern's build included:

● Enough space to live in for long periods of time without feeling uncomfortable

● A vehicle that could fit into a normal parking space and easily navigate city streets

● Something they could build themselves

● A reliable engine and drivetrain, and minimal rust

● An affordable purchase price so money could be focused on the conversion work

## Rooftop deck

The space advantages of a bus aren't limited only to the interior. To maximise Fern's usable space, Ben and Mande built a rooftop deck to function as a hangout space, accessible via a ladder mounted to the rear door. To make the space more comfortable, the couple designed a system for attaching a series of supports to allow them to hang a pair of hammocks – the perfect spot to read a book, take a nap or simply enjoy an elevated view of the surroundings.

Built from cedar to reduce weight (the roof is the worst location for adding weight due to an increased centre of gravity) the

platform includes a roof rack for storing and transporting larger equipment such as their paddleboards. Rainwater and debris are able to flow freely from beneath the floating deck thanks to it being mounted on 4x4in posts.

## Comfort and convenience

One of the key criteria on the wishlist for Ben and Mande's conversion was to create something that felt like home wherever they were parked, and this started with the bed. 'We decided against a folding or stowable option, instead dedicating the entire back of the bus to a permanent bed and blowing the budget on a good mattress.'

With a likelihood of extreme temperatures on their trip, a roof fan was installed. Combined with several drop-down windows and screens, the fan pulls enough air through the bus to keep things cool, while using a fraction of the electricity of a more industrial solution like air conditioning.

A unique advantage of a bus is the sheer number of windows it possesses, allowing for an unrivalled panoramic view of the surroundings. However it also means extra work when it comes to privacy and light reduction at night. To this end the couple have installed copper curtain rods, and hand-sewn curtains with magnets in the seams, making for an extremely quick and straightforward transition from day to night.

## Storage

For many people, vanlife is about simplifying and de-cluttering, but even the most free-spirited traveller needs a certain amount of essentials for daily living. Add in the kit required for sports and hobbies and space can quickly become a challenge. 'It was important to find a good balance of simplifying our lives while still having the stuff we wanted to fully experience the places we'd go.'

Bikes are among the most space-consuming items to carry, but thanks to the dimensions of Fern the couple found a way to hang them vertically using front fork-mounts. The front wheels are stowed in custom mounts beneath the bus, alongside the water tanks.

The 'garage' of the bus, which is accessible from both inside and outside, contains dozens of deliberately organised, labelled totes, with a bungee-cord ceiling holding items including life jackets, camp chairs, waders and paddles. Even the oven is used for storing items when not in use.

## Kitchen

With plans to remain on the road for as long as possible, Ben and Mande also planned to cook on board the bus as often as possible to save money. As such, the kitchen is particularly well supplied, starting with a solid butchers block countertop with an under-mounted sink and a faucet supplied by 25 gallons of on-demand freshwater. Overhead, the couple built pantry space for food and dishes, while beneath the counter are three large drawers and a double-door cabinet. The main feature of the kitchen is an old propane stove/oven combo salvaged from a 1950s travel trailer, and a Yeti cooler keeps everything cold.

Like most vanlifers, Ben and Mande also love cooking outdoors, and so they keep a portable grill in the garage. Hot-dog forks and cast-iron cookers are always on hand for when the campfire is burning.

## Outdoor shower

Experience quickly teaches most vanlife fans about the transformative powers of a hot shower. 'On extended trips, if too much time passed between showers, we noticed that we became increasingly irritable. At times, our wellbeing seemed to directly correlate with the frequency of our showers. We love to bathe in lakes and streams, but sometimes the water is frigid or we just don't have ready access. We knew that a shower would be an important part of the bus.'

Not wishing to give up living space inside the bus, Ben and Mande chose to rig an outdoor shower comprising a tank-less portable water heater, propane tank, freshwater pump and a 25-gallon freshwater storage tank mounted under the floor. A custom curtain rod attaches to the open back door of the bus, creating a cosy enclosed space while allowing the sensation of showering in the elements.

*Left, top to bottom: 1. Conversion required gutting Fern's interior; 2. A custom sink and countertop give space for cooking; Right, top to bottom: 1. The outdoor shower runs on the 25-gallon storage tank; 2. Many windows mean great views*

# Q&A

**Has the van worked out as you expected?**
The bus has worked better than we ever dreamed. Since completing the build, Fern has carried us over 10,000 miles, and everything is holding up great despite all the potholes and bumps in the road. Her engine hasn't required any extra attention outside of routine and preventative maintenance, which validates our decision to wait until we found a good low-mileage example.

**With hindsight, is there anything you'd have done differently?**
We currently rely on shore power to charge our house batteries, and so we plan to install solar panels to keep us off-grid for longer durations.

**What is it about vanlife that has most surprised you?**
We're endlessly surprised by the kindness and hospitality of strangers. Getting on the road and meeting people has shattered stereotypes and refreshed our optimism. Society can feel divided and angry if you're viewing it through a screen, but face to face with real people, all we find is kindness and smiles.

**What further plans do you have for the van?**
Creating the bus was such a gratifying experience, but we can't help but miss that process of creating. The feedback we receive about Fern is always so positive, so we have decided to keep at it. We'll continue adventuring in Fern, while also building more buses for other people.

**What are your three top tips for vanlife?**
**1.** Never pass up the opportunity to meet a stranger. We love this lifestyle because we get to meet so many amazing people we wouldn't otherwise cross paths with.
**2.** Travel with friends. Experiencing the road with like-minded folks makes for the best kind of adventures.
**3.** Slow down. When we first hit the road, we thought we should see everything as quickly as possible. After a couple of months of keeping up that pace we were exhausted. Now we take it slow, even if that means missing out on other things.

*Left: A rooftop deck allows for lounging in a hammock up top*

# Mercedes Sprinter

**Tired of the corporate life and with a shared passion for the great outdoors, Ohio natives Emilie Johnson and Joe Neiheisel took the bold decision to leave their jobs, sell their house and live in a van for two years, exploring the western United States in pursuit of adventure.**

Vanlife is about the outdoors, and while hardcore wild campers may snipe at the relative comforts of a vehicle, if you are interested in adventure sports, you may need something to transport you and your kit.

Before buying their van, marketeer Emilie Johnson and corporate finance executive Joe Neiheisel tent camped 100 nights a year to accommodate their love for riding, skiing, climbing, and kayaking. After falling for a converted Sportsmobile on a trip in 2012, they began planning their own vanlife journey – one that rapidly escalated into a multi-year voyage.

## Type of van

The choice of vans for conversion can be bewildering – especially in North America – but there is one model that is becoming ubiquitous among the current generation of outdoor sports enthusiasts: the Mercedes Sprinter.

The first Mercedes van to launch with a name instead of a number, the Sprinter debuted in 1995 with the most powerful diesel engine in its class, and won plaudits as the International Van of the Year. Its North American lineage was more complex, with variants available from 2001 under both Dodge and Freightliner brands.

The second generation Sprinter broke cover in a more conventional fashion in 2006 and continued selling with revisions and facelifts through to 2018, with over 3 million vans now on the road in more than 130 countries. Such is its popularity that many colloquially refer to the 3.5-tonne van category simply as 'sprinters'.

When searching for their base vehicle, Emilie and Joe knew that they wanted a cargo van with as few bells and whistles as possible, since they planned a complete bespoke conversion.

'After careful research and determining what was most important to us, we chose the MB 144 Sprinter hi-roof for its legendary 500,000 mile diesel engine, fantastic fuel economy, the ability to stand up inside, its ability to fit in a standard parking spot, and the clearance to navigate almost any dirt road. We were going to put a lot of time, energy and money into the project, so we wanted the best engine we could get.'

After two different Sprinters slipped through their fingers, Joe took a risk and drove a 12-hour round trip to buy the current van, sight unseen. 'On the drive home, I have to admit that buyer's remorse sank in,' he says. 'The empty cargo space whistled and echoed every bit of road noise, and the hot sun beating through the huge windshield and side windows was relentless.'

Needless to say, once the conversion work began in earnest, that remorse soon turned into excitement and joy.

**Vehicle model:** 2014 Mercedes Benz Sprinter 144in high roof cargo van
**Seats:** 2 plus our dog Uschi's perch
**Sleeps:** 2 plus floor space
**Engine/mpg:** 2500 4-cylinder diesel/23-28 mpg
**Cost of van:** $35,000
**Cost of conversion:** $20,000
**Longest trip:** 48,000 miles since Dec 2016
**Favourite trip:** Western United States
**Dream trip:** Pan-American trip
**Instagram:** @permanentroadtrip

*Left: The Mercedes Sprinter is a vanlife classic for its high ceiling and extensive garage for storage; Next page: The double slider doors significantly add to the living space*

# How they did it...

## The conversion

Outdoor activity fans Emilie and Joe wanted to build a van that would handle extreme conditions and transport them – and their equipment – down the bumpiest of roads. This meant:

● Having everything stored inside the van, including sporting equipment, water, propane, tools and batteries
● Rock-solid insulation and ventilation to handle temperature extremes
● All-terrain tyres
● The ability to stand upright in the van
● A fully equipped kitchen with running water, 12v appliances and solar power

## Aesthetics and functionality

With so much functionality required from such a small (and mobile) space, aesthetics are often at best a secondary consideration with vans. Sometimes, however, form can follow function. 'When we began the conversion, we weren't designing it for showroom appeal. However, our friends who did most of the build are master carpenters, and so they immediately raised the bar.'

The cabinetry throughout Emilie and Joe's Sprinter was custom built, featuring a combination of dark and light wood accents. But functionality and simplicity was always kept front-of-mind. 'We have open cabinets for food and storage of lightweight items such as window shades and coats, tall wardrobes for clothing, a medicine cabinet and kitchen cabinets with doors that latch with magnets.'

Wanting to add an artistic touch, the couple commissioned a local artisan to create a laser-cut mountain scene on the four wardrobe cabinet doors that occupy one entire wall. 'Our van has appeared in numerous online publications and even won second place in the Mercedes Benz "My Van" contest as a result!'

## Double slider door

The double slider door was a rare and lucky find. 'It is one of, if not the standout features of the van, and it was a game changer for us.'

Not only did the door allow Emilie and Joe to incorporate built-in shoe cubbies (enough for 12 pairs, accessible from the outside) and provide a second access point to the kitchen cabinets, but it also offers spectacularly framed views of the surroundings. 'We often joke that if we run out of money we should sell coffee or tacos from the window.'

The double slider also provides the perfect dust-free location for the main power shut-off and additional venting for the fridge, as well as supplying natural privacy and extra insulation when required.

'More often than not, when we are parked somewhere with the double slider doors open, people are innately drawn to the van and ask if they can take a look around.'

© Courtesy of Emilie Johnson and Joe Neiheisel

## Living space

The best van conversions will allow the user to open up the interior of the van as much as possible and with as little effort as possible when parked, and Emilie and Joe have made a number of changes to enable this. 'The van came with a bulkhead and bench seat, which we removed and replaced with a Sprint Ride passenger seat, adding swivels for both front seats at the same time. Since we travel with our dog we also built a multifunctional rectangular perch, which fits snugly between the seats with her dog bed on top while also storing items like our double-burner propane cooker.'

The van is able to host up to six people comfortably for a visit or a meal, and the addition of ceramic tint on the three front windows plus a ceiling fan helps to moderate internal temperatures and glare when parked.

## Garage

Unsurprisingly for a vehicle custom-designed by two outdoor sport enthusiasts, the garage is the beating heart of the van, with everything neatly tucked away in its own space. 'Because every inch counts, we knew for ease of access that having two LED-lit 500-pound slide-out drawers was essential.'

Since their main pursuits including skiing and mountain biking, Emilie and Joe have designed one drawer to hold all of their bike gear, and a second wider drawer for large duffels containing ski gear as well as one for backcountry camping. There is also a space for dirty laundry, camp chairs and yoga mats.

With three cubbies extending the full depth of

the garage, it's also home to a 25 gallon water tank, three pairs of skis, skins and poles, an extra foldout table and shade tent, a longboard, straps, tools and other essentials such as the extension for the clever rear door bike stand.

## Cooking and cleaning

Conscious of the varied weather conditions on their journey, Emilie and Joe have created two kitchen areas – one inside and one outside. 'During inclement weather, we set up our propane stove inside. However, as often as possible, we flip down our built-in table mounted to the rear of our sink cabinet and cook outside. We installed an amber light bar for cooking at night to mitigate bugs, and cut a hole through the back of the sink cabinet for easy access to our propane. This comes in handy not only for cooking, but also to fuel our on-demand heated outdoor shower. Throw down our teak shower step, and presto, we're in business. '

Counters are made from food-safe butchers block, and a 4.5 cubic foot, 12V marine fridge provides ample room for fresh food.

'With 25 gallons of filtered water, we have enough to last up to 10 days in the warmer months and three weeks in the winter, meaning we can stay off-grid as much as possible.'

*Left, top to bottom: 1. The build includes a wide butcher block; 2. Modifications allow for cooking outdoors; 3. Off the road; Right, top to bottom: 1. The garage allows for extra storage; 2. The dog bed platform also doubles as storage; Next page: The water tank is crucial for desert trips*

# Q&A

**Has the van worked out as you expected?**

Our van has honestly exceeded our expectations, mainly because we designed and purchased every single part and component and were intimately involved in the conversion process from start to finish.

**With hindsight, is there anything you'd have done differently?**

Being able to sit up straight in bed was important to us since it accounts for half of the living space, but we could have achieved this with the bed platform set at 33 or 34in from the floor instead of 31in. We also would have created better airflow from the main living space into the gear garage to mitigate condensation in cold weather, although we have since found a work-around for this.

We would also have positioned the main outlet in the living space in a more convenient spot, and would eliminate the two-burner induction cooktop and convection oven, which performs best with AC power. Before we set out, we assumed we would plug in on average once a week, but out of 450 days on the road we have plugged in less than a dozen times.

**What has most surprised you most about vanlife?**

The generosity and curiosity of people never cease to amaze us. On more than 20 occasions, we've met perfect strangers at trailheads who, within a 15-minute conversation and a tour of our van, have invited us back to their homes for a meal, showers, access to laundry, and a driveway to park our van overnight. Many of these people will likely be lifelong friends, and in some cases we've already met up with them multiple times for fun and adventures on the road.

**Do you have further plans for the van?**

Our primary plan is simply to keep the van on the open road with us in it for as long as possible. While we have explored a lot already, our list of places to visit and those to return to is growing every day.

**What are your three top tips for vanlife?**

**1.** Design your van based on how you intend to use it. Living in your van full time versus being a weekend warrior will determine how extensive your build is.
**2.** If the idea of vanlife is appealing to you, why not get started today? Get a plan together and work towards it one step at a time.
**3.** Generate goodwill, be respectful of the Earth and other people, and mindful that your actions are a reflection not only on you but also on the vanlife movement.

# Toyota Land Cruiser

**Australian couple Mark and Jolie gave up their jobs in building design and construction to follow their dream of circumnavigating the globe in a modified Toyota Land Cruiser.**

Like many vanlife enthusiasts, construction manager Mark Firkin came to love vehicle-based travel at a young age, journeying around Australia for a year with his family as a child. In 2011 he and six friends drove from New York to Panama, buying vans for around AUD$1000 each and spending two weeks fitting them out in a Home Depot car park.

Fast forward to 2016 and Mark and his building designer partner Jolie King decided to change their life direction completely, leaving their home in Perth, Australia to take an epic road trip from Asia to London, passing through Indonesia, Malaysia, Thailand, Cambodia, Laos, Myanmar, India, Nepal, China, Pakistan, Tajikistan, Kyrgyzstan, Uzbekistan, Turkmenistan, Iran and Turkey, before finally crossing Europe.

## Type of van

The Toyota Land Cruiser has been on sale in relatively unchanged form since 1984, with 4WD and a rugged, no-nonsense off-road focus putting it in a similar category to the Land Rover Defender. Like the Defender, the van is slow, noisy and uncomfortable, but it also shares its sheer resilience and go-anywhere attitude, making it perfect for people intending to spend a lot of time off the beaten track.

'The goal was simple: to build a vehicle that would be comfortable to live in while camping in the most remote places, and with the ability to get us there, and back, confidently,' says Mark. Australia is the leading market for the Toyota Land Cruiser, meaning there was plenty of choice when finding a base vehicle.

With several different cab options available, the Troop Carrier or 'Troopy' is the pick of the bunch for a camper conversion, with a sizeable rear cab and no side passenger doors, meaning maximum space for seating, storage and fitted units.

It's also an ideal platform for a roof conversion – something that was essential for Mark and Jolie. 'One of the vans we drove across the Americas had a hi-top, which showed how beneficial it is being able to stand fully upright when inside. Coupled with 4WD capabilities due to the terrain we'd be crossing, this narrowed the vehicle search options considerably.'

Mark and Jolie aimed to complete the fit-out themselves, partly to ensure they knew how everything went together – essential if you plan to head into wilder locations where you might need to manage running repairs yourself. But with Mark still in near full-time employment, the process wasn't totally painless. 'I was away for three weeks out of four,' he says. 'So we spent a lot of time on Skype and sending plans back and forth to each other, which at one point led to us having an unexpected internal shower!'

**Vehicle model:** Toyota Land Cruiser troop carrier
**Model year:** 2006
**Seats:** 2
**Sleeps:** 3
**Engine/mpg:** 4.2L Straight 6 Cylinder Turbo Diesel/19mpg
**Cost of van:** AUD$31,000
**Cost of conversion:** AUD$18,000
**Longest trip:** Perth to Indonesia via West Coast, Central + Northern Australia and Timor Leste – currently seven months and approx 30,000km
**Favourite trip:** The current one – Perth to London
**Dream trip:** A continuation of our current route, which would either include shipping the van from London to North Africa to complete the West Coast to Cape Town route, or from London to eastern Canada to complete the Americas

# How they did it...

## The conversion

With a huge distance to cover across some of the most rugged terrain in the world, it was clear that something beyond the standard camper van would be required for Mark and Jolie's journey.

The key items on their hit list included:

● Ability to have a roof conversion
● Serious off-road capability
● Long-range fuel tanks
● Good parts availability
● Strong, reliable engine and drivetrain

## The roof

Apart from the vehicle itself, a roof conversion is typically the next biggest investment, and not an area in which to cut corners.

The conversion Mark installed is a full-length aluminium kit, which includes heavy-duty canvas walls, three windows (one of which features a small awning), insulation and a bed, which folds neatly into the roof on gas struts — something Mark was especially keen on. 'The ability to simply lift a completely made bed when not in use to create a standing area in its place is easily one of the best things about the vehicle,' he says.

The roof also has the ability to fit a roof rack to hold surfboards, a solar panel, dive equipment and winter gear, with the whole roof assembly opening and closing in under a minute. This means it can be used as easily for short stops en-route to a destination as it can for longer stays.

## The awning

Having some form of external shade was compulsory for Mark and Jolie when planning their build. With such a wide variety of terrain on their planned route, the ability to escape the elements without being forced to retreat inside was extremely important, be it the monsoon rains of Southeast Asia or the beating desert sun. 'We needed something that was going to last the entire journey, be sturdy and durable, and preferably easy to erect,' says Mark.

The awning covers the side and rear of the vehicle in one structure, and — with the added benefit of not requiring supporting poles — takes one person around 30 seconds to put up or down.

Clever use of light bars fixed above the drop-down table and under the awning ensures that they can make use of the external space at all times of the day and night.

## Living space

Several factors formed the basis of the internal design concept in order to make the space more practical and usable for the trip. These included the ability to sit at a table and face each other; a second bed in the lower area for emergency use; and the ability to cook/clean/wash when needed.

As with most campervan conversions, the best designs incorporate several functions in one, and Mark and Jolie's interior is no exception. The bench seat can be transformed

© Courtesy of Mark Firkin and Jolie King

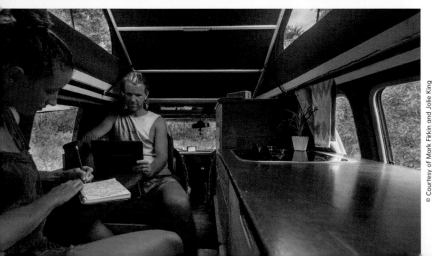

into a seat and table for four, or extended laterally to make a second bed.

The fridge is also built directly into the kitchenette, resulting in a longer bench space. Coupled with the full head height and integrated sink, this makes for a highly functional cooking area, and the waterproof vinyl floorboards make cleaning spills and muddy footprints extremely easy.

## Cooking and cleaning

For day vans and shorter trips, cooking arrangements can be fairly flexible. But for longer journeys where cooking is an essential act, something more integrated and considered is desirable.

The full-length kitchenette in Mark and Jolie's van stores all the necessary cooking and cleaning equipment and food supplies, and meals are cooked on a twin petrol-powered cooker, with the majority of meals prepared externally on the fold-down table hinged inside the rear door. 'We chose petrol as the fuel source because of its universal availability.'

Food is stored in an 80L fridge/freezer plus a small pantry cabinet for dry-stored goods, and the kitchenette also features a stainless-steel sink, electric pump and inline water filter fed from a stainless 60L tank housed on the underside of the vehicle. Like fuel, water is not something you want to run short on in the middle of nowhere.

'We use a solar shower for all cleaning and washing duties, which is an easy way to manage water usage, and is simple but effective,' says Mark.

## Electrical

As someone used to constructing homes, 12v power was one aspect of the van that Mark needed to understand in order to carry out repairs on the road. All rear cab appliances run through a fuse board installed behind the driver's seat, with only the laptops requiring the use of a 400w inverter. Real-time battery information is shown on a dashboard display, minimising the risk of a flat battery.

'We installed a removable 180w solar panel to the roof, meaning the vehicle can be in the shade while the panel sits in the sun,' he says.

Lighting is also important when you're in the wilderness, and the roof conversion includes three two-tone LED lights – two in the rear space and one in the overhead console. There are also two flexible LED reading lights in the bed space itself, and USB and cigarette lighter sockets have been installed above the pantry for charging.

*Left, top to bottom: 1. Before the build; 2. Constructing a custom solution; 3. The full length kitchenette; Right, top to bottom: 1. The awning provides crucial shade; 2. Food prep outdoors helps reduce built-up heat; 3. The rooftop conversion in action*

# Q&A

**Has the van worked out as you expected?**
Definitely. We've pushed the vehicle into some very remote locations over thousands of kilometres of difficult terrain, and so far we've always arrived at our destination and felt comfortable once we got there. Upgrading the wheels and suspension has proven to be one of our better choices.

**With hindsight, is there anything you'd have done differently?**
A larger water tank would probably be beneficial. We currently carry around 80L, and while it sounds like a lot, in hot or humid environments even this amount can be exhausted quickly.

Around 100L would be a good compromise between the amount of weight carried and the typical water requirements.

**What has most surprised you about vanlife?**
Just how many superfluous items we had gathered previously in our lives because we thought we needed them.

**What further plans do you have for the van?**
At this stage we are happy with the current arrangement, although on completion of the trip it will need a new paint job and we may splurge on some subtle engine mods.

**What would be your three top tips for vanlife?**
**1.** Respect your environment and leave no trace.
**2.** Don't rush your journey.
**3.** You don't need lots of money, equipment or a high-end van to enjoy the lifestyle.

*Right: The roof assembly can be opened or closed in under a minute*

# Volkswagen Transporter T4

Author, art curator and cycling fanatic Ed Bartlett had a wide range of requirements but only space for one vehicle. Taking the compact yet functional Swiss Army Knife as a template, he set out to create the ultimate 'do it all' van.

Growing up on the South West coast of England, where every other vehicle seemed to be a camper van or surf bus, it was perhaps only a matter of time before Ed Bartlett purchased one. In the end it was 40 years before 'Izzy' – a red Volkswagen Transporter T4 Multivan – joined the family. Sport and lifestyle played a large part in the decision. 'As a mountain biker living in London, it was essential to have transport to get you, your bike and your mates to the trails.' After leaving London, Ed decided to spend a year having adventures. 'It didn't take long for the vanlife bug to take hold', he says.

## Type of Van

Manufactured from 1990 to 2003, the Volkswagen T4 modernised the Transporter platform, moving the engine and drive to the front of the vehicle. With styling cues taken from the Mk2 Golf, the T4 offered a variety of wheelbases, body types and engines, including a sporty 2.8 VR6 petrol and a gutsy 2.5tdi turbo diesel with 88bhp and 102bhp variants. The mechanical aspects of the T4 were an improvement from the Type 25 that preceded it, and build quality, reliability, an award-winning cockpit design and almost car-like drivability are still close to modern standards, making regular use surprisingly easy and enjoyable.

After exploring various options – from a basic panel van through to full blown camper conversions – Ed was considering compromise before stumbling across the rare Multivan: 'For some reason – possibly the fact VW only built around 700 in right-hand drive configuration – my research didn't throw up the Multivan. Then one day I pulled into a petrol station behind one. Intrigued by the badging and rear-facing seats, I spoke to the owner, who kindly slid the side door open to let me have a look. Within seconds, I knew I'd found my vehicle!'

The Multivan - known as the Eurovan in the US domestic market – has a number of features that make it interesting both as a standalone 'day van' but also as a base for further conversion work. In default configuration it can seat seven, with useful touches like multiple 12v power sockets, folding coffee table, sliding side window and reading light in the rear cabin as standard. However, the magic is in the flexibility of the seating, with rear-facing buddy seats that fold up and clip out in seconds, as well as a full-width bench seat that converts into a double bed. 'There were a few things about the van I loved immediately. The first was the washable vinyl floor, because I'm always carting muddy bikes and gear around. The second was the ability to just park up and sit in the back with the coffee table out and a nice view within seconds.'

**Vehicle:** Volkswagen Transporter T4 Multivan (Eurovan)
**Seats:** 7
**Sleeps:** 4
**Engine/mpg:** 2.5tdi/ 34mpg
**Cost of van:** £8250
**Cost of conversion:** £6500
**Longest trip:** UK to Tuscany via the Cote D'Azur, returning via the Alps
**Favourite trip:** West Coast of Scotland
**Dream trip:** Via ferry to Iceland
**Instagram:** @edbartlett

*Clockwise from top left: 1. The pop-top roof was a conversion must; 2. View from the side-view mirror; 3. A retractable awning provides shade and extra living space*

# How he did it...

## The Conversion

Before buying the van, Ed set out to create the ultimate 'Swiss Army Knife' vehicle – a daily driver that could switch easily between 7-seat people carrier, load-lugging work van, bike shuttle, day van and yet still do a turn as a 'proper' campervan for longer trips abroad. This meant:

- No fixed internal camper conversion
- Maximising internal storage space and options
- Leveraging additional external space via fixed awning
- Modular solutions for camping and cooking essentials

## The Roof

The single biggest decision for most van owners is deciding whether or not to add a pop-top roof, which requires significant cutting and remodeling the structure of the vehicle.

'There are some who said it was sacrilege to modify such a limited run vehicle, and others who feel equally passionately that this is silly, pointing to VW's own official conversions. I didn't want to risk devaluing the vehicle, however the Austops roof looks factory-fit and even has a panoramic canvas option.'

Although the Multivan already features a folding bed, Ed's plan to regularly transport bikes inside the vehicle meant that the additional sleeping space became essential.

'Once I got used to the knack of using the roof, I found myself popping it up in all sorts of situations. Having the extra height to be able to stand fully upright is very useful when getting changed and anyone regularly using their van for sporting activities will see the benefits.'

As part of the roof conversion, Ed also had LED lights installed into the new interior roof lining, giving near-daylight conditions for very little power draw.

## The Awning

With interior space extended via a moveable roof, the other major consideration was how to harness the external space around the van.

'Most van owners seemed to be using separate awning structures next to their vehicles, but I knew that I wasn't likely to spend huge amounts of time in campsites – I like to wild camp where possible, and I rarely stay in one spot for long. I also really wanted to minimise the amount of objects I carried loose in the vehicle, or that I'd have to load for each trip.'

Ed decided to go with a retractable awning permanently fixed to the side of the vehicle.

'Above all, this van is about convenience. A Swiss Army Knife wouldn't be what it is if you kept all the different tools separately, and it was the same thinking with the awning.'

'Having the ability to pretty much double the vehicle footprint in less than a minute, in almost any location or situation is very useful, and I've had much more use than I first expected. I was initially slightly worried about the wind noise and fuel economy impact when driving, but both have proven to be a non-issue.'

© Courtesy of Ed Bartlett

## Living space

With numerous seating options possible from the Multivan, one of the first jobs was to experiment with different combinations. 'Flexible load space was essential, so my first change was to remove the rear-facing buddy seat on the passenger side and fit a swivel base to the passenger seat. This gives much easier access to the rear when using the sliding side door, but I still have a second rear-facing seat option when camping.' A storage sorter hanging over the back of the passenger seat keeps smaller items sorted and accessible.

Staying with the storage theme, the minimalist frame of the remaining buddy seat creates an ideal cubby space where it meets the drivers' seat, and this is used to store camping essentials including leveling blocks and a sleeping bag. The space beneath the rear bench seats holds a thin inflatable mattress as well as tea and coffee-making facilities, accessed via a front drawer.

## Cooking and cleaning

With no fixed internal solution for cooking or storage, dining demanded a creative approach. 'My goal was to be able to pack for any length of time away with a maximum of two trips in and out of my apartment, but still keep the van interior as uncluttered as possible at other times.'

With cooking duties shared between a collapsible barbecue, gas-powered portable stove and a Jet Boil water heater, Ed went with a two box system for the remainder – one for food supplies and one for cooking paraphernalia. 'The

supplies and one for cooking paraphernalia. 'The food box is far from a new idea – it's a mainstay of most camper vans. But it was especially important for me, and took a lot of refining.' Both dishes and personal hygiene are taken care of using a combination of a folding bowl and a flexible fabric water cylinder pressurised via an inbuilt hand pump, although a pop-up shower cubicle is another tool in the van's armory.

## Electrical

Although the T4 Multivan is well appointed as standard, there was one area that Ed knew he would need to improve. 'I'm fanatical about music so I blew the budget on a proper audio build, including DAB radio, hands-free calling and a decent dock connector to allow me to use the navigation app on my phone.'

While the interior was stripped, Ed added a marine-spec gel leisure battery and split-charge system, and wired the audio and 12v sockets to draw power from this to ensure no unexpected dead-start scenarios. Warmth is another important consideration when camping, but the previous owner had installed an Eberspacher heater complete with timer, rounding off the Swiss Army Knife functionality of the van.

---

*Previous page: A permanently affixed awning deploys in under a minute; Left, top to bottom: 1. The bed gets set up from a stored inflatable mattress; 2. The front passenger swivel seat; 3. The remaining buddy seat; Right, top to bottom: 1. Inside the pop-top roof; 2. Bike storage was a top priority; Next page: Ed Bartlett in his converted T4*

© Courtesy of Ed Bartlett

# Q&A

**Has the van worked out as expected?**
I can't honestly think of a single moment where it's not been able to handle something I have asked of it. I've used it as a 6-seater for a few daytrips with friends, wild camped my way around Scotland, used it as a van to move big pieces of art for work, and taken my motorbike, road bike and mountain bike to the Alps, all without missing a beat. I don't feel like there are many comfortable and practical daily drivers that could manage that.

**Is there anything you'd have done differently with hindsight?**
I would have held out longer for a base van with air conditioning, but they are pretty rare for the Multivan, which is already a very limited model in right-hand drive. I once sat in a three-hour traffic jam in the South of France in a pair of flip-flops and not much else!

I also wouldn't have gone with the side exit exhaust. The idea was to keep the fumes away from the rear tailgate and sliding door when camping, but it's rare that's ever an issue. What it does do is put the fumes nearer the driver's side window, which can obviously be less than ideal when sitting in traffic. It looks cool though, I guess.

**What about vanlife has most surprised you?**
The community. Regardless of the kind of van you drive, or how you use it, there's a huge network of people willing to share tips, locations and general advice.

**Do you have further plans for the van?**
More trips! I've had a busy last 12 months and so it hasn't been used as much as I would like, but I've been doing more regular weekend cycling trips just recently. I really want to get back to Scotland again this year and also to plan another big European road trip. My ultimate dream is to take it to Iceland and Norway. On the hardware side, everything is set up pretty much how I want it right now, although if I start doing longer trips I might consider a solar setup with a fridge, and maybe a custom pullout cooker build in the tailgate.

**What are your top 3 tips for vanlife?**
**1.** Merino: Staying on top of dirty clothing can be a pain. Merino helps to regulate your body temperature, and can sometimes go days without needing a wash. It also dries really quickly once you do.

**2.** Get organised: When you're away on a trip, you don't want to waste too much time searching for things or setting up. Plan your storage well from the start, and keep things in their place. You'll enjoy trips so much more.

**3.** Water: You can never really have too much. Essential for drinking, cooking and cleaning, and it will always run out at the most inconvenient moment if you don't bring enough.

# On the Road

The best part of vanlife is the up-close access it gives to some of the world's most scenic drives and destinations. Look no further for inspiration than these epic routes across the globe, from the mountains to the coasts and everywhere inbetween.

Argentina

Canada

©kovgabor/Shutterstock

Australia

©Artie Photography (A-tie Ng)/Getty Images

Germany

Ireland

New Zealand

Italy

Scotland

Nepal

USA

# Freetown to Accra

West Africa is an extraordinary sweep of iconic terrain. There are many views that will define your journey: an oasis-like clearing in the heart of a rainforest; stirring sand dunes sculpted to perfection by the wind; a gloriously deserted arc of sand along a gloriously deserted coastline... The wildlife is pretty spectacular too, with more here than initially meets the eye if you know where to look, including elephants, primates, big cats and some of the world's best birdwatching. And unlike in eastern or southern Africa, you're likely to have whatever you find all to yourself.

## 1. Freetown

For the traveller, Sierra Leone is still West Africa's secret beach destination. Sweet sands rise from the soft waters of the Atlantic, with the backdrop dressed in sun-stained hues, rainforest green and the red, red roads of the north. Its capital, strung between the mountains and the sea, is a cheeky, quicksilver city bubbling with energy, colour and charm. But it's real, all of it – the chatter and the chaos and the colour and the dirt and the lush lobster dinners and the devastating history of war and Ebola – and those lovely white sands too.

While you're here, stop in at the Sierra Leone National Museum (022-223555; Siaka Stevens St), with its collection of cultural and historical artefacts, including Temne Guerrilla leader Bai Bureh's drum, clothes and sword.

Make your way east along the Masiaka-Yonibana Hwy, which at Yonibana changes to the Bo-Kenema Hwy; dip south at Bo and follow signs to Potoru (85km/53 miles from Bo) for a detour to Tiwai Island.

## 2. Tiwai Island

One of the few remaining tracts of ancient rainforest in West Africa, Tiwai Island, meaning 'Big Island' in the Mende language, is Sierra Leone's most popular and accessible nature reserve. Set on the Moa River, the entire island is run as a conservation research project – known as the Tiwai

Island Wildlife Sanctuary. Tiwai covers a mere 12 sq km, but teems with an astonishing range of flora and fauna, and is most famous for its primate population. Although not part of the island, Gola Rainforest National Park shares the same tract of rainforest as Tiwai Island. (Visits must be booked in advance through www.tiwaiisland.org; you park in Kambama and continue with a guide.) Head north again toward the town of Makeni; nearby are several places where it's possible to wild camp. Continue north to the town of Kabala, 137km (85 miles) from Makeni.

## 3. Kabala

One of the larger cities in northern Sierra Leone, Kabala is surrounded by mountains and is known for its clothing – browse the markets for the traditional rust-red ronko gown.

Continuing northeast of Kabala, you'll cross the border into Guinea at Gberia-Fotombu. The first significant town on the Guinea side of the border is Faranah, gateway to the Parc National de Haut Niger.

## 4. Parc National de Haut Niger

Covering some 1200 sq km, the Parc National de Haut Niger is one of West Africa's last significant stands of tropical dry forest and one of the most important protected areas in Guinea. The forest, which is pockmarked with areas of tall grassland savannah and run through by the River Niger,

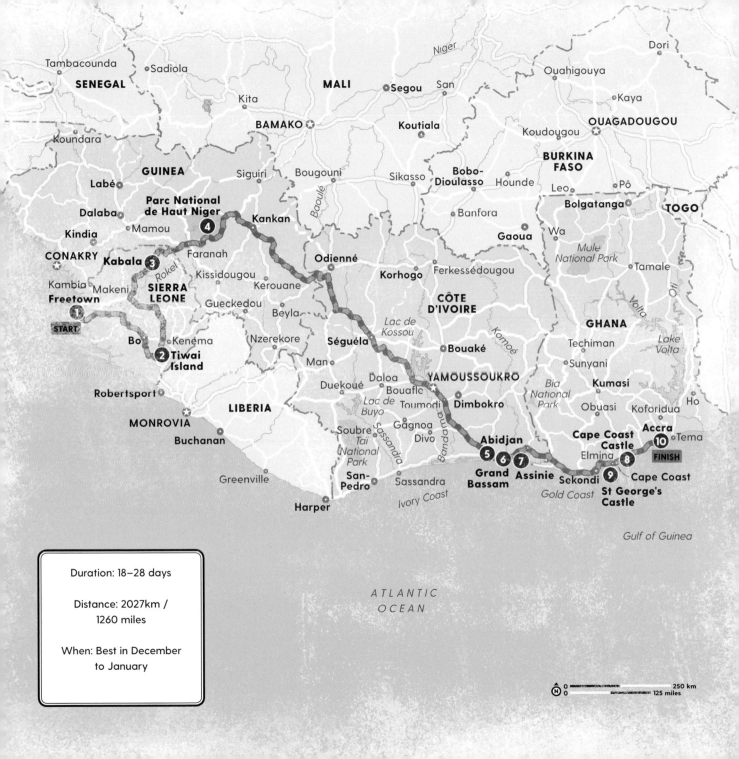

Duration: 18–28 days

Distance: 2027km /
1260 miles

When: Best in December
to January

© Felix Lipov / Shutterstock

© Universal Images Group North America LLC / DeAgostini / Alamy Stock Photo

**Park life**
To get to the Parc National de Haut Niger, take the dirt road leading east from Faranah to the tiny village of Sanbaya (Sambonya) via Beindou. This is where you will collect your obligatory guide and the park itself starts just to the north of the village. You must make arrangements for visiting in advance at the Ministère de l'Agriculture in Faranah.

has plenty of wildlife, including significant numbers of chimpanzees, buffalo, duikers and waterbuck as well as crocodiles and hippos. However, you would be very lucky indeed to actually see much wildlife thanks to the dense foliage, a general sense of caution of most of the animals and a near total lack of visitor facilities. Dedicated birders though will likely find the forest highly rewarding.

From the park, make your way southeast into Cote d'Ivoire and to the buzzing city of Abidjan.

## 5. Abidjan

Côte d'Ivoire's economic engine is strapped between lagoons and waterways, overlooking the crested waves of the Atlantic. At first glimpse, you wonder if these shiny skyscrapers can really be West Africa, but once you walk around Abidjan's neighbourhoods, local life comes alive and the city's vibrant tropical mood is revealed. Abidjan is a challenging city to move around in – it's vast and connected by mini-motorways. But each neighbourhood's distinct feel gives you an insight into the vast scope of Abidjan's character and contradiction; it's quite common for sharp luxury to exist right next to painful poverty. Make sure to dip into the markets, street-food stops, art galleries and a sleek bar or two.

## 6. Grand Bassam

Arty and bathed in faded glory, beachside Bassam was Côte d'Ivoire's French colonial capital until a yellow-fever epidemic broke out in 1896, prompting the French to move their capital to Bingerville. The town, named a Unesco World Heritage Site in 2012, had a glittery image as the top resort in the country until a March 2016 terrorist attack killed 16 people, many of them foreigners. The town is now safe, but the attack caused a slump in the local tourism industry and Grand Bassam is working hard to recover its flair.

## 7. Assinie

Quiet little Assinie tugs at the heartstrings of overlanders, washed-up surfers and rich weekenders from Abidjan who run their quad bikes up and down its peroxide-blonde beach. It actually comprises a triumvirate of villages: Assinie village, Assinie Mafia and Assouindé, all of which are laid out along the beaches and flow into each other, unified by their uniquely holiday atmosphere.

Continue east along coastal roads and across the border into Ghana, aiming for the unmissable castle at Cape Coast.

## 8. Cape Coast Castle

Cape Coast's imposing, whitewashed castle (033 213 2529; Victoria Rd) commands the heart of town, overlooking the sea. Once one of the world's most important slave-holding sites, it provides horrifying insight into the workings of the trade. Staff conduct hour-long tours, during which you'll visit the dark, damp dungeons where slaves waited for two to 12 weeks, contemplating rumours that hinted at their fate. A visit to the dungeons contrasts sharply with the governor's bedroom, blessed with floor-to-ceiling windows and panoramic ocean views.

There's also an excellent museum on the first floor, detailing the history of Ghana, the slave trade, Akan culture and the castle itself; converted by the Dutch in 1637, expanded by the Swedes in 1652, and captured by the British, who ruled from here for two centuries until Accra was declared the new capital in 1877.

## 9. St George's Castle

Not quite enough castle for you? Backtrack a smidge to Elmina, where you'll find St George's Castle, a Unesco heritage site built as a trading post by the Portuguese in 1482, and captured by the Dutch in 1637. It was expanded when slaves replaced gold as the major object of commerce, with storerooms converted into dungeons. The informative tour (included in the entry fee) takes you to the grim dungeons, punishment cells, Door of No Return and the turret room where the British imprisoned the Ashanti king, Prempeh I, for four years.

The Portuguese church, converted into slave auctioning rooms by the Protestant Dutch, houses a museum with simple but super-informative displays on the history and culture of Elmina.

Continue east along paved road N1 about 160km (100 miles) to Accra.

## 10. Accra

Ghana's beating heart probably won't inspire love letters, but you might just grow to like it. The capital's hot, sticky streets are perfumed with sweat, fumes and yesterday's cooking oil. Like balloons waiting to be burst, clouds of dirty humidity linger above stalls selling mangoes, banku (fermented maize meal) and rice. The city's tendrils reach out towards the beach, the centre and the west, each one a different Ghanaian experience.

Stop by the Makola Market for sensory overload, then head to Bojo Beach to chill out. On arrival there's a small entrance fee to pay, and you'll then be rowed across a clear strip of water to a pristine strip of beach, where there are sun loungers and refreshments. It's a worthy alternative to hectic Labadi Beach.

*Previous spread, clockwise from left: Finding balance at Côte d'Ivoire's Grand Bassam; Ghana's Cape Coast Castle; another golden reason to stop off at Grand Bassam Opposite: the views from Cape Coast Castle stretch along the sand*

# Crossing the Kathmandu Loop

A mountain drive with plains appeal, this dusty circuit from Kathmandu to the Terai serves up everything from medieval villages to rhinos and Himalayan views. There are fuel stops and tyre-repair stands all along the route. Keep in mind, we're talking about some rough roads and extremely steep mountain passes; make certain that your vehicle is road-worthy.

### 1. Kathmandu

Road blocks, traffic jams, irate crowds protesting this and that, and a gauntlet of sacred cows, street dogs and suicidal chickens. Leaving Kathmandu is a test of both driving skill and patience. Faced by the magnitude of the task, many drivers balk, and limp back to Thamel to settle in with a good book and a falafel wrap.

However, those willing to go the distance receive ample rewards. You don't have to go far beyond the Kathmandu Ring Road to find yourself surrounded by the pristine mountain scenery that first drew travellers to Nepal. Indeed, you're likely to find more peace and privacy on a country drive through the Himalayan foothills than at Everest Base Camp.

The Nepali capital is both blessed and cursed by its location; blessed, because of the scenery, but cursed because of the sheer impracticality of getting anywhere else by road. Most traffic still chokes its way along the hugely overcrowded Prithvi Hwy, which punches east past a forest of brick kilns towards Pokhara and the turn off to the lowlands.

### 2. Trisuli River

Even if you start the journey at first light, it will take several hours to get clear of the police checkpoints and escape the relentless snarl of buses, jeeps and trucks before breathing easy in the winding valley of the Trisuli River. This may be the busiest road in Nepal – and it's reputedly the fifth-most dangerous road in the whole world – but it passes through a fantasy landscape of cascading terraced fields and isolated farmhouses clinging improbably to sheer mountainsides.

Leaving the main pack behind, you'll enjoy what by Nepali standards counts as a peaceful ride, close encounters with oncoming buses notwithstanding. Savour the clean air after the smog of Kathmandu and be sure to pause occasionally to snap photos of scenic banyan trees and suspension bridges and to sip chiya (tea) at dusty roadside canteens.

### 3. Bandipur

There's plenty to see on the way to Pokhara – the Manakamana cablecar, the palace and birthplace of Prithvi Narayan Shah (the king who unified Nepal in the 1700s) at Gorkha – but your destination lies off the main highway at Bandipur, a precariously balanced Newari village that has changed only superficially since the days when yak caravans were the main form of transport into the Kathmandu Valley.

Bandipur is an ideal place to wander around, admiring tottering temples and tall timber and mudbrick townhouses – several now converted into hotels – flanking the main bazaar. After a blissful night in the cool air, freewheel downhill to another favourite detour, the millpond-calm lake of Begnas Tal, reflecting the sawtooth ridge of the Annapurnas to the north.

130

N
0 ___ 50 km
0 ___ 25 miles

CHINA (TIBET)

Duration: 15–20 days

Distance:
466km / 290 miles

When:
Best in October to
November or March to April

Manang

Ghorepani

Ranipauwa

Beni

Baglung

Kusma

Pokhara

Siswa

Ghanpokhara

Besi Sahar

Karelung

Kunchha

Damauli

Bartar

Labsibot

Jiwadanda

Syabru

Trisuli River

Dhunche

Burathum

Betrawati

Putalikhet

Bathala

Jharkham

Dumrichaur

Waling

Ramdighat

Mariphant

Birkot

Bandipur 3

Gorkha

NEPAL

Devghat

Mugling

Benighat

Trisuli River

Kakani

Tansen 4

2

Trisuli
River

Malekhu

Duireni

Kathmandu

1 START

Butwal

Somnath

Bharatpur

Ratnanagar

Naubise

Daman

Parasi

Patlahara

FINISH 5

Debichaur

Bhimphedi

Siddharthanagar

Thuthibari

Dibni

Chitwan
National Park

Bhagaura

Hetauda

Nautanwa

Nichlaul

Gobardhana

Amlekhganj

Pathalia

Simara

Juribela

Sanduria

Gandak River

INDIA

Ramnagar

Nakartiagar

Maharajganj

Bayaha

Bhaunra

Birganj

Kalaiya

Lauriya
Mandangarh

Champapur

For most travellers, the logical next stop would be Pokhara, the starting point for treks to Annapurna and Mustang. However, first head for Tansen, another historic hill town to the south. Branching at Pokhara, the Siddhartha Hwy winds through a series of narrow gorges, twisting like a snake with indigestion. Even better, the rough terrain deters much of the four-wheeled traffic, making driving here a real pleasure.

## 4. Tansen

Once the capital of a powerful Magar kingdom, Tansen is an agreeable jumble of royal relics and traditional shophouses. It invites aimless wandering, with its scores of inquisitive children and cheerful old men in topis (Nepali caps), puffing reflectively on beedi cigarettes. Tansen's greatest treasure though is a hike north of town, on the banks of the Kali

*Clockwise from opposite: The city of Kathmandu remains a challenging place in which to drive; Tansen's many sights include this tomb; the village of Bandhapur has become a popular place to overnight*

# Nepal

Gandaki River. Here, the crumbling remains of the baroque Rani Mahal palace recall the lonely exile of Khadga Shamsher Rana, driven from Kathmandu after plotting against the monarchy.

The Siddhartha Hwy collides with the Terai at Butwal, a hectic bazaar that feels as if it's been transplanted from India, right down to the stalls heaped with glass bangles and piles of blood-red tilaka powder. The next step of the Kathmandu Loop is perhaps the most challenging – not because of winding mountain roads, but because of winding plains traffic.

## 5. Chitwan National Park

Drivers take advantage of the flat Mahendra Hwy – the main transect through the Terai – for some of their most death-defying overtaking. Expect many near misses before you reach Sauraha, the gateway to Chitwan National Park.

The third spike on Nepal's tourism trident, after Kathmandu and the Himalaya, Chitwan is one of the last refuges of the one-horned Indian rhino and the royal Bengal tiger. You have a reasonable chance of spotting either, or both, on guided walks through the jungle. Keep in mind you'll need at least two days in the park to fully appreciate everything it offers.

From Chitwan, many travellers choose to charge south to the Indian border or north to Kathmandu on the choked highway to Mugling, but the wise caravanner will skip this in favour of the Tribhuvan Rajpath, which wriggles through the high ridge southwest of Kathmandu. Forking off the Mahendra Hwy at the nondescript Terai town of Hetauda, this is another low-traffic delight, rising in tight switchbacks through handsome stands of pine, sal and rhododendron trees to Daman at the crest of the ridge.

*Above: Indian rhinos cross the river in Chitwan National Park, which is one of the animal's last refuges; Opposite: the Himalayan valley drive offers some world-beating vistas – and some equally testing roads*

# Great Ocean Road

One of the most beautiful coastal road journeys on Earth, this world-famous road hugs the western Victorian coast, passing beaches, iconic landforms and fascinating seaside settlements. It's wildly popular and very commercial, so don't expect to find yourself all alone in the middle of nowhere. The crowds are here for good reason: it's a truly spectacular drive.

### 1. Torquay

The undisputed surfing capital of Australia is a brilliant place to start your journey. The town's proximity to world-famous Bells Beach, and status as home of two iconic surf brands – Rip Curl and Quicksilver – have assured Torquay's place at the pinnacle of mainstream surf culture. Torquay's beaches lure everyone from kids in floaties to backpacker surf-school pupils. Fishermans Beach, protected from ocean swells, is the family favourite. Ringed by shady pines and sloping lawns, the Front Beach beckons lazy bums, while surf lifesavers patrol the frothing Back Beach during summer.

Famous surf beaches include nearby Jan Juc and Winki Pop. Visit the Surf World Museum (www.surfworld.com.au), home to the Australia's Surfing Hall of Fame, then start working on your legend by taking surf lessons with Westcoast Surf School (03-5261 2241; www.westcoastsurfschool.com) or Torquay Surfing Academy (035261 2022; www.torquaysurf.com.au).

Pass the turn-off to Jan Juc, then take the next left (C132) and follow the signs to Bells Beach.

### 2. Bells Beach

A slight detour off the Great Ocean Road takes you to famous Bells Beach, the powerful point break that is part of international surfing folklore (it was here, albeit in name only, that Keanu Reeves and Patrick Swayze had their ultimate showdown in the film *Point Break*). When the right-hander is working, it's one of the longest rides in the country. If you're here just to take a look, park up in the car park and head for the lookout, from where stairs lead down to the beach (not for swimming).

Return to the Great Ocean Road (B100), and soon after doing so consider taking the turn-off to spectacular Point Addis, a vast sweep of pristine beach. Anglesea is a further 10km (6 miles) down the Great Ocean Road, with dense woodland lining the road as you descend into town.

### 3. Anglesea

Mix sheer orange cliffs falling into the ocean with hilly, tree-filled 'burbs and a population that booms in summer and you've got Anglesea, where sharing fish and chips with seagulls by the Anglesea River is a decades-long family tradition for many. Main Beach is good for surfers, while sheltered Point Roadknight Beach is for families. In addition to such quintessentially Australian summer pastimes, Anglesea is famous for those seeking to spy their first kangaroos – at Anglesea Golf Club (03-5263 1582; www.angleseagolfclub.com.au) you can watch the marsupials graze on the fairways.

The B100 follows the coast (although it does sidestep attractive Point Roadknight) for 11km (7 miles) to Aireys Inlet, and then to Fairhaven, with a historic lighthouse and wonderful beaches. From Aireys it's 18km (11 miles) of glorious coast-hugging road into Lorne – stop for photos at the Great Ocean Road memorial archway.

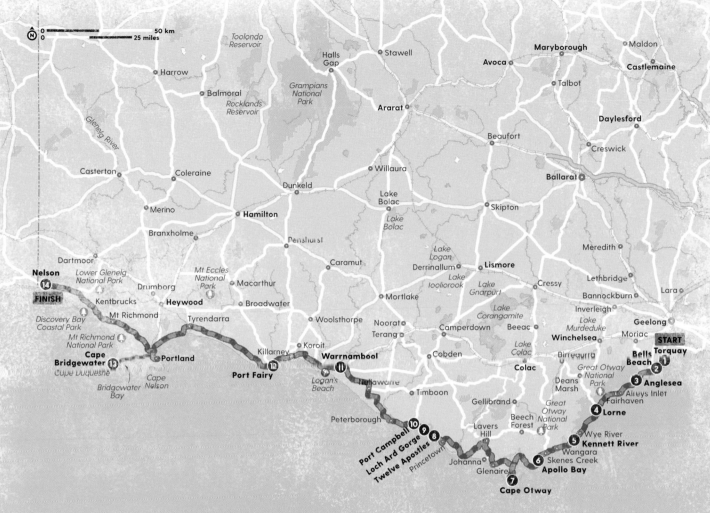

**N** 0 ———— 50 km
0 ———— 25 miles

Toolondo Reservoir
Harrow
Halls Gap
Stawell
Maryborough
Maldon
Castlemaine
Avoca
Balmoral
Rocklands Reservoir
Grampians National Park
Talbot
Daylesford
Ararat
Beaufort
Creswick
Casterton
Coleraine
Dunkeld
Willaura
Ballarat
Skipton
Merino
Hamilton
Lake Bolac
Lake Bolac
Meredith
Branxholme
Penshurst
Lethbridge
Lara
Dartmoor
Lower Glenelg National Park
Macarthur
Caramut
Lake Logan
Derrinallum
Lismore
Cressy
Inverleigh
Bannockburn
Lake Gnarput
Lake Murdeduke
Geelong
Nelson **14** FINISH
Kentbrucks
Mt Richmond
Drumborg
Heywood
Broadwater
Woolsthorpe
Mortlake
Terang
Camperdown
Beeac
Winchelsea
Lake Corangamite
Lake Murdeduke
Moriac
START
Torquay
Discovery Bay Coastal Park
Mt Richmond National Park
Tyrendarra
Killarney
Koroit
Noorat
Birregurra
Great Otway National Park
Bells Beach **1**
**2**
Cape Bridgewater **13**
Portland
Port Fairy
Warrnambool **11**
Logan's Beach
Cobden
Colac
Lake Colac
Deans Marsh
Anglesea **3**
Aireys Inlet
Cape Nelson
**1h**
Nullawarre
Timboon
Gellibrand
Beech Forest
Great Otway National Park
Fairhaven
Lorne **4**
Bridgewater Bay
Cape Duquesne
Peterborough
Lavers Hill
Wye River
Kennett River **5**
Port Campbell **10**
Loch Ard Gorge **9**
Twelve Apostles **8**
Princetown
Johanna
Glenaire
Wangara
Skenes Creek
Apollo Bay **6**
**7** Cape Otway

*Bass Strait*

SOUTHERN OCEAN

KING ISLAND

---

Duration: 5–7 days

Distance: 378km / 235 miles

When: Year-round but October to March has the best weather

## 4. Lorne

There's something about Lorne... For a start, this is a place of incredible natural beauty, something you see vividly as you drive into town from Aireys Inlet: tall old gum trees line its hilly streets, and Loutit Bay gleams irresistibly. Kids will love the beachside swimming pool, trampolines and skate park, and there's more than 50km (31 miles) of bushwalking tracks around Lorne. Up in the hilly hinterland behind town, seek out the Erskine Falls (Erskine Falls Access Rd); it's an easy walk to the viewing platform, or 250 slippery steps down to its base. Back in town, the Great Ocean Road National Heritage Centre (15 Mountjoy Pde) tells the story of the construction of the Great Ocean Road.

Although the winding nature of the road makes it feel longer – by now you know the

*Above: The famed Twelve Apostles; Following spread, clockwise: Bells Beach, as seen in Point Break; spot koalas at Cape Otway from its Treetop Walk; the shipwrecking rocks of Loch Ard Gorge*

© Maciej Nadstazik / 500px

pose (well, they're often asleep) in the tree forks, sometimes at eye level. Local parrots and lorikeets are also known to swoop down and perch on heads and outstretched arms if you stay still enough.

The road could hardly get closer to the coast for the 22km (14 miles) from Kennett River to Apollo Bay.

## 6. Apollo Bay

At Apollo Bay, one of the Great Ocean Road's largest towns, rolling hills provide a postcard backdrop to the town, while broad, white-sand beaches dominate the foreground. Local boy Mark Brack, son of the Cape Otway Lighthouse keeper, knows this stretch of coast better than anyone around – both his Otway Shipwreck Tours (0417 983 985; msbrack@bigpond.com) and Mark's Walking Tours (0417 983 985; www.greatoceanwalk. usn.au/markstours) are outstanding. Another worthwhile excursion is the kayak expedition out to an Australian fur seal colony in a double kayak with Apollo Bay Surf & Kayak (0405 495 909; www.apollobaysurfkayak.com.au).

The turn-off for Lighthouse Rd (ie Cape Otway), which leads 12km (7.4 miles) down to the lighthouse, is 21km (13 miles) from Apollo Bay. Those 12km are through dense woodland pretty much all the way.

## 7. Cape Otway

Cape Otway is the second most southerly point of mainland Australia (after Wilsons Promontory) and this coastline is particularly beautiful, rugged and historically treacherous for passing ships despite the best efforts of the Cape Otway Lightstation (03-5237 9240; www.lightstation.com). The oldest surviving lighthouse on mainland Australia, it was built in 1848 by more than 40 stonemasons without

deal: dense forests to your right, uninterrupted sea views to your left – it's just 20km (12 miles) from Lorne to Kennett River.

## 5. Kennett River

Kennett River is one of the easiest places to see koalas in Australia. In the trees immediately west of the general store and around the excellent caravan park, koalas

mortar or cement. The forested road leading to Cape Otway is a terrific spot for koala sightings. Can't find any? Look for the cars parked on the side of the road and tourists peering up into the trees.

The road levels out after leaving the Otways and enters narrow, flat scrubby escarpment lands that fall away to sheer, 70m-high cliffs along the coast between Princetown and Peterborough – a distinct change of scene. The Twelve Apostles are after Princetown.

## 8. Twelve Apostles

The most enduring image for most visitors to the Great Ocean Road, the Twelve Apostles jut from the ocean in spectacular fashion. There they stand, as if abandoned to the ocean by the retreating headland, all seven of them... Just for the record, there never were 12, and they were once called 'Sow and Piglets' until some bright spark in the 1960s thought they might attract tourists with a more venerable name. The two stacks on the eastern (Otway) side of the viewing platform are not technically Apostles – they're Gog and Magog. And the soft limestone cliffs are dynamic and changeable, with constant erosion from the waves: one 70m-high stack collapsed into the sea in July 2005 and the Island Archway lost its archway in June 2009. The best time to visit is sunset, partly to beat the tour buses, and to see little penguins returning ashore. For the best views, take a chopper tour with 12 Apostles Helicopters (03-5598 8283; www.12apostleshelicopters.com.au).

When you can finally tear yourself away, continue northwest along the Great Ocean Road and in no time at all you'll see the signpost to Loch Ard Gorge.

## 9. Loch Ard Gorge

Close to the Twelve Apostles, Loch Ard Gorge is a gorgeous U-shaped canyon of high cliffs, a sandy beach and deep blue waters. It was here that the Shipwreck Coast's most famous and haunting tale unfolded: the iron-hulled clipper Loch Ard foundered off Mutton Bird Island at 4am on the final night of its long voyage from England in 1878. Of 37 crew and 19 passengers on board, only two survived. Eva Carmichael, a non-swimmer, clung to wreckage and was washed into a gorge – since renamed Loch Ard Gorge – where apprentice officer Tom Pearce rescued her. Despite rumours of a romance, they never saw each other again and Eva soon returned to Ireland. There are several walks in the area taking you down to the cave where the shipwreck survivors took shelter, plus a cemetery and rugged beach.

It's around 6km (4 miles) along the B100 from Loch Ard Gorge into Port Campbell.

## 10. Port Campbell

Strung out around a tiny bay, Port Campbell is a laidback coastal town and the ideal base from which to take your time exploring the areas around Twelve Apostles and Loch Ard Gorge. It has a lovely, sandy, sheltered beach, one of the few safe places for swimming along this tempestuous stretch of coast.

There is a feeling of crossing a high clifftop plateau on the first stretch out of Port Campbell. After the Bay of Islands, it turns inland through green agricultural lands.

## 11. Warrnambool

Warrnambool means whales, at least between May and September, when whales frolic off shore on their migration. Southern right whales

**Good to know:** Driving in Australia requires a valid driver's licence. You can drive with a foreign (English language) licence for three months. Longer than that, you need to get a licence from an Australian state. If your licence is not in English, you need to get an International Driving Permit from the Automobile Association in your home country before arriving.

(named due to being the 'right' whales to hunt) are the most common visitors, heading from Antarctica to these more temperate waters. Undoubtedly the best place to see them is at Warrnambool's Logans Beach whale-watching platform – they use the waters here as a nursery. Call ahead to the visitor centre to check if whales are about, or see www.visitwarrnambool.com.au for latest sightings. Otherwise, take the time to visit top-notch historic buildings of Flagstaff Hill Maritime Village (03-5559 4600; www.flagstaffhill.com), with its shipwreck museum, heritage-listed lighthouses and garrison, and its reproduction of a historical Victorian port town. It also has the nightly Shipwrecked, an engaging 70-minute sound-and-laser show telling the story of the Loch Ard's plunge.

The road – the Princes Hwy (A1), and no longer the Great Ocean Road – loops around to Port Fairy, just 29km (18 miles) from Warrnambool.

## 12. Port Fairy

Settled in 1833 as a whaling and sealing station, Port Fairy retains its historic 19th-century charm with a relaxed, salty feel, and a winning mix of architecture that encompasses heritage bluestone and sandstone buildings and whitewashed cottages, colourful fishing boats and wide, tree-lined streets; in 2012 it was voted the world's most liveable community. Across the bridge from the picturesque harbour, Battery Hill has cannons and fortifications. To guide your steps through the town's heritage, pick up a copy of the popular Maritime & Shipwreck Heritage Walk from the visitor centre. And there's a growing foodie scene here too – Basalt Wines

(0429 682 251; www.basaltwines.com), just outside Port Fairy in Killarney, is a family-run biodynamic winery that has tastings in its shed.

The road hugs the coast into Portland (75km/46 miles) and then the traffic lessens as you leave the main highway and drive northwest along the C192 for 67km (41 miles) into Nelson.

*Above: Port Fairy, once voted the world's most liveable community*
*Right: head to Australia's second-most southerly point to clap eyes on the Cape Otway Lightstation, built in 1848*

Forest on the cliff top. A longer two-hour return walk takes you to a seal colony where you can see dozens of fur seals sunning themselves on the rocks; to get a little closer, take the exhilarating Seals by Sea tour (03-5526 7247; www.sealsbyseatours.com.au), a 45-minute Zodiac cruise.

### 14. Nelson

Tiny Nelson is the last vestige of civilisation before the South Australian border – just a general store, a pub and a handful of places to stay. We like it especially for its proximity to the mouth of the Glenelg River, which flows through Lower Glenelg National Park. The leisurely 3½ hour trips run by Nelson River Cruises (0448 887 1225, 08-8738 4191; www.glenelgrivercruises.com.au) head along the Glenelg River and include the impressive Princess Margaret Rose Cave (08-8738 4171), with its gleaming underground formations – along this coastline of towering formations, these are surely the most surprising. If you prefer to explore under your own steam, try Nelson Boat & Canoe Hire (08-8738 4048).

### 13. Detour: Cape Bridgewater

Cape Bridgewater is an essential 21km (13 mile) detour off the Portland–Nelson Rd. The stunning 4km arc of Bridgewater Bay is perhaps one of Australia's finest stretches of white-sand surf beach. The road continues on to Cape Duquesne, where walking tracks lead to a spectacular blowhole and the eerie Petrified

# Outback Queensland

From the tropical coast of Far North Queensland to the deepest outback, this 2WD odyssey crosses stirring outback country and has all the ingredients for a fine adventure without leaving the tarmac. It all begins in the lush, tropical surroundings of Cairns and the Atherton Tablelands, where dramatic Undara Volcanic National Park offers a parched preview, onwards to Croydon, Normanton, Cloncurry and Mt Isa, each getting remoter by degrees.

## 1. Cairns

Cairns is an unlikely gateway to the outback, but therein lies its charm. Above all else, swim in the ocean (you won't see it again for a while), stock up on your favourite snacks for the long drive ahead (most shops from here on will only stock the basics), and dive into the culinary scene (it's pub food and not much else until Mt Isa).

Follow the coastal Bruce Hwy for 24km (15 miles) south to Gordonvale, then veer inland at the Gillies Hwy. The road bucks and weaves southwest through rain-forested hillsides and rocky outcrops to Yungaburra close to the shores of Lake Tinaroo, 12km (7.4 miles) before reaching Atherton. It's then 18km (11 miles) southwest to Herberton.

## 2. Herberton

A must-see on any comprehensive trip into the Tableland is the fascinating and fun Historic Village Herberton (07-4097 2002; www.herbertonhistoricvillage.com.au), comprising over 50 heritage buildings, restored and relocated to the sweet, sleepy Tableland town of Herberton. Exhibits range from the school to the sawmill, the bank to the bishop's house and everything in between. There's nothing quite like it anywhere else in Australia. It's 18km (11 miles) back to the Kennedy Hwy, a further 19km (12 miles) south to Ravenshoe, then 142km (88 miles) to Undara Volcanic National Park, with the views either side of the road getting drier with each passing kilometre. Undara is 15km (9 miles) south off the Gulf Developmental Road on a sealed road.

## 3. Detour: Atherton Tableland Waterfalls

Climbing back from the coast between Innisfail and Cairns is the fertile food bowl of the far north, the Atherton Tableland. Quaint country towns, eco-wilderness lodges and luxurious B&Bs dot greener-than-green hills between patchwork fields, pockets of rainforest, spectacular lakes and waterfalls, and Queensland's highest mountains, Bartle Frere (1622m) and Bellenden Ker (1593m). From Herberton it's 39km (24 miles) to Millaa Millaa, which lies along the Palmerston Highway; 1km east of Millaa Millaa, turn north on to Theresa Creek Rd. Surrounded by tree ferns and flowers, the Millaa Millaa Falls, 1.5km (0.9 miles) along, are easily the best for swimming and have a grassy picnic area. Almost ridiculously picturesque, the spectacular 12m-high falls are reputed to be the most photographed in Australia. Zillie Falls, 8km (5 miles) further on, are reached by a short walking trail that leads to a lookout peering down (with some vertigo) on the falls from above, while Ellinjaa Falls have a 200m walking trail down to a rocky swimming hole at the base of the falls.

## 4. Undara Volcanic National Park

About 190,000 years ago, the Undara shield volcano erupted, sending molten lava coursing through the surrounding landscape. While the surface of the lava cooled and hardened, hot lava continued to race through the centre of the flows, eventually leaving the world's longest continuous lava tubes from a single vent. There are over 160km (99

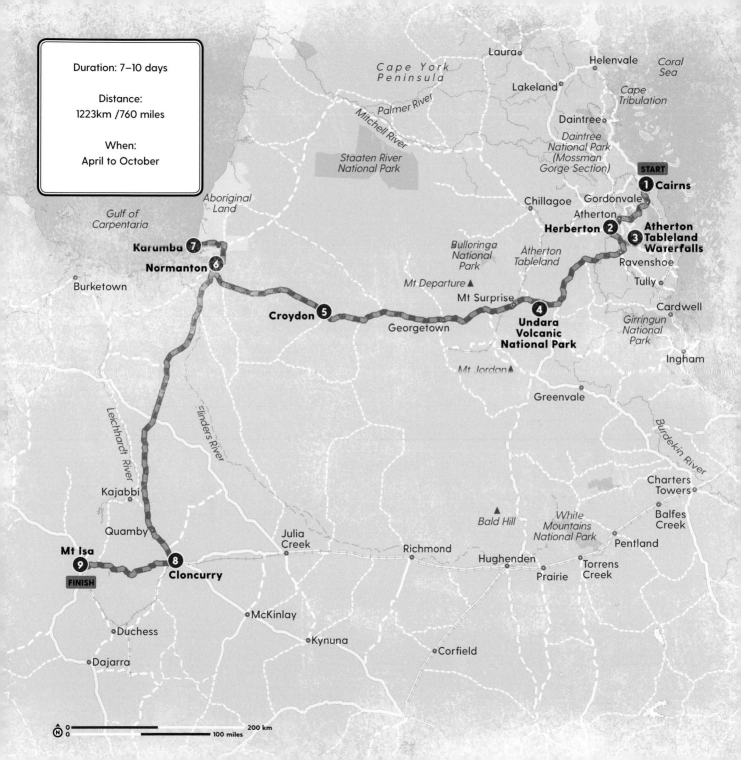

Duration: 7–10 days

Distance:
1223km /760 miles

When:
April to October

Laura
Helenvale
*Coral Sea*

*Cape York Peninsula*

Lakeland

*Cape Tribulation*

*Palmer River*

Daintree

*Mitchell River*

*Daintree National Park (Mossman Gorge Section)*

**START**
**1** **Cairns**

Gordonvale

Chillagoe

Atherton

**Herberton** **2**

**3** **Atherton Tableland Warerfalls**

Ravenshoe

Tully

*Staaten River National Park*

*Aboriginal Land*

*Bulloringa National Park*

*Atherton Tableland*

Mt Departure ▲

Mt Surprise

*Girringun National Park*

Cardwell

*Gulf of Carpentaria*

**Karumba** **7**

**Normanton** **6**

**Croydon** **5**

Georgetown

**4** **Undara Volcanic National Park**

Ingham

Burketown

Mt Jordan ▲

Greenvale

*Burdekin River*

*Leichhardt River*

*Flinders River*

Kajabbi

Quamby

Charters Towers

Balfes Creek

*Bald Hill* ▲

*White Mountains National Park*

Pentland

**Mt Isa**
**9**

**FINISH**

**8**
**Cloncurry**

Julia Creek

Richmond

Hughenden

Torrens Creek

Prairie

McKinlay

Kynuna

Corfield

Duchess

Dajarra

N

0          100 miles          200 km

miles) of tubes here, but only a fraction can be visited as part of a guided tour. Most of these are operated by Undara Experience (07-4097 1900, 1800 990 992; www.undara.com.au), which runs daily two-hour tours, including 'Wildlife at Sunset', where you'll see tiny microbats swarm out of a cave and provide dinner for lightning-fast hanging tree snakes, known as night tigers. Under your own steam, a worthwhile detour is the signposted drive to Kalkani Crater. The crater rim walk is an easy 2.5km (1.5 mile) circuit from the car park.

Return to the Gulf Developmental Road (Savannah Way) and then tick off the tiny settlements that loom like mirages in this empty land – such as Georgetown after 127km (79 miles)– before pulling into dusty Croydon, a further 149km on.

© Chris Putnam / Alamy Stock Photo

© Michael Willis / Alamy Stock Photo

© Hilke Maurder / Alamy Stock Photo

**Good to know:**
Just outside the Undara Volcanic National Park, Undara Experience (1800 990 992; www. undara.com.au) has a great range of accommodation, from a shady campground to nifty little swag tents on raised platforms. Staying here puts you close to the caves and surrounding bushwalks, and there's a good restaurant, a bar and barbecue areas. There's a small shop on site and pricey fuel.

## 5. Croydon

If you haven't already felt it on the road in, Croydon is where that sense of having fallen off the map and emerged into the outback really takes hold. It's a dusty, red-earth kind of place that was, incredibly, once the biggest town in the Gulf of Carpentaria thanks to a short but lucrative gold rush. Gold was discovered here in 1885, and in its heyday there were 30 pubs – just one, the Club Hotel, built in 1887, survives. Croydon's visitor information centre (07-4748 7152; Samwell St) has details of the historic precinct and shows a short film (free) about the gold-rush days. At the timber Croydon General Store (07-4745 6163; Sircom St) the sign declares this the 'oldest store in Australia, established 1894'.

The Savannah Way (which continues, much of it unsealed, beyond Normanton into the Northern Territory) carries you across the red-and-yellow countryside for 148km (92 miles) into Normanton.

## 6. Normanton

The port for Croydon's gold rush, Normanton boasts a broad long main street lined with some colourful old buildings. It's a quiet place that occasionally springs into life: at Easter the Barra Bash lures big crowds, as do the Normanton Rodeo & Show (mid-June) and the Normanton Races (September). In the historic Burns Philp building, the visitor information and heritage centre (07-4745 8444) has lots of information. Everyone stops to take a photo of Krys the Crocodile on Landsborough St. It's a supposedly life-sized statue of an 8.64m saltie shot by croc hunter Krystina Pawloski on the Norman River in 1958 – the largest recorded croc in the world.

As the crow flies Karumba is just a hop across the Mutton Wetlands, but by road it's 37km (23 miles) north to Maggieville, then 42km (26 miles) west to Karumba on the shores of the Gulf.

## 7. Karumba

When the sun sinks into the Gulf of Carpentaria in a fiery ball of burnt ochre, Karumba is transformed into a little piece of outback paradise. It's the only town accessible by sealed road on the entire Gulf coast, and it's a great place to kick back for a few days. The actual town is on the Norman River, while Karumba Point is about 6km (3.7 miles) away by road on the beach. Karumba's visitor information centre (074745 9582; www.carpentaria.qld.gov.au) has details of fishing charters and cruises, plus crab-catching and croc-spotting on the river.

Tearing yourself away from the Gulf, the Burke Developmental Road is a quiet outback road, crossing the dry Gulf hinterland. After 192km (119 miles), pause for some company at the Burke & Wills Roadhouse, then it's 181km (112 miles) south to Cloncurry.

## 8. Cloncurry

Compared with where you're coming from, Cloncurry (population 2313) will seem like the heights of civilisation. Known to its friends as 'the Curry', Cloncurry is renowned as the birthplace of the Royal Flying Doctor Service (RFDS) and today it's a busy pastoral centre with a reinvigorated mining industry. The outstanding John Flynn Place (07-4742 4125; www.johnflynnplace.com.au) celebrates Dr John Flynn's work setting up the invaluable and groundbreaking RFDS, which gave hope, help and health services to people across the remote outback.

You're almost there and, having come so far, you'll barely notice the final 122km (76 miles) along the more heavily trafficked Barkly Hwy.

## 9. Mt Isa

You can't miss the smokestacks as you drive into Mt Isa, one of Queensland's longest-running mining towns and a travel and lifestyle hub for central Queensland. The sunset view from the City Lookout of the twinkling mine lights and silhouetted smokestacks is strangely pretty and very Mt Isa. Strange rock formations – padded with olive-green spinifex – line the perimeter of town, and deep-blue sunsets eclipse all unnatural light. Try to visit in mid-August for Australia's largest rodeo (www.isarodeo.com.au; 2nd weekend in Aug).

Don't miss the award-winning Outback at Isa (1300 659 660; www.outbackatisa.com.au), which includes the Hard Times, an authentic underground trip to give you the full Isa mining experience; the Isa Experience & Outback Park, a hands-on museum providing a colourful and articulate overview of local history; and the fascinating Riversleigh Fossil Centre.

*Previous spread, from left: idyllic Millaa Millaa Falls; a Normanton pitstop; a farrier gets to work in Historic Village Herberton Right: cruising the Norman River near the town of Karumba*

© Ian Beattie / Alamy Stock Photo

# Western Australia's Southwest Coast

A road trip down to and along Western Australia's southwest coast is one of the continent's most rewarding drives, with wineries, gorgeous national parks and a postcard-perfect coastline. Most visitors make a beeline for Margaret River, but there's so much more to explore on this wild and dramatic shore, where beaches stretch to eternity and dolphins swim in the shallows. And the further you go, the quieter the roads and the more thrilling the sense of this vast continent.

### 1. Bunbury

Once purely industrial, Bunbury is on the up. The port area has been redeveloped (especially just north of the compact city centre, where you'll find numerous waterside restaurants) and the city now draws a growing crowd of nature-lovers. The real stars are the roughly 60 bottlenose dolphins that live in Bunbury's Koombana Bay; their numbers swell to more than 250 in summer. The Dolphin Discovery Centre has a beachside zone where dolphins regularly come to interact with people in the shallows, and you can wade in alongside them, under the supervision of trained volunteers. A close encounter is more likely in the early mornings between November and April – you may find yourself giggling in childish delight as the dolphins nuzzle up to your toes.

From Bunbury, the main route south branches to the Bussell Hwy (for Margaret River), and the South Western Hwy (to the southern forests and south coast). Take the latter, passing through Donnybrook and Greenbushes in the 96km (59 mile) run into Bridgetown.

### 2. Bridgetown

Lovely little Bridgetown is a quintessential rural Aussie town, surrounded by karri forests and rolling farmland with some lovely Blackwood River frontage that turns yellow, red and orange in autumn. It's garnering something of a reputation as a popular weekender and the town comes alive from Friday evening to Sunday lunch. Wander its historic main street and watch in particular for Bridgedale House (Hampton St), built of mud and clay by the area's first settler in 1862, and since restored by the National Trust.

Forest crowds the road south of Bridgetown, particularly around the truffle-and-timber town of Manjimup (36km/22 miles). Around 15km (9 miles) south of it, take the turn-off right (southwest) for the last 19km (12 miles) into Pemberton.

### 3. Pemberton

It's hard not to fall in love with drowsy little Pemberton, hidden deep in the karri forests that are such a feature of this corner of the country. To get out among the tall timbers, aim to spend a day or two driving the well-marked Karri Forest Explorer tracks, walking the trails and picnicking in the green depths; check in at the visitor centre (08-9776 1133; www.pembertonvisitor.com.au) in town for maps and advice.

Wineries, too, are a big part of Pemberton's star appeal. If Margaret River is WA's Bordeaux, Pemberton is its Burgundy, producing excellent chardonnay and pinot noir, among other varietals. One option is to visit Mountford (www.mountfordwines.com.au), where the wines and ciders produced are all certified organic, plus there's a gallery on site. Pemberton Wine Centre (www.marima.com.au), in the heart of Warren National Park, is another appealing option.

Return 19km (12 miles) northeast through the forests to the South Western Hwy, where you turn right. From here, the road angles southeast through more wonderfully dense forests.

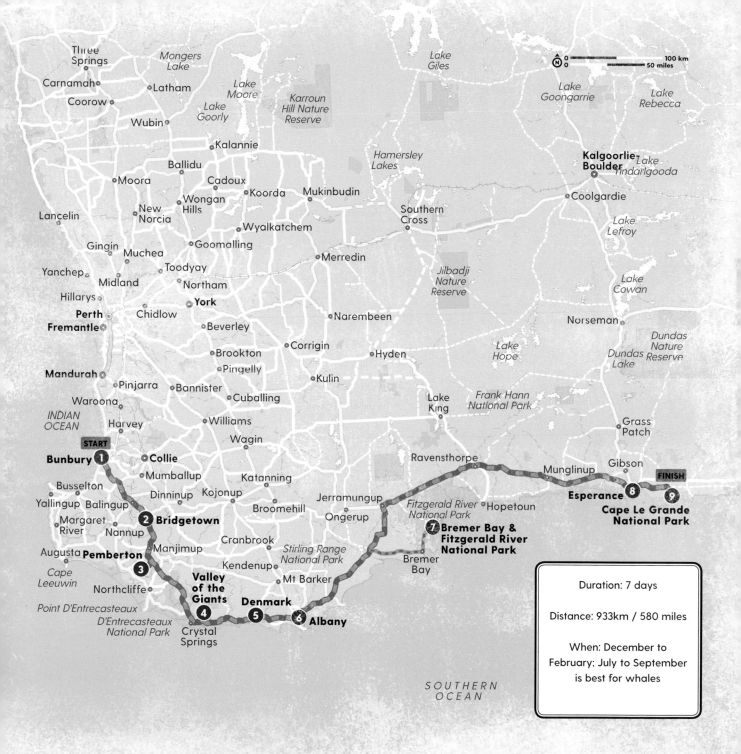

Three Springs
Carnamah
Coorow
Mongers
Lake
Latham
Lake
Moore
Wubin
Lake
Goorly
Karroun
Hill Nature
Reserve
Lake
Giles
Lake
Goongarrie
Lake
Yindarlgooda
Lake
Rebecca
Kalannie
Ballidu
Cadoux
Koorda
Mukinbudin
Moora
Wongan
Hills
Hamersley
Lakes
**Kalgoorlie
Boulder**
Lancelin
New
Norcia
Goomalling
Wyalkatchem
Southern
Cross
Coolgardie
Gingin
Muchea
Toodyay
Merredin
Lake
Lefroy
Yanchep
Midland
Northam
Jilbadji
Nature
Reserve
Lake
Cowan
Hillarys
**York**
Chidlow
**Perth**
**Fremantle**
Beverley
Narembeen
Norseman
Dundas
Nature
Reserve
Brookton
Corrigin
Hyden
Lake
Hope
Dundas
Lake
**Mandurah**
Pingelly
Kulin
Pinjarra
Bannister
Cuballing
Lake
King
Frank Hann
National Park
Grass
Patch
Waroona
Williams
*INDIAN
OCEAN*
Harvey
Wagin
Gibson
**START**
Ravensthorpe
Munglinup
**FINISH**
**Bunbury** ① **Collie**
Mumballup
**Esperance** ⑧
⑨
Busselton
Dinninup
Katanning
Jerramungup
*Fitzgerald River
National Park*
Hopetoun
**Cape Le Grande
National Park**
Yallingup
Balingup
Kojonup
② **Bridgetown**
Broomehill
Ongerup
Margaret
River
Nannup
Cranbrook
⑦ **Bremer Bay &
Fitzgerald River
National Park**
Augusta
**Pemberton**
Manjimup
*Stirling Range
National Park*
Kendenup
Bremer
Bay
*Cape
Leeuwin*
③
**Valley
of the
Giants**
Mt Barker
Northcliffe
*Point D'Entrecasteaux*
④
**Denmark**
⑤
⑥ **Albany**
*D'Entrecasteaux
National Park*
Crystal
Springs

Duration: 7 days

Distance: 933km / 580 miles

When: December to
February; July to
September
is best for whales

*SOUTHERN
OCEAN*

© EAGiven / Getty Images

From the turn-off, it's 103km (64 miles) into the seaside hamlet of Walpole; watch for big ocean views opening up on the final approach.

## 4. Valley of the Giants

Peaceful little Walpole (pop 320) makes a good base from which to explore the heavily forested Walpole Wilderness Area, which covers a whopping 3630 sq km. The undoubted (and most accessible) highlight of this fabulously wild corner is the Valley of the Giants (www. valleyofthegiants.com.au) and its irresistible Tree Top Walk. Here, a 600m-long ramp rises from the valley, allowing visitors access high into the canopy of the giant tingle trees. Good walking

tracks include a section of the Bibbulmun Track, which passes through Walpole to Coalmine Beach. Scenic drives include the Knoll Drive, 3km (2 miles) east of Walpole.

At Walpole, the South Western Hwy (Rte 1) becomes the South Coast Hwy. It occasionally emerges from the forests soon after passing the turn-off to Peaceful Bay, with some wonderful ocean views away to the south as you near Denmark, 66km (41 miles) from Walpole.

## 5. Denmark

The first of the medium-sized towns you come to along WA's south coast, Denmark has a truly lovely setting with long sandy beaches and

which offers all-day tours to the wineries or further afield to Porongurup National Park or Mt Barker.

It's just 50km (31 miles) from Denmark to Albany and you know the deal – forests to the left of you, ocean to the right, and it's all really rather beautiful.

## 6. Albany

Established in 1826, Albany is Western Australia's oldest town, a bustling commercial centre with a stately and genteel decaying colonial quarter and a waterfront in the midst of redevelopment. Take a stroll down Stirling Terrace and up York St for fine Victorian-era architecture. But it's Albany's waters where we recommend you spend most of your time. Southern right and humpback whales gather near the bays and coves of King George Sound from July to mid-October. You can sometimes spot them from the beach, but going with Albany Whale Tours (08-9845 1068; www. albanywhaletours.com.au) or Albany Ocean

sheltered inlets to the south and forests hard up against its back on the inland side. It's slowly earning a reputation as something of a sustainable and artsy place, and the result is a community, both permanent and transitory, of farmers, fishers and families. Denmark is located in the cool-climate Great Southern wine region, with Howard Park (www.burchfamilywines.com.au) and Forest Hill (www.foresthillwines.com.au) among the better wineries nearby. To really get the most of these wineries and Denmark's natural hinterland, book ahead with Denmark Wine Lovers Tour (0410 423 262; www.denmarkwinelovers.com.au),

Adventures (0428 429 876; www.whales.com.au) will increase your chances. Diving and snorkelling is another Albany speciality, thanks to the 2001 scuttling of the warship HMAS Perth to create an artificial reef for divers; contact Southcoast Diving Supplies (08-9841 7176; www.divealbany.com.au). East of the town centre, the beautiful Middleton and Emu Beaches face King George Sound.

The road and coastline turns northeast, arcing up and over the Great Australian Bight. It's 292km (181 miles) to the Hopetoun turn-off, from where it's another 49km (30 miles) down to the coast.

## 7. Detour: Bremer Bay & Fitzgerald River National Park

Far enough off the main road to remain a secret, sleepy Bremer Bay is fringed with brilliant white sand and translucent green waters. It's quiet and very beautiful. From July to November the bay is a cetacean maternity ward for southern right whales, while the town also serves as a gateway to Fitzgerald River National Park.

Walkers will discover beautiful coastline, sand plains, rugged coastal hills (known as 'the Barrens') and deep, wide river valleys. In season, you'll almost certainly see whales and their calves from the shore at Point Ann, where there's a lookout and a heritage walk that follows a short stretch of the 1164km (723 miles) No 2 rabbit-proof fence, one of the longest fences on earth. Entry to the park from Bremer Bay is via Swamp and Murray Rds, and all roads are gravel and passable in 2WD vehicle except after rains – check locally before you set out.

To get here, drive 117km (73 miles) northwest of Albany along Rte 1 to Boxwood Hill. Bremer Bay lies 62km (38 miles) due east of Boxwood Hill.

*Previous spread, clockwise from left: Tree Top Walk, Valley of the Giants; Elephant Rocks off Denmark; hiking in Warren National Park; Albany is WA's oldest town; Right: Who could resist a detour to beautiful Bremer Bay?*

### 8. Esperance

Framed by turquoise waters and utterly pristine white beaches, Esperance sits in solitary splendour on the Bay of Isles. It's such an appealing place that families still travel from Perth or Kalgoorlie just to plug into the easygoing vibe and great beach life. Picture-perfect beaches dot the even more remote national parks to the town's southeast, and the pristine environment of the 105 islands of the off-shore Recherche Archipelago are home to fur seals, penguins and sea birds; a tour to Woody Island is highly recommended, ask at the visitor centre (08-9083 1555; www.visitesperance.com) in Esperance for details. Wreck-diving is also possible with Esperance Diving & Fishing (08-9071 5111; www.esperancedivingandfishing.com.au).

Take the Condingup road that runs northeast, then follow the signs along sealed roads first to Gerbryn, then Cape Le Grand National Park.

### 9. Cape Le Grand National Park

Starting 60km (37 miles) east of Esperance, Cape Le Grand National Park boasts spectacular coastal scenery, dazzling beaches and excellent walking tracks. There's good fishing, swimming and camping at Lucky Bay and Le Grand Beach, and day-use facilities at gorgeous Hellfire Bay.

Make the effort to climb Frenchman Peak (a steep 3km (2 mile) return, allow two hours), as the views from the top and through the rocky 'eye', especially during the late afternoon, are superb. To explore further, your best bet is a 4WD tour along the sand and two-hour circuits of Great Ocean Dr with Eco-Discovery Tours (0407 737 261; www.esperancetours.com.au).

# Northland & Bay of Islands

Known as the 'Winterless North' because of its mild weather, this area combines historical charm with marine adventures. Further north the attractions become even more remote and spectacular, leading all the way to the very top of the North Island at Cape Reinga.

### 1. Auckland

Framed by two harbours, NZ's most cosmopolitan city spreads vibrantly across a narrow coastal isthmus. Explore Auckland's ocean-going personality at the New Zealand Maritime Museum, or take a ferry across the Waitemata harbour to the heritage Edwardian and Victorian architecture of the seaside suburb of Devonport, or a sea-kayaking excursion to Rangitoto island, a forested volcanic cone. Back on land, for the best view of Rangitoto, stroll along Takapuna Beach on Auckland's North Shore or ride a bike around the bays along Tamaki Drive.

For the first leg of 104km (65 miles), depart across the Auckland Harbour Bridge heading north on SH1. North of Warkworth, turn into Wayby Valley Rd continuing on to Mangawhai Heads. Pay tolls for the Northern Gateway Toll Road on SH1 online at www.nzta.govt.nz.

### 2. Mangawhai Heads

Mangawhai village lies on a horseshoe-shaped harbour, but it's Mangawhai Heads, 5km (3 miles) further on, that's really special. A narrow sandspit stretches for kilometres to form the harbour's south head, sheltering a seabird sanctuary. There's an excellent surf beach, best viewed while traversing the Mangawhai Cliff Top Walkway. Starting at Mangawhai Heads, this walking track (around two to three hours) offers extensive views of the ocean and the coast. Make sure you time it right to return down the beach at low tide.

From Mangawhai Heads continue along Cove Rd to Waipu Cove (around 13km/8 miles); it's a very pretty rural and coastal route away from the busier main roads. During summer, Langs Beach en route is enlivened by the scarlet blooms of the pohutukawa, often dubbed 'NZ's Christmas tree'.

### 3. Waipu

The arcing beach at Waipu Cove looks out to Bream Bay. On the near horizon, islands include the Hen and Chickens. Waipu Cove is excellent for swimming – and body surfing if there are good waves – and there are shaded spots for a picnic. A further 8km (5 miles) along a coastal road, Waipu is a sleepy village with excellent cafes that comes to life on summer weekends. The area was originally colonised by Scottish settlers – via Nova Scotia in Canada – who arrived between 1853 and 1860. The Waipu Museum (09-432 0746; www.waipumuseum.co.nz) tells their story.

Rejoin SH1 from Waipu via Nova Scotia Dr, and continue north to Whangarei (39km/24 miles). En route, Ruakaka and Uretiti both offer excellent beaches. Marsden Point announces the entrance to Whangarei Harbour.

### 4. Whangarei

Northland's only city has a thriving local art scene, and an attractive riverside area with excellent museums. Explore Clapham's Clocks (09438 3993; www.claphamsclocks.com) where more than 1400 ticking, gonging and cuckooing timepieces fill the National Clock Museum in Town Basin.

**Cape Reinga** ⑩

*North Cape*

Te Paki

*Te Paki Recreation Reserve*

*Great Exhibition Bay*

Te Kao

*Ninety Mile Beach*

Pukenui

*Karikari Peninsula*

*Doubtless Bay*

*SOUTH PACIFIC OCEAN*

Awanui

Taipa

⑨ **Mangonui**

Kaitaia

Kaeo

*Matauri Bay*

*Cape Brett*

*Tauroa Point*

⑪ **Ahipara**

Herekino

*Omahuta Forest*

**Kerikeri**
⑧

⑥ **Russell**
⑦
**Paihia**

*Warawara Forest*

⑫ **Rawene**

Kaikohe

Kawakawa

*Russell Forest*

Helena Bay

*Poor Knights Islands*

**Opononi & Omapere** ⑬

Whakapara

Matapouri

⑤ **Tutukaka**

**NORTH ISLAND**

Whakapara

Hikurangi

*Wairua River*

**Waipoua State Forest** ⑭

*Maunganui Bluff (460m)*

④ **Whangarei**

*Hen & Chicken Islands*

Ruakaka

Uretiti

*Bream Bay*

Dargaville

**Waipu** ③

*Baylys Beach*

Brynderwyn

② **Mangawhai Heads**

*TASMAN SEA*

⑮
**Matakohe** FINISH

Wellsford

*Kaipara Harbour*

Warkworth

Pouto

*North Head*

*Dome Forest*

Waiwera

*South Head*

*Woodhill Forest*

Helensville

Waimauku

Muriwai Beach

Te Henga (Bethells Beach)

Piha

① **Auckland**
START

**Duration:** 6–8 days

**Distance:** 1057km / 658 miles

**When:** February to April for the best weather, but try to avoid the busy Easter period

0 ———— 50 km
0 ———— 25 miles
N

This harbourside area is also a good place for shopping. A 1904 Māori portrait by artist CF Goldie is a treasure of the adjacent Whangarei Art Museum (09-430 4240; www.whangareiart museum.co.nz).

Depart Whangarei via Bank St, Mill St and Ngunguru Rd to Tutukaka (30km/19 miles). Worthy short stops include Whangarei Falls, a spectacular 26m-high cascade 6km (4 miles) from Town Basin, and Ngunguru, a sleepy estuary settlement just before Tutukaka.

## 5. Tutukaka

Filled with yachts, gamefishing charter boats and dive crews, Tutukaka's marina presents opportunities to explore the stunning above- and below-water scenery in the surrounding area. Many travellers are here to go diving at the Poor Knights Islands, but the underwater thrills are also accessible for snorkelling fans. Surfing lessons are available at O'Neill Surf Academy (09-434 3843; www. oneillsurfacademy.co.nz), and one of the best walks is a blissful 20-minute coastal one from Matapouri to the compact cove at Whale Bay.

Allow two hours for this 106km/66 mile-leg. Leaving Tutukaka and heading north, the coastal road veers inland before reaching the coast again at Matapouri. From Matapouri, continue west to SH1 at Hikurangi. Head north on SH1, and turn right into Russell Rd just before Whakapara. Featuring coastal scenery, this winding road – take care – continues via Helena Bay to Russell.

## 6. Russell

Once known as 'the hellhole of the Pacific', Russell is a historic town with cafes and genteel B&Bs. Russell was originally Kororareka, a fortified Ngāpuhi village. In the early 19th

century the local Māori tribe permitted it to become NZ's first European settlement. It quickly attracted roughnecks like fleeing convicts, whalers and drunken sailors, and in 1835, Charles Darwin described it as full of 'the refuse of society'. After the signing of the Treaty of Waitangi in 1840, nearby Okiato was the country's temporary capital before the capital was moved to Auckland in 1841. Okiato, then known as Russell, was abandoned, and the name Russell eventually replaced Kororareka. Historical highlights now include Pompallier Mission (09-403 9015; www.pompallier.co.nz), an 1842 Catholic mission house, and Christ Church (1836), NZ's oldest church. It's 8km (5 miles) to Okiato, and a car ferry crosses regularly from Okiato to Opua (5km/3 miles from Paihia).

## 7. Paihia

Connected to Russell by passenger ferries across a narrow harbour, Paihia is more energetic than its sleepier sibling. The waterfront hosts maritime excursions including island sightseeing, dolphin-watching and sailing. A coastal road meanders 3km (2 miles) to the Waitangi Treaty Grounds (09-402 7437; www.waitangi.org.nz). Occupying a headland draped in lawns and forest, this is NZ's most important historic site. On 6 February 1840, the first 43 of more than 500 Māori chiefs signed the Treaty of Waitangi with the British Crown. Admission to the Treaty Grounds includes guided tours, Māori cultural performances and entry to the Museum of Waitangi, a showcase of the treaty in NZ's past, present and future.

From Paihia, continue on SH11 (Black Bridge Rd) to Kerikeri, a meandering 24km (15 miles) through citrus orchards. Around 4km (2.5 miles) from Paihia, Haruru Falls can be reached by turning off Puketona Rd on to Haruru Falls Rd.

## 9. Mangonui

Doubtless Bay gets its name from an entry in Captain James Cook's logbook, where he wrote that the body of water was 'doubtless a bay'. The main centre, Mangonui ('Big Shark'), retains a fishing-port ambience, and cafes and galleries fill its historic waterfront buildings. They were constructed when Mangonui was a centre of the whaling industry (1792–1850) and exported flax, kauri (a native coniferous tree) timber and gum.

At Hihi, 15km (9 miles) northeast of Mangonui, the Butler Point Whaling Museum (0800 687 386; www.butlerpoint.co.nz) showcases these earlier days. The nearby settlements of Coopers Beach, Cable Bay and Taipa are all pockets of beachside gentrification and well-tanned retirees with golf habits.

This leg is 132km (82 miles). From Mangonui, drive west on SH10 to rejoin SH1 at Awanui. From Awanui head to NZ's northernmost point, Cape Reinga. An interesting stop is at the Nga-Tapuwae-o-te-Mangai Māori Ratana temple at Te Kao, 58km (36 miles) north of Awanui. Look out for the two green-and-white domed towers.

Campervans can park free of charge at the Mangonui Lions Park for up to three nights.

For stunning beaches facing all directions, take a quick detour on to Karikari Peninsula, well-signposted about 9km (6 miles) west of Taipa off SH10.

## 8. Kerikeri

Famous for its oranges, Kerikeri also produces kiwifruit, vegetables and wine. It's increasingly popular with retirees and hosts some of the Northland's best restaurants. A snapshot of early Māori and Pākehā (European New Zealander) interaction is offered by a cluster of historic sites centred on Kerikeri's picturesque river basin. Dating from 1836, the Stone Store (09-407 9236; www.historic.org.nz) is NZ's oldest stone building, and tours depart from here for the nearby Mission House (www.historic.org.nz), NZ's oldest surviving building, from 1822. There's an ongoing campaign to have the area recognised as a Unesco World Heritage Site.

From Kerikeri, head north on SH10, turning east to Matauri Bay Rd to complete a stunning 41km (25 mile) loop back to SH10 just north of Kaeo. This coastal road takes in Matauri Bay, Tauranga Bay and the Whangaroa Harbour. Back on SH10, continue 30km (19 miles) north to Mangonui, 90km (56 miles) from Kerikeri, and Doubtless Bay.

## 10. Cape Reinga

In the waters surrounding windswept Cape Reinga Lighthouse (a rolling 1km walk from the car park), the Tasman Sea and Pacific Ocean meet, crashing in waves up to 10m high in stormy weather. Māori consider Cape Reinga (Te Rerenga Wairua) the jumping-off point for souls as they depart on the journey to their spiritual homeland. Out of respect to the most sacred site of Māori people, refrain from eating or drinking anywhere in the area.

It is possible to drive down Ninety Mile Beach, but every year several tourists – and their hire cars – get stuck in the sand. Join a 4WD bus tour or drive south to Kaitaia from Cape Reinga on SH1 (111km/69 miles) and continue 13km (8 miles) west to Ahipara on the Ahipara Rd.

## 11. Ahipara

All good things must come to an end, and Ninety Mile Beach does at this relaxed Far North beach town. A few holiday mansions have snuck in, but mostly it's just the locals keeping it real with visiting surfers. The area is known for its huge sand dunes and massive gum field where 2000 people once worked. Adventure activities are popular on the dunes above Ahipara and further around the Tauroa Peninsula. Ahipara Adventure Centre (09-409 2055; www.ahiparaadventure.co.nz; 15 Takahe St) can hook you up with sand toboggans, surfboards and mountain bikes, and Ahipara-based NZ Surf Bros (09-945 7276, 021 252 7078; www.nzsurfbros.com) offers surfing lessons.

From Ahipara, drive 64km (40 miles) through the verdant Herekino forest to the sleepy harbour settlement of Kohukohu. Around 4km (2.5 miles) past Kohukohu, a car ferry crosses the Hokianga Harbour to Rawene. Payment is cash only and the ferry leaves Kohukohu on the hour from 8am to 8pm.

## 12. Rawene

During the height of the kauri timber industry Kohukohu was a busy town with a sawmill, shipyard, two newspapers and banks. These days it's a very quiet harbour backwater dotted with well-preserved heritage buildings. Have a coffee and one of NZ's best pies at the local cafe, before catching the ferry across the harbour to Rawene. Founded as NZ's third European settlement, a number of historic buildings (including six churches) remain from a time when the harbour was considerably busier than it is now. Information boards outline a heritage trail of the main sights. Built in the bustling 1860s by a trader, stately Clendon House (09-405 7874; www.historic.org.nz) is now managed by the New Zealand Historic Places Trust.

After crossing on the ferry from Kohukohu to Rawene, another winding road and scenic road travels 20km (12 miles) to reach Opononi, near the entrance of the Hokianga Harbour.

## 13. Opononi & Omapere

The twin settlements of Opononi and Omapere lie on the south head of Hokianga Harbour. Views are dominated by mountainous sand dunes across the water at North Head. Starting at the car park at the end of Signal Station Rd – right off SH12 at the top of the hill leaving Omapere – the Arai te Uru Heritage Walk (roughly 30 minutes return) follows the cliffs and passes through manuka scrub before continuing to the Hokianga's southern headland. At the headland are the remains of an old signal station built to assist ships making the

© Mark Read / Lonely Planet

treacherous passage back into the harbour.

Climbing south out of Omapere – don't miss the spectacular views back across the harbour – SH12 continues to the Waipoua State Forest – a meandering journey of around 20km (12 miles).

## 14. Waipoua State Forest

This superb forest sanctuary – proclaimed in 1952 after public pressure – is the largest remnant of the once-extensive kauri forests of northern NZ. The forest road (SH12) stretches for 18km (11 miles) and passes huge trees. Near the northern end of the park stands mighty Tane Mahuta, named for the Māori forest god. At 51.5m high with a 13.8m girth, he's the largest kauri alive, and has been growing for between 1200 and 2000 years. Stop at the Waipoua Forest Visitor Centre (09-439 6445; www.teroroa.iwi.nz/visitwaipoua) for an exhibition on the forests, guided tours, flax-weaving lessons, and a cafe. You can also plant your own kauri tree, complete with GPS coordinates.

From Waipoua Forest Visitor Centre, it's 107km (65 miles) on SH12, via the riverine town of Dargaville, to Matakohe. About 4km (2.5 miles) north of Dargaville, Baylys Coast Rd runs 9km (5.5 miles) west to the wild surf at Baylys Beach.

## 15. Matakohe

Apart from the charms of the village, the key reason for visiting Matakohe is the superb Kauri Museum (09-431 7417; www.kaurimuseum.com). The giant cross-sections of trees are astounding, but the entire timber industry is brought to life through video kiosks, artefacts, fabulous marquetry, and reproductions of a pioneer sawmill, boarding house, gumdigger's hut and Victorian home. The Gum Room holds a weird and wonderful collection of kauri gum, the resinous amber substance that can be carved, sculpted and polished to a jewel-like quality. The museum shop stocks mementoes crafted from kauri wood and gum.

From Matakohe, travel east on SH12 to join SH1 again at Brynderwyn. Drive south to Wellsford and then take SH16 for the scenic route southwest back to Auckland (163km/101 miles in total from Matakohe). From Wellsford to Auckland on SH16 is around 110km (68 miles), taking in views of Kaipara Harbour and West Auckland's vineyards.

© Mark Read / Lonely Planet

# The Southern Alps Circuit

**Nothing defines the South Island like the Southern Alps, the 500km-long series of ranges stretching from Nelson Lakes to Fiordland. This trip offers the chance to admire a vast swathe of them on such quintessential New Zealand experiences as glacier ice hikes, scenic flights, cross-country bike rides and nature walks – or by staring out of the van window, if you prefer.**

## 1. Christchurch

Nowhere in NZ is changing as fast as post-earthquake Christchurch, and visiting the country's second-largest city during its rebuilding phase is both interesting and inspiring. What's more, the majority of Christchurch's pre-quake attractions are open for business, including the must-visit Canterbury Museum (03-366 5000; www.canterburymuseum.com). Not only does it provide a well-rounded introduction to the city and region, it's also particularly strong on the natural history of wider NZ.

Head out of the city limits on SH73, which strikes out across Canterbury Plains and heads into the Southern Alps. The Big Ben, Torlesse and Craigieburn Ranges are but a prelude to the mega-peaks of Arthur's Pass National Park, around two hours (148km/92 miles) from Christchurch.

## 2. Arthur's Pass National Park

Straddling the Southern Alps, Arthur's Pass National Park encompasses a seriously rugged landscape, riven with deep valleys and ranging in altitude from 245m (804ft) at the Taramakau River to 2408m (7900ft) at the top of Mt Murchison. It's popular with alpinists and backcountry trampers, but its dramatic wilderness can readily be appreciated on brief forays close to the highway. There are multiple walking options from the village, including one of the best day hikes in the country. The strenuous 7km (4.3 mile) climb up Avalanche Peak should only be attempted in fine weather by fit, well-equipped and experienced walkers.

Those who do make the effort, however, will be rewarded with staggering views of the surrounding mountains, valleys and hanging glaciers. The village itself, home to a permanent population of around 60, sports a couple of cafes and the Arthur's Pass Visitor Centre (03-318 9211; www.doc.govt.nz). Pop in here for walking track information and local weather forecasts.

Continue west on SH73. Beyond the actual pass (920m/3018ft), craggy mountain vistas give way to rural scenes as the highway winds down to meet SH6, the West Coast Rd. At Kumara Junction head south to Hokitika, 22km (14 miles) away for a total of 100km (62 miles, some 90 minutes) driving.

## 3. Hokitika

Just one of scores of West Coast towns founded on gold, Hokitika boasts an admirable array of historic buildings, including the 1908 Carnegie Building housing Hokitika Museum. An exemplary provincial museum and easily the best on the Coast, its wide-ranging displays cover such topics as the gold rushes, the region's natural and social history, and traditional Māori use of pounamu. Hokitika today is a stronghold of this indigenous and highly prized stone, judiciously gathered from nearby rivers. It is fashioned into pendants and other personal treasures by master carvers who jostle for position alongside jewellers, glass-blowers and various other craftspeople. Art-lovers will find the town a delight. Keep your fingers crossed for a clear

evening, because five minutes' walk from the town centre is Sunset Point – a prime place to watch the light fade with a feed of fish and chips, seagulls circling, and big Tasman Sea waves crashing on the driftwood-strewn shore.

Just south of Hokitika are a couple of scenic walks – the historic Mananui Tramline and the commercial Treetop Walkway, a canopy-level construction built from steel. The rest of the 27km (17 mile) drive to Ross cuts inland through a mixture of pasture and patches of forest. If you're ready for a shower and sauna, the Shining Star Holiday Park (03-755 8921; 16 Richards Dr) is an attractive beachside spot complete with a menagerie.

## 4. Ross

Ross was the scene of a major kerfuffle in 1907 when NZ's largest gold nugget (the 2.772kg 'Honourable Roddy') was unearthed. The Ross Goldfields Heritage Centre (www.ross. org.nz; 4 Aylmer St) displays a replica Roddy, along with a scale model of the town in its glittering years. Starting near the museum, the Water Race Walk (one hour return) passes old gold diggings, caves, tunnels and a cemetery. Apparently there's still gold in them thar hills, so you might like to try a spot of gold panning in Jones Creek. The $10 pan hire fee is a small outlay for the chance to find Roddy's great, great grand-nuggets, don't you think?

The 131km (81 mile), two-hour drive south to Fox Glacier meanders inland crossing numerous mighty West Coast river systems, cutting through dense rainforest and passing tranquil lakes. The 30-minute section between Franz Josef Glacier and Fox Glacier townships will blow your socks off (if it's not raining...).

## 5. Fox Glacier

Fox Glacier is the smaller and quieter of the twin glacier townships, and is set in more rural surrounds. While you should linger in both if your itinerary allows, Fox is our pick of the two. Scenic helicopter flights are offered by a raft of operators touting for business on the main road. There is also a choice of independent or guided walks up into the glacier valley, as well as glacier hikes with Fox Glacier Guiding.

Allow 90 minutes to reach Ship Creek, 103km (64 miles) away along a scenic stretch of highway chopped through lowland forest and occasional pasture with intermittent views seaward. Stop at Knights Point, 5km (3 miles) south of Lake Moeraki, a spectacular lookout commemorating the opening of this stretch of highway in 1965.

**Cromwell thrills**
Petrolheads will love
Cromwell's Highlands
Motorsport Park (03-445
4052; www.highlands.
co.nz), a first-rate 4km
racing circuit offering a
range of high-octane
experiences. Start out
on the go-karts before
taking a 200km/h ride
in the Highlands Taxi,
then completing three
laps of the circuit as a
passenger in a Porsche
GT, or behind the wheel
of a V8 muscle car.

## 6. Ship Creek

For a taste of the wilderness that qualifies the
Haast region for inclusion in Te Wāhipounamu–
South West New Zealand World Heritage Area,
you can't go past Ship Creek. The car park
alongside the highway is the trailhead for two
fascinating walks. We suggest starting with
Kahikatea Swamp Forest Walk, a 20-minute
amble through a weird bog, before heading on
to the beach for the Dune Lake Walk. This salty,
sandy amble is supposed to take half an hour
but may well suck you into a vortex of beachcombing, wave-watching, seabird-spotting
and perhaps even a spot of tree-hugging in the
primeval forest around the reedy lake.

SH7 sticks close to the coast before crossing
the Haast River on NZ's longest single-lane
bridge. At Haast Junction, around half an hour
from Ship Creek, take SH6 to Haast township –
a chance to stock up on food and fuel – before
continuing on towards Haast Pass. This 97km
(60 mile) leg will take just under two hours.

## 7. Makarora

The first sign of life after crossing Haast
Pass into Central Otago, middle-of-nowhere
Makarora survives as a road-trip stop and
a base for adventure into Siberia. No, not
that Siberia. We're talking about the remote
wilderness valley within Mt Aspiring National
Park, reached on one of the South Island's
adventure tours – the Siberia Experience
(03-443 4385; www.siberiaexperience.co.nz).
This thrill-seeking extravaganza combines
a 25-minute small-plane flight, a three-hour
tramp through the remote mountain valley and
a half-hour jetboat trip down the Wilkin and
Makarora Rivers. There may be better ways to
spend four hours, but it's tough to think of any.

© Matteo Colombo / Getty Images

Classic Central Otago scenery – wide, open,
and framed by schist peaks – welcomes you
as SH6 snakes away from Makarora and sidles
along the convoluted edges of Lake Wanaka
and Lake Hawea. This glorious 64km (40 mile)
drive to Wanaka takes around an hour.

## 8. Wanaka

Though certainly more laidback than its amped-
up sibling Queenstown, Wanaka is not a sleepy
hamlet anymore. Its lakeside setting is sublime,
its streets less cluttered and clogged with traffic.
Combine this with a critical mass of shops,
restaurants and bars, and you've got an arguably
more charming (and slightly cheaper) rival.
There's also an endless array of adrenalising
and inspiring outdoor activities. Wanaka is the
gateway to Mt Aspiring National Park, as well
as Cardrona and Treble Cone ski resorts. Closer
to town, however, are heaps of easier and more
accessible adventures. A classic walkway hoofs
it up to the summit of Mt Iron (527m/1729ft, 1½
hours return), revealing panoramic views of Lake
Wanaka and its mind-boggling surrounds.

Head to Queenstown via the well-signposted
Crown Range, NZ's highest sealed road at
1121m/3677ft. Pull over at designated lookout
points to admire the view on the way down
to the Wakatipu Basin, and at the junction
with SH6 head right towards Queenstown. This
68km (42 mile) drive will take just over an hour.

## 9. Queenstown

New Zealand's premier resort town is an
extravaganza of shopping, dining and tour
booking offices, packaged up together in the
midst of inspiring mountain surrounds. Ease
your way into it on foot, taking in major sites
such as Skyline Gondola and Steamer Wharf,

and following Queenstown Gardens' lakeshore path, revealing ever-changing panoramas of Lake Wakatipu and the Remarkables. Add to this backdrop the region's other mountain ranges, tumbling rivers, hidden canyons and rolling high country, and it's not hard to see why Queenstown is the king of outdoor adventure.

The dramatic 60km (37 mile) drive through the Kawarau Gorge will take around an hour. Drive on SH6A out of Queenstown past the airport and then onwards beyond Lake Hayes and the turn-off for Arrowtown. There are numerous temptations on the way to Cromwell including Gibbston Valley wineries and the original AJ Hackett bungee jump.

## 10. Cromwell

The hot, dry, highly mineral soils around Cromwell account for the town's claim to fame as a fruit bowl – celebrated in the giant, gaudy fruit sculpture that greets visitors as they arrive. Among many luscious specimens are the grapes grown around Bannockburn, Central Otago's finest wine-growing subregion, just south of Cromwell. A dozen or so wineries are open to the public, with several offering notable dining.

From Cromwell cross the bridge over Lake Dunstan and drive north on SH8 along the lake, through Tarras, and on to Lindis Pass before passing into Mackenzie Country. Around 9km (5.5 miles) after Twizel is the turn-off for Aoraki/ Mt Cook on SH80. This 204km (127 mile) journey should take less than three hours.

## 11. Aoraki / Mt Cook National Park

The spectacular 700 sq km Aoraki/Mt Cook National Park, along with Fiordland, Aspiring and Westland National Parks, forms part of the

*Previous spread; looking over Queenstown from the Skyline Gondola Right, from top: Lake Tekapo's 1935 Church of the Good Shepherd; the irresistibly open road towards Mt Cook*

Te Wāhipounamu–South West New Zealand World Heritage Area, which extends from Westland's Cook River down to Fiordland. Fenced in by the Southern Alps and the Two Thumb, Liebig and Ben Ohau Ranges, more than one-third of the national park has a blanket of permanent snow and glacial ice. The highest maunga (mountain) in the park is mighty Aoraki/Mt Cook – at 3754m (12,316ft) it's the tallest peak in Australasia. Unless you're an able alpinist, the best way to view this mountain majesty is on a scenic flight. Helicopter Line (03-435 1801; www.helicopter. co.nz) at Glentanner Park and Mount Cook Ski Planes (03-430 8026; www.mtcookskiplanes. com) at Mt Cook Airport will buzz you around the peaks on a variety of trips; all but the shortest include a landing in the snow.

Return along SH80, pausing at lookout points along the 55km (34 mile) stretch to soak up more of the mesmerising lake and mountain scenery. At the junction with SH8 turn left and drive a further 47km (29 miles) northeast over the Mary Range to Lake Tekapo.

## 12. Lake Tekapo

The mountain-ringed basin known as the Mackenzie Country – lined with surreal blue hydro lakes and canals, surrounded by golden tussock – is one of the South Island's most celebrated landscapes. Towards its northern

© Lingxiao Xie / Getty Images

© Ramiro Torrents / Getty Images

boundary is Lake Tekapo township, born of a hydropower scheme completed in 1953. Perched on the shore of the opalescent, turquoise lake, with a backdrop of the snow-capped Southern Alps, it's no wonder the Church of the Good Shepherd is one of NZ's most photographed buildings. Built of stone and oak in 1935, it features a picture window that frames a distractingly divine view of lake and mountain majesty. Arrive early morning or late afternoon if you want to avoid the crowds. The view is indeed divine, but still no match for the epic, 360-degree panorama from the top of Mt John (1029m/3376ft). A winding but well-sealed road leads to the summit, home to astronomical observatories and the fabulous Astro Café. You can also reach the summit via the circuit track (2¼ hours return). Supremely situated on terraced, lakefront grounds is Tekapo Motels & Holiday Park (03-680 6825; www.laketekapoaccommodation.co.nz).

Climb away from the lake on SH8 over the Burkes Pass (709m/2326ft) and on to the rural town of Fairlie, home of super-fine pies. From here, drive on SH79 through rolling countryside to Geraldine, the cheese and pickle capital of New Zealand. Total distance is 89km (55 miles).

## 13. Geraldine

With a touch of quaint English village about it, Geraldine is a pleasant place to break a journey amid the rural Canterbury Plains. On the town's northwestern fringe, stretch your legs at Talbot Forest Scenic Reserve (www.doc.govt.nz) and hug some magnificent trees, including lofty kahikatea (white pine) and a massive totara estimated to be around 800 years old.

Drive north on SH72, crossing the braided Rangitata River after 6km (3.7 miles), and passing through flat, irrigated land along Roman-straight roads. Continue on SH72 as it traces around the eastern edge of the mountains. Turn right on to SH77, 72km (45 miles) from Geraldine, and drive the last 10km (6 miles) to Methven.

## 14. Methven

Methven is busiest in winter, when it fills up with snow bunnies heading to nearby Mt Hutt ski field. At other times tumbleweeds don't quite blow down the main street – much to the disappointment of the wannabe gunslingers arriving for the raucous October rodeo. Over summer it's a low-key and affordable base for explorations into the spectacular mountain foothills. The town itself can be explored on a heritage trail and the Methven Walk/Cycleway. Maps are available from the i SITE (03-302 8955; www.methvenmthutt.co.nz).

Drive north on Mt Hutt Station Rd, then turn right on to SH72, passing through Mt Hutt village before reaching the blue and braided river at Rakaia Gorge, 16km (10 miles) from Methven.

## 15. Rakaia Gorge

One of NZ's most voluminous braided rivers, the Rakaia starts out deep and swift in the mountains before gradually widening and separating into strands over a gravel bed. The half-day Rakaia Gorge Walkway is a good opportunity to survey the river's milky blue waters and take in other sites, including the historic ferryman's cottage and old coal mines.

Drive east on SH72 (Route 77) for 41km (25 miles) to Darfield, leaving the mountains in the rear-view mirror as you reach the patchwork Canterbury Plains. Continue east on SH73 to the outskirts of Christchurch, then follow signs for the city centre. Total distance is 88km (55 miles).

# Circling the Canadian Rockies Coast

**Taking you through Kootenay, Banff and Yoho National Parks and dipping into Alberta, this trip shows off Mother Nature at her best: lofty snowy peaks, deep forests and natural hot springs. This is where mountains stretch up to the stars and waterfalls, and canyons and gem-coloured lakes lie deep in the forest, waiting to be discovered... as do bears, moose and other critters.**

### 1. Radium Hot Springs

Set in a valley just inside the southern border of Kootenay National Park, the outdoor Radium Hot Springs (250-347 9485; www.pc.gc.ca/hotsprings) has a hot pool simmering at 39°C (102°F) and a second pool to cool you off at 29°C (84°F). Originally sacred to First Nations peoples for the water's curative powers, these springs are uniquely odourless and colourless. The large tiled pool can get crowded in summer. You can rent lockers, towels and even swimsuits.

From Radium Hot Springs, it's a lovely 83km (52 mile) drive on Hwy 93 through the park to Ochre Ponds and Paint Pots.

### 2. Ochre Ponds & Paint Pots

As the road delves down into the woods along Hwy 93, a signpost leads to a short, flat interpretive trail. Follow this to the intriguing red-and-orange Ochre Ponds. Drawing Kootenay First Peoples for centuries – and later European settlers – this iron-rich earth was collected, mixed with oil and made into paint. Further along the trail are three crystal-blue springs that are known as the Paint Pots. Continue north along Hwy 93 for 3km (2 miles) to the next stop.

### 3. Marble Canyon

This jaw-dropping stop is not for the faint-of-heart. An easy 15-minute trail zigzags over Tokumm Creek, giving phenomenal views deeper and deeper into Marble Canyon below. The limestone and dolomite walls have been carved away by the awesome power of the creek, resulting in plunging falls and bizarrely shaped cliff faces. The trail can be slippery. Take sturdy shoes and your camera.

Marble Canyon Campground (off Hwy 93, Kootenay National Park) is a high-country 61-pitch campground situated near the Marble Canyon trail, and has flush toilets but no showers. Most sites have tree cover to shelter from the wind. The eastern side has the best views.

Continue north along Hwy 93 and across the provincial border into Alberta to the junction with Hwy 1 (Castle Junction). Head west.

### 4. Banff National Park

More of a drive than a stop, the stretch of Hwy 1 running from Castle Junction to Lake Louise is one of the most scenic routes through Banff National Park. The highway runs through the Bow Valley, following the weaving Bow River and the route of the Pacific Railway. The craggy peaks of the giant Sawback and Massive mountain ranges sweep up on either side of the road. The resulting perspective is much wider than on smaller roads with big open vistas. There are several viewpoint pull-offs where gob-smacked drivers can stop to absorb their surroundings. Watch for the unmissable Castle Mountain looming in its crimson glory to the northwest. The Panorama Ridge then rises in the south, after which the enormous Mt Temple comes into view, towering at 3542m (11,620ft). Stop at the Mt Temple Viewpoint for a good gander. This stretch of the highway is only two lanes with no fencing to stop wandering animals from venturing into the road. Drive with caution.

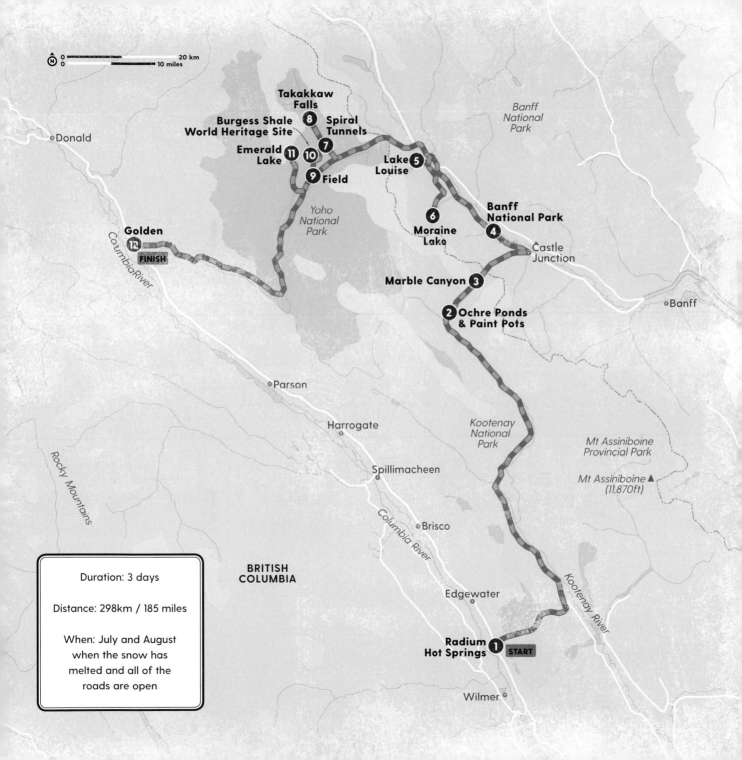

Takakkaw
Falls

**8**

Burgess Shale
**World Heritage Site**

Spiral
Tunnels

**7**

Emerald
Lake

**11** **10**

**9** Field

Lake
Louise

**5**

Banff
**National Park**

**6**

Moraine
Lake

**4**

Castle
Junction

Donald

*Yoho
National
Park*

Golden

**12**
**FINISH**

*Banff
National
Park*

Banff

Marble Canyon **3**

**2** Ochre Ponds
**& Paint Pots**

Parson

*Kootenay
National
Park*

*Mt Assiniboine
Provincial Park*

*Mt Assiniboine* ▲
*(11,870ft)*

Harrogate

Spillimacheen

*Rocky
Mountains*

Columbia River

Brisco

**BRITISH
COLUMBIA**

Edgewater

*Kootenay
River*

Radium
**Hot Springs**

**1**
**START**

Wilmer

0 ——————————— 20 km
⊕N
0 ——————————— 10 miles

Duration: 3 days

Distance: 298km / 185 miles

When: July and August
when the snow has
melted and all of the
roads are open

**Tip:** In general, you'll want to rely mostly on established campgrounds, and should make reservations ahead of time in peak season; boondocking on private land is generally frowned upon. As a last resort, WalMart parking lots allow overnight stays.

*Left: Hwy 93, which on this route will take you from Kootenay National Park into Alberta, runs through some soaring Rocky Mountains scenery and evolves into the Icefields Parkway further north*

The turnoff for Lake Louise Village is 24km (15 miles) from Castle Junction.

## 5. Lake Louise

With stunning emerald-green water and tall, snowy peaks that hoist hefty Victoria Glacier up for all to see, Lake Louise has captured the imaginations of mountaineers, artists and visitors for over a century. You – and the enormous numbers of other visitors – will notice the lake's colour appears slightly different from each viewpoint. Follow the Lakeshore Trail, a 4km (2.5 mile) round trip, or head up the gorgeous (though somewhat more difficult) route to Lake Agnes and its sun-dappled teahouse, perched 7km (4.3 miles) from Lake Louise's shore.

For a more relaxed experience, rent a canoe from Lake Louise Boathouse (403 522 3511) and paddle yourself through the icy waters. Or take to the skies – the Lake Louise Gondola (403 522 3555; www.lakelouisegondola.com) lands you at a lofty 2088m (6850ft) for a view of the lake and the surrounding glaciers and peaks. En route you'll sail over wildflowers and possibly even a grizzly bear. At the top is the Wildlife Interpretation Centre, which hosts regular theatre presentations and guided walks. Travel the 14-minute ascent in either an open ski lift or an enclosed gondola.

From Lake Louise Dr, head south along Moraine Lake Rd for 14km (9 miles).

## 6. Moraine Lake

You'll be dazzled by the scenery before you even reach Moraine Lake, set in the Valley of the Ten Peaks. En route, the narrow, winding road gives off fabulous views of the imposing Wenkchemna Peaks. Look familiar? For years this scene was carried on the back of the Canadian $20 bill. In 1894, explorer Samuel Allen named the peaks with numbers from one to 10 in the Stoney Indian Language (wenkchemna means '10'); all but two of the mountains have since been renamed. You'll quickly notice the Tower of Babel, ascending solidly toward the heavens at the northeastern edge of the range.

With little of Lake Louise's hustle or bustle and lots of beauty, many people prefer the more rugged and remote setting of Moraine Lake to Lake Louise. The turquoise waters are surprisingly clear for a glacial reservoir. Take a look at the surrounding mountains through telescopes secured to the southern shore (free!) or hire a boat and paddle to the middle for a 360-degree view. There are also some great day hikes from here, and, to rest your weary legs, a cafe, dining room and lodge. The road to Moraine Lake and its facilities are open from June to early October.

Return to Hwy 1 and continue westwards, across the provincial border and into Yoho National Park.

## 7. Spiral Tunnels

Upon completion of the railway in 1885, trains struggled up the challenging Kicking Horse Pass, which you'll cross soon after the Alberta–British Columbia provincial border. This is the steepest railway pass in North America and wrecks and runaways were common. In 1909 the Spiral Tunnels were carved into Mt Cathedral and Mt Ogden and are still in use today. If you time it right, you can see a train exiting from the top of the tunnel while its final cars are still entering at the bottom. Watch from the main viewing area on the north side of the highway.

Continue west on Hwy 1 and then turn north on to Yoho Valley Rd (open from late June to October). Be prepared – this road climbs a number of tight switchbacks.

## 8. Takakkaw Falls

Named 'magnificent' in Cree, Takakkaw Falls (Yoho National Park) is one of the highest waterfalls in Canada (245m/804ft). An impressive torrent of water travels from the Daly Glacier, plunges over the edge of the rock face into a small pool and jets out into a tumbling cloud of mist. En route to the falls you'll pass a second Spiral Lookout and the Meeting of the Rivers, where the clear Kicking Horse runs into the milky-coloured Yoho.

Return to Hwy 1 and continue west to Field.

## 9. Field

In the midst of Yoho National Park, on the southern side of the Kicking Horse River, lies the quaint village of Field. This historic but unfussy railroad town has a dramatic overlook of the river. While Field may be short on amenities, it's a beautiful place to wander. It's also the place to come if you want to organise an activity in the park – from dog-sledding in winter to canoeing and white-water rafting in summer.

## 10. Burgess Shale World Heritage Site

In 1909 Burgess Shale was unearthed on Mt Field. The fossil beds are home to perfectly preserved fossils of marine creatures, dated at over 500 million years old and recognised as some of the earliest forms of life. The area is now a World Heritage site and accessible only by guided hikes, led by naturalists from the Yoho Shale Geoscience Foundation (800-343

3006; www.burgess-shale.bc.ca). Reservations well in advance are essential, as is stamina: it's an impressive 19.3km (12 mile) round trip, ascending 762m (2500ft).

Continue west on Hwy 1 and take the first right. Continue north for 10km (6 miles).

## 11. Emerald Lake

Gorgeously green Emerald Lake gains its colour from light reflecting off fine glacial rock particles that are deposited into the lake by grinding glaciers. It's a highlight of the park, so the lake attracts visitors year-round, either to simply admire its serenity or to fish, skate, hike or horseback ride. In summer, the water warms up just enough to have a very quick dip. En route to the lake watch for the impressive natural bridge stretching across the Kicking Horse River.

Return to Hwy 1 and continue to Golden, 54km (33 miles) from the turnoff.

*Clockwise from far left: Glacial Moraine Lake in the Valley of the Ten Peaks; the Takakkaw Falls off Yoho Valley Rd plunge 245m; crossing the Cascade River on horseback in Banff National Park*

© Dennis Cox / Alamy Stock Photo

© Justin Foulkes / Lonely Planet

## 12. Golden

Boasting six national parks in its backyard, little Golden is a popular base. It's also the centre for white-water rafting trips on the turbulent Kicking Horse River. Powerful grade III and IV rapids and breathtaking scenery along the sheer walls of Kicking Horse Valley make this rafting experience one of North America's very best. Full-day trips on the river cost roughly CAN$165; half-day trips CAN$65. Operators include Alpine Rafting (250-344 6778; www.alpinerafting.com).

Back on dry land, the Northern Lights Wolf Centre (250-344 6798; www.northernlightswildlife.com) is a refuge for this misunderstood animal, promoting respect for the role of wolves in the wild. Meet a resident wolf or two and learn about their routines and survival.

© Justin Foulkes / Lonely Planet

# Nova Scotia & Cape Breton's Cabot Trail

**Encounter Nova Scotia's windblown coastline, a rich blend of Gaelic, Acadian and Mi'kmaq cultures, vibrant autumnal foliage and a stunning national park on Canada's Cabot Trail. The route is circular, so you can head in either direction, and driving here is a pleasant, leisurely experience. Though the maximum speed on the Cabot Trail is a stately 50mph, the trail has a pace of its own; locals regularly stop their vehicles in the middle of the highway – for a pedestrian, a moose or simply a friendly chat with a neighbour heading in the oncoming direction.**

### 1. Cape Breton

Life on the island of Cape Breton, in the far eastern corner of Canada, goes with the flow. Lobster boats chug into the horizon; whales rise and fall beyond the shore; bears lumber through the island's boreal forests; the Atlantic wind carries the rhythmical notes of Gaelic fiddles.

Surrounded by the Gulf of St Lawrence on one side, and the Atlantic Ocean on the other, Cape Breton's northern half is home to the Cabot Trail, a beautiful 297km (185 mile) road that hugs cliffs, then winds and climbs over the Cape Breton highlands before dropping down to grass-covered sand dunes and tranquil hamlets. Alexander Graham Bell, he of telephone-invention fame and a regular visitor to the island, declared that of the many natural places he'd seen around the world, 'Cape Breton out-rivals them all.'

But the Cabot Trail is more than a drive with stunning geography, ocean vistas, wilderness and wildlife. It's also a cultural circuit enriched by colourful inhabitants and centuries-old traditions. The Mi'kmaq people inhabited the island when the first Europeans, led by explorer John Cabot, arrived in 1497. In later centuries, many Scottish, Irish and English settled. So did Acadians, descendants of the French, all contributing to a colourful Gaelic mélange.

### 2. Cape Breton Highlands National Park

Many fishing villages were not accessible by land until as late as the 1930s, when car travel over the Cape Breton highlands became possible. In 1936, the Cape Breton Highlands National Park was created in the northern section of the island, preserving 949 sq km (366 sq miles) of coastal wilderness, forests and mountains. The road – which encompasses much of the park – was gradually paved in sections between 1940 and 1961.

### 3. Baddeck

Officially, the Cabot Trail starts and ends in Baddeck, which is a pretty harbour town on Bras d'Or Lake. Take a quick pre-drive look into the Alexander Graham Bell National Historic Site, which displays Bell's fascinating inventions, including his hydrofoil.

From Baddeck, head north to St Anns, home of the Colaisde na Gáidhlig, North America's only Gaelic college, where you can learn to speak the language, step-dance or play the bagpipes. The road then winds through corridors of pine and spruce, before emerging at a cliff edge to a view of the icy ocean. In its northern section the road heads around the national park, whose hiking trails and campgrounds make it the perfect stop for vanlife adventurers.

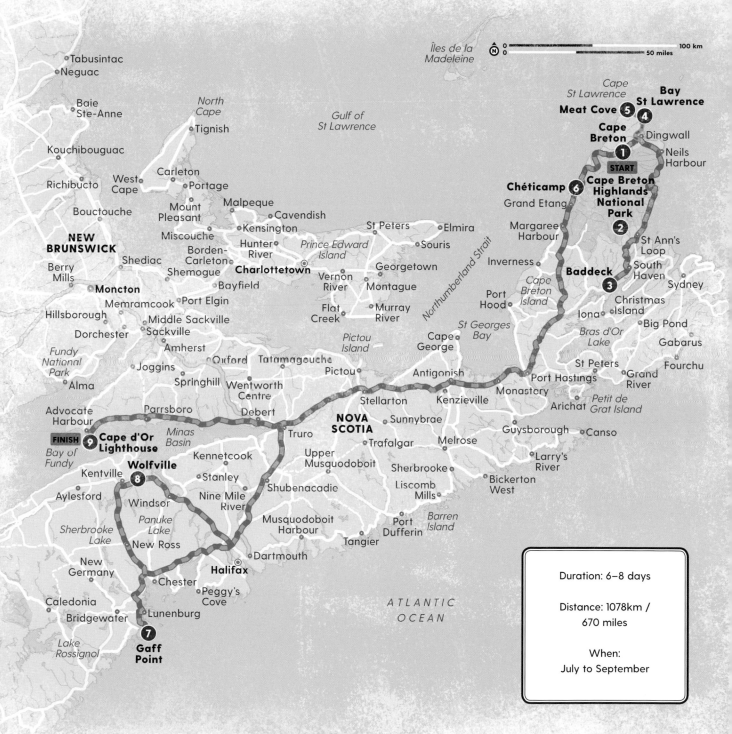

Îles de la
Madeleine

0 ———————————— 100 km
N
0 ———————————— 50 miles

*Cape
St Lawrence*

**Bay
St Lawrence**

**Meat Cove** ⑤
④

*Cape
St Lawrence*

**Cape
Breton**
① Dingwall

**START**

Neils
Harbour

**Chéticamp** ⑥ **Cape Breton
Highlands
National Park**

Grand Etang ②

Margaree
Harbour

St Ann's
Loop

South
Haven

Inverness

*Cape
Breton
Island*

**Baddeck**
③

St Peters Elmira
Souris

Georgetown

Montague

Port
Hood

Iona

Christmas
Island

Sydney

*North
Cape*

*Gulf of
St Lawrence*

Tignish

Carleton

Portage

West
Cape

Mount
Pleasant

Malpeque
Cavendish

Kensington

Miscouche

Borden-
Carleton

Hunter
River

*Prince Edward
Island*

**Charlottetown**

Shemogue

Bayfield

Vernon
River

Port Elgin

Shediac

Flat
Creek

Murray
River

*Northumberland Strait*

Big Pond

*Bras d'Or
Lake*

Gabarus

St Peters

Fourchu

Grand
River

*Petit de
Grat Island*

Tabusintac
Neguac

Baie
Ste-Anne

Kouchibouguac

Richibucto

Bouctouche

**NEW
BRUNSWICK**

Berry
Mills

**Moncton**

Memramcook

Hillsborough

Dorchester

*Fundy
National
Park*

Alma

Joggins

Springhill

Oxford

Amherst

Tatamagouche

Middle Sackville

Sackville

Wentworth
Centre

Pictou
Island

Pictou

Stellarton

*St Georges
Bay*

Cape
George

Antigonish

Kenzieville

Monastery

Port Hastings

Arichat

Guysborough

Canso

Larry's
River

Bickerton
West

Liscomb
Mills

Sherbrooke

Melrose

Trafalgar

**NOVA
SCOTIA**

Sunnybrae

*Minas
Basin*

Parrsboro

Advocate
Harbour

**FINISH** ⑨ **Cape d'Or
Lighthouse**

*Bay of
Fundy*

Kentville

Aylesford

**Wolfville**
⑧

Windsor

*Panuke
Lake*

*Sherbrooke
Lake*

New Ross

New
Germany

Caledonia

Bridgewater

*Lake
Rossignol*

Chester

Lunenburg

⑦
**Gaff
Point**

Peggy's
Cove

**Halifax**

Dartmouth

Debert

Truro

Kennetcook

Stanley

Nine Mile
River

Shubenacadie

Upper
Musquodoboit

Musquodoboit
Harbour

Tangier

Port
Dufferin

*Barren
Island*

**ATLANTIC
OCEAN**

Duration: 6–8 days

Distance: 1078km /
670 miles

When:
July to September

© Justek16 / Shutterstock

You'll quickly get used to stopping. At North River, you can jump in a kayak and paddle up an inlet while keeping an eye out for whales and otters. At Ingonish Beach, enjoy a round of golf at Highlands Links, a stunning course designed by Stanley Thompson in 1939.

## 4. Detour: Bay St Lawrence

Back on the trail, at Cape North on the northernmost tip, take a detour to the tiny fishing port of Bay St Lawrence for a whale-watching cruise alongside the bay's rugged coastline, whose numerous waterfalls and sea caves are just as beautiful as the pilot whales and dolphins that swim around the boat.

## 5. Meat Cove

Back on land, head from Cape North to the remote settlement of Meat Cove, so named because in the 1700s, European settlers slaughtered moose, deer and bear there for antlers and hides. It's a must-visit for the cove's only chowder hut, which whips up seafood chowder, lobster rolls and crab sandwiches.

As you drive along the northwestern shore of Cape Breton – between Cape North and Pleasant Bay – be sure to stop at the magnificent 'look-offs,' viewing points that frequently dot the route. Among other things, these showcase the island's deciduous trees – birch and maple – which transform into an

Pignons (www.lestroispignons.com).

Another cultural event is the annual Celtic Colours International Festival in October, when local and international artists fiddle, pipe and dance in churches and school halls. But whatever the time of year, it's worth the drive just to kick up your heels at a ceilidh (pronounced cay-lee), a Gaelic gathering where all are welcome to eat, drink and be merry to a backdrop of local folk music, and Cape Breton's exceptional hospitality.

From Chéticamp, continue south along Rt 19, leaving the cape behind as you make your way toward the capital. A popular, family-friendly beach experience can be had at Rainbow Haven Provincial Park. And there's plenty to do in Halifax, including dozens of parks, art galleries, farmers markets and museums.

## 7. Gaff Point

Sandy beaches and sea-kayaking opportunities abound along the south shore; stop in Mahone Bay to soak up the cute, casual waterfront

*From left: The west side of the Cabot Trail through Cape Breton Highlands; autumnal roadside views; lobster fishing has a proud history in Cape Breton; Overleaf: the Cabot Trail winds onwards around the coast*

explosion of colour each autumn. Bald eagles frequently soar overhead.

## 6. Chéticamp

Heading south at Pleasant Bay, steep cliffs morph into lowlands comprising grass-covered dunes and sandy beaches. A shock of striped red, white and blue flags (and even buildings) signifies your arrival into Chéticamp, a village that proudly proclaims its French Acadian roots. A sign also states cheekily that the locals are 'Proud to be Hookers,' a nod to Chéticamp's expert hooked-rug makers. The best examples of their work are exhibited in the hooked-rug museum called Les Trois

atmosphere; nearby, there's a good hiking trail at Gaff Point, a 7km (4 mile) loop starting at Hirtle's Beach in Kingsburg. It's a great way to get an up-close view of the rugged coastal geography.

## 8. Wolfville

From here, you can drive straight north or, if you have more time, take the long way, following the south shore and then the northern coastline around to Wolfville. The coastal route offers any number of developed campgrounds, including The Islands Provincial Park (902-875 4304) near Shelburne.

Wolfville is a college town with bags of historic small-town atmosphere, and lots of vineyards in the surrounding area. Don't miss a visit to the Grand-Pré National Historic Site, an interpretive museum that explains the historical context for the deportation of the French-Acadian people from Acadian, Mi'kmaw and British perspectives and traces the many routes Acadians took from, and back to, the Maritimes.

## 9. Cape d'Or Lighthouse

Head along Hwy 215 toward Truro, where you'll make a nearly 180-degree turn to hop on Hwy 2 heading west again. At Parrsboro, look for a turnoff to the Cape d'Or scenic area (Hwy 209), another 48km (30 miles) along partially unpaved roads. The spectacular cape of sheer cliffs was misnamed Cape d'Or (Cape of Gold) by Samuel de Champlain in 1604 – the glittering veins he saw in the cliffs were copper. Mining took place between 1897 and 1905 and removed the sparkle, but the scenery remains epic. The present lighthouse was added in 1922.

From here, retrace your steps to Truro, from where it's a straightforward dash along the TransCanada Hwy (104) back to Cape Breton.

Tip: In summer, Parks Canada (www.pc.gc.ca) offers a range of activities in the Cape Breton Highlands National Park. You can hike at sunset along the scenic Skyline Trail with a park interpreter, enjoy the gourmet contents of a Parks Canada picnic basket, or learn to cook, crack and feast on a lobster. At night, rub shoulders with the region's ghosts on a lantern walk or wander through the park with a guide to view the star-filled sky.

# Vancouver Island's North Trail Coast

Throw yourself head-first into Vancouver Island's natural side. Ancient forests, diving orca, wild sandy beaches, quaint villages and a peek into First Nations cultures make it a well-rounded trip. It's a bit like following Alice down the rabbit hole – you'll feel you've entered an enchanted land that's beyond the reach of day-to-day life. Ancient, moss-covered trees will leave you feeling tiny, as bald eagles swoop above and around you like pigeons. You'll see bears munching dandelions and watching you inscrutably. And totem poles, standing like forests, will seem to whisper secrets of the past. Go on. Jump in.

### 1. Tofino

Packed with activities and blessed with stunning beaches, the former fishing town of Tofino sits on Clayoquot (clay-kwot) Sound, where forests rise from roiling waves that batter the coastline. Visitors come to surf, whale-watch, kayak, hike and hug trees. For the scoop on what to do, hit the visitor centre (250-725 3414; www.tourismtofino.com).

The area's biggest draw is Long Beach, part of Pacific Rim National Park. Accessible by car along the Pacific Rim Hwy, this wide sandy swathe has untamed surf, beachcombing nooks and a living museum of old-growth trees. There are plenty of walking trails; look for swooping eagles and huge banana slugs. Tread carefully over slippery surfaces and never turn your back on the mischievous surf.

Kwisitis Visitor Centre houses exhibits on the region, including a First Nations canoe and a look at what's in the watery depths. While you're in Tofino, don't miss Roy Henry Vickers' Eagle Aerie Gallery (250-725 3235; www.royhenryvickers.com), housed in an atmospheric traditional longhouse. Vickers is one of Canada's most successful and prolific Aboriginal artists. Also visit Tofino Botanical Gardens (250-725 1220; www.tbgf.org), 4.8 hectares of forest and coast complete with pocket gardens, art installations and a historic homestead. A short trip from town is the Maquinna Marine Provincial Park (www.bcparks.ca), where 2km (1.25 miles) of boardwalks lead to natural hot springs. Also accessible from Tofino is mesmerising Meares Island, home to the Big Tree Trail, a 400m boardwalk through old-growth forest that includes a stunning 1500-year-old red cedar.

Follow Pacific Rim Hwy 4 southeast, and then north as it turns into the Mackenzie Range. Mountains rise up on the right as you weave past the unfathomably deep Kennedy Lake (there are a number of vehicles resting unreachable at its bottom). The road carries on along the racing Kennedy River. Continue to the next stop, just past Port Alberni.

### 2. Cathedral Grove

To the east of Port Alberni, Cathedral Grove is the spiritual home of tree huggers and the mystical highlight of MacMillan Provincial Park. Look up – way, waaaaay up – and the vertigo-inducing views of the swaying treetops are likely to leave you swooning. Extremely popular in summer, Cathedral Grove's accessible forest trails wind through dense woodland, offering glimpses of some of British Columbia's oldest trees, including centuries-old Douglas firs more than 3m (10ft) in diameter. Try hugging that.

First-timers should drop by the Pacific Rim Visitors Centre

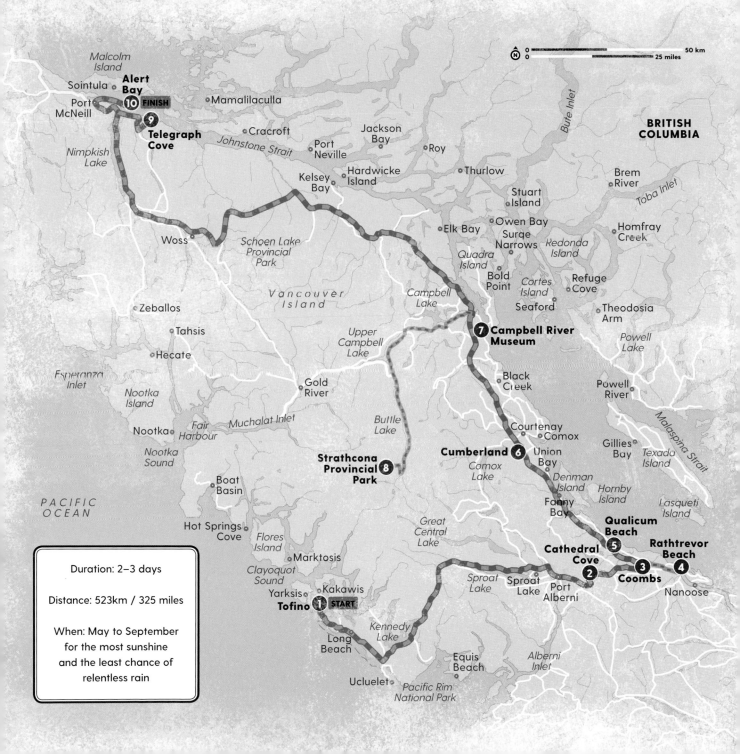

**BRITISH COLUMBIA**

Malcolm Island
Sointula
**Alert Bay**
**10** **FINISH**
Port McNeill
**9**
**Telegraph Cove**
Mamalilaculla
Cracroft
Jackson Bay
Roy
Nimpkish Lake
Johnstone Strait
Port Neville
Hardwicke Island
Kelsey Bay
Woss
Schoen Lake Provincial Park
Elk Bay
Owen Bay
Surge Narrows
Bute Inlet
Brem River
Thurlow
Stuart Island
Toba Inlet
Quadra Island
Redonda Island
Homfray Creek
Bold Point
Cortes Island
Refuge Cove
Vancouver Island
Campbell Lake
Seaford
Theodosia Arm
Zeballos
Upper Campbell Lake
**7** **Campbell River Museum**
Powell Lake
Tahsis
Black Creek
Powell River
Hecate
Esperanza Inlet
Gold River
Buttle Lake
Courtenay
Comox
Gillies Bay
Texada Island
Malaspina Strait
Nootka Island
Muchalat Inlet
**Strathcona Provincial Park** **8**
**Cumberland** **6**
Union Bay
Denman Island
Hornby Island
Lasqueti Island
Nootka
Fair Harbour
Comox Lake
Nootka Sound
Fanny Bay
Boat Basin
Great Central Lake
**Qualicum Beach**
**5**
**PACIFIC OCEAN**
Hot Springs Cove
Flores Island
**Cathedral Cove**
**Rathtrevor Beach**
**4**
Marktosis
Sproat Lake
**2**
**3**
**Coombs**
Clayoquot Sound
Sproat Lake
Port Alberni
Nanoose
Yarksis
Kakawis
**Tofino** **1** **START**
Equis Beach
Long Beach
Kennedy Lake
Alberni Inlet
Ucluelet
Pacific Rim National Park

Duration: 2–3 days

Distance: 523km / 325 miles

When: May to September for the most sunshine and the least chance of relentless rain

0 ————— 50 km
0 ————— 25 miles
N

## Canada / Vancouver Island

(250-726-4600; www.pacificrimvisitor.ca) for maps and advice on exploring this spectacular region. If you're stopping in the park, you'll need to pay and display a pass, which you'll find is available here.

Continue east on Hwy 4, past Cameron Lake, with swimming beaches and supposedly a resident monster. From Hwy 4, follow Hwy 4A for Coombs.

### 3. Coombs

The mother of all pit stops, Coombs Old Country Market (250-248-6272; www. oldcountrymarket.com) attracts huge numbers of visitors almost year-round. You'll get inquisitive looks from a herd of goats that spends the summer season on the grassy roof, a tradition here for decades. Nip inside for giant ice-cream cones, heaping pizzas and all the deli makings of a great picnic, then spend an hour or two wandering around the attendant stores, which are filled with unique crafts, clothes and antiques.

### 4. Detour: Rathtrevor Beach

It's only around 20 minutes from Coombs, but Rathtrevor Beach feels like it's a million miles away. Visit when the tide is out and you'll face a huge expanse of sand. Bring buckets, shovels and the kids, who'll spend hours happily engrossed in digging, catching crabs and hunting for shells. The beach is in a provincial park just east of Parksville, and is backed by a forested picnic area. To get there from Coombs, drive east on Hwy 4A, connecting to Hwy 19 northwest and then turning off at Rathtrevor Rd.

Continue east on Hwy 4A, crossing Hwy 19 to Parksville on the coast. Turn left and follow

the coastline west past pretty French Creek and on to Qualicum Beach.

### 5. Qualicum Beach

A small community of classic seafront motels and a giant beachcomber-friendly bay, Qualicum Beach is a favourite family destination. This coastline is thick with shellfish; many of the scallops, oysters and mussels that restaurants serve up come from here. Wander the beach and look for sand dollars – readily found here.

settlements, home to workers from Japan, China and the American South. While it's retained that small-town feel, with a main street that's still lined with turn-of-the century wooden stores, it's also moved with the times. Instead of blacksmiths and dry-goods shops, you'll find cool boutiques, espresso bars and even tattooists. Stop by Dark Side Chocolates (250-336-0126; www.darksidechocolates. com) for truffles and bars, and be sure to visit the evocative and very impressive Cumberland Museum (250-336-2445; www. cumberlandmuseum.ca). Explore more than 40 exhibits, including a replica coal mine and company store, brought to life by colourful stories of Cumberland's early residents.

Head north on Hwy 19, with mountain and island views. Turn right on Hamm Rd, east across farmland and passing a bison farm. Turn left on Hwy 19A, which skirts Oyster Bay. The next stop is on your left, on the outskirts of Campbell River.

While it's slower than Hwy 19, Hwy 19A is a scenic drive, following the coast north past the Fanny Bay Oyster Farm (stop in for a cookbook) and Denman Island (site of a famous chocolate factory). Just north of Union Bay, turn left to connect with Hwy 19. Turn right, continue north and take the exit for Cumberland.

## 6. Cumberland

Founded as a coal mining town in 1888, Cumberland was one of BC's original pioneer

## 7. Campbell River Museum

Stretch your legs and your curiosity with a wander through the award-winning Museum

## Canada / Vancouver Island

at Campbell River (250-287 3103; www. crmuseum.ca). Hop behind the wheel of an early logging truck, explore a settler's cabin, see First Nations masks and watch footage of the removal of the legendary, ship-destroying Ripple Rock, which was blasted with the largest non-nuclear explosion in history.

From Campbell River, head northwest on Hwy 19. As you inch into Vancouver Island's north, follow the signs and an increasingly narrow road for 16km (10 miles) to Telegraph Cove. En route, you'll pass Beaver Cove with its flotilla of logs waiting to be hauled away for milling. It's a beautiful drive, but isolated. Fuel up before you head out.

### 8. Detour: Strathcona Provincial Park

BC's oldest protected area and also Vancouver Island's largest park, Strathcona (250-474-1336; www.bcparks.ca) is a 40km (25 mile) drive west on Hwy 28 from Campbell River. Centred on Mt Golden Hinde, the island's highest point (2200m/7218ft), it's a pristine wilderness crisscrossed with trail systems that deliver you to waterfalls, alpine meadows, glacial lakes and looming crags. On arrival at the main entrance, get your bearings at Strathcona Park Lodge & Outdoor Education Centre. It's a one-stop shop for a range of park activities, including kayaking, guided treks and rock climbing for all ages.

### 9. Telegraph Cove

Built on stilts over the water in 1912, Telegraph Cove was originally a station for the northern terminus of the island's telegraph. A salmon saltery and sawmill were later added. Extremely popular with summer day-trippers,

the boardwalk and its many houses have been charmingly restored, with plaques illuminating their original residents. During the season, the waters off the cove are also home to orcas. See (and hear!) them with Stubbs Island Whale Watching (250-928-3185; www.stubbs-island. com). You might also encounter minke and humpback whales as well as dolphins and

porpoises. Return to Hwy 19 and carry on to Port McNeill, from where you can catch a BC Ferries vessel to Alert Bay on Cormorant Island.

## 10. Alert Bay

This welcoming village has an ancient and mythical appeal underpinned by its strong First Nations culture and community. In some respects,

it feels like an open-air museum. On the southern side is an old pioneer fishing settlement and the traditional Namgis Burial Grounds, where dozens of gracefully weathering totem poles stand like a forest of ageless art.

Next to the site of the now-demolished St Michael's Residential School is a much more enduring symbol of First Nations community. The must-see U'mista Cultural Centre (250-974-5403; www.umista.ca) houses ceremonial masks and other potlatch items that were confiscated by the Canadian government in the 1920s and have now been repatriated from museums around the world.

Continue over the hill to the Big House, where traditional dance performances are held for visitors. One of the world's tallest totem poles is also here. Alert Bay is home to many professional carvers of these magnificent towers and you'll see their work in galleries around the village. Head to the visitor centre (250-974-5024; www.alertbay.ca) for more information.

# The Long Way Round

There's a strong case to be made that Ireland's top sites are closest to its dramatic coastlines: the splendid scenery, the mountain ranges (geographically, Ireland is akin to a bowl, with raised edges) and most of its major towns and cities – Dublin, Belfast, Galway, Sligo and Cork. The western edge, between Donegal and Cork, corresponds to the Wild Atlantic Way driving route.

### 1. Dublin

From its music, art and literature to the legendary nightlife that has inspired those same musicians, artists and writers, Dublin has always known how to have fun and does it with deadly seriousness. Should you tire of the city's more highbrow offerings, the Guinness Storehouse (www.guinnessstorehouse. com) is the most popular place to visit in town; a beer-lover's Disneyland and multimedia bells-and-whistles homage to the country's most famous export and the city's most enduring symbol. The old grain storehouse is a suitable cathedral in which to worship at the altar of the black gold; shaped like a giant pint of Guinness, it rises seven impressive storeys high around a stunning central atrium.

From Dublin, it's 165km (102 miles) of motorway to Belfast – M1 in the Republic, A1 in Northern Ireland – but remember that the speed limit changes from kilometres to miles as you cross into the North.

### 2. Belfast

Belfast is in many ways a brand-new city. Once lumped with Beirut, Baghdad and Bosnia as one of the four 'Bs' for travellers to avoid, in recent years it has pulled off a remarkable transformation from bombs-and-bullets pariah to a hip-hotels-and-hedonism party town. The old shipyards on the Lagan continue to give way to the luxury apartments of the Titanic Quarter, whose centrepiece, the stunning, star-shaped edifice housing the Titanic Belfast Centre (www. titanicbelfast.com), covering the ill-fated ocean liner's

construction here, has become the city's number-one tourist draw. New venues keep popping up – already this decade, historic Crumlin Road Gaol (028-9074 1501; www. crumlinroadgaol.com) and the SS Nomadic have opened to the public, and WWI warship HMS Caroline became a floating museum in 2016. They all add to a list of attractions that includes beautifully restored Victorian architecture, a glittering waterfront lined with modern art, a fantastic foodie scene and music-filled pubs. If you're keen on learning more about the city's troubled history, take a walking tour of West Belfast.

From here, take the A8 to Larne and follow the coast through handsome Cushendall and popular Ballycastle to the Giant's Causeway.

### 3. Giant's Causeway

When you first see it you'll understand why the ancients believed the causeway was not a natural feature. The vast expanse of regular, closely packed, hexagonal stone columns dipping gently beneath the waves looks for all the world like the handiwork of giants. This spectacular rock formation – a national nature reserve and Northern Ireland's only Unesco World Heritage Site – is one of Ireland's most impressive and atmospheric landscape features, but it can get very crowded. If you can, try to visit midweek or out of season to experience it at its most evocative. Sunset in spring and autumn is the best time for photographs.

From Giant's Causeway there's an excellent opportunity to get out of the van and stretch your legs a bit: Between

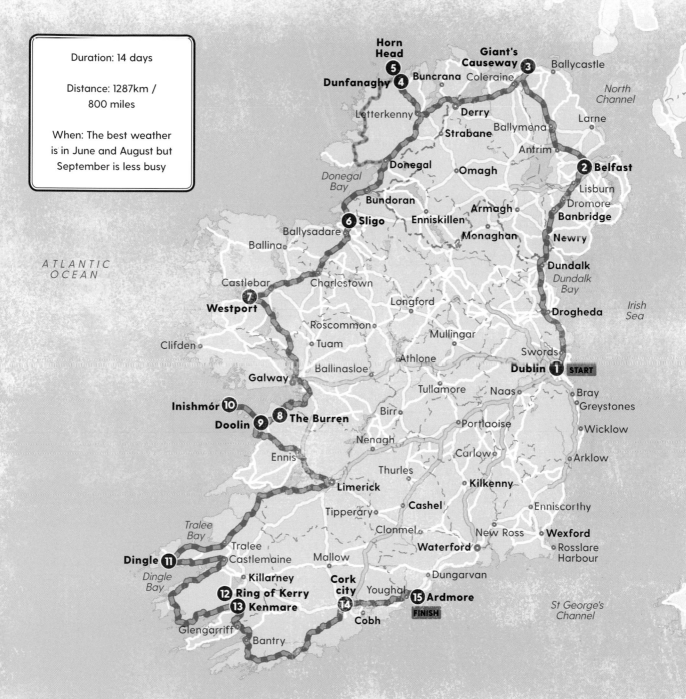

Duration: 14 days

Distance: 1287km / 800 miles

When: The best weather is in June and August but September is less busy

# Ireland

the Giant's Causeway and Ballycastle lies the most scenic stretch of the Causeway Coast, with sea cliffs of contrasting black basalt and white chalk, rocky islands, quaint harbours and broad sweeps of sandy beach. It's best enjoyed on foot, following the 16.5km (10 miles) of Causeway Coast Way (www.walkni.com).

About 8km (5 miles) east of the Giant's Causeway is the meagre ruin of 16th-century Dunseverick Castle, spectacularly sited on a grassy bluff. Another 1.5km (9 miles) on is the tiny seaside hamlet of Portbradden, with half a dozen harbourside houses and the tiny blue-and-white St Gobban's Church, said to be the smallest in Ireland. Visible from Portbradden and accessible via the next junction off the A2 is the spectacular White Park Bay, with its wide, sweeping sandy beach. The main attraction on this stretch of coast is the famous Carrick-a-Rede Rope Bridge (www.nationaltrust.org.uk).

Back at the Causeway, follow the A29 and A37 as far as Derry/Londonderry, then cross the invisible border into the Republic and take the N13 to Letterkenny before turning northwest along the N56 to Dunfanaghy. It's a total of 136km (85 miles).

## 4. Dunfanaghy

Huddled around the waterfront beneath the headland of Horn Head, Dunfanaghy's small, attractive town centre has some of the finest dining options in the county's northwest. Glistening beaches, dramatic coastal cliffs, mountain trails and forests are all nearby.

## 5. Detour: Horn Head

This alluring peninsula has some of Donegal's most spectacular coastal scenery and plenty of birdlife. Its dramatic quartzite cliffs, covered with bog and heather, rear over 180m high, and the view from their tops is heart-pounding. The road circles the headland; the best approach by car is in a clockwise direction from the Falcarragh end of Dunfanaghy. On a fine day, you'll encounter tremendous views of Tory, Inishbofin, Inishdooey and tiny Inishbeg islands to the west; Sheep Haven Bay and the Rosguill Peninsula to the east; Malin Head to the northeast; and the coast of Scotland beyond. Take care in bad weather as the route can be perilous.

It's a scenic 145km (90 miles) stretch through Letterkenny and south to Sligo town; you'll hop

*Above: The road weaves around Slea Head on the Dingle Peninsula for no more than 50km but there are so many potential stop-offs that you best take your time*

© Marco Bottigelli / Getty Images

flanked by fields, hedge rows and clusters of farmhouses. Castlebar, 15km before Westport, is a busy county town worth a wander.

## 7. Westport

There's a lot to be said for town planning, especially if 18th-century architect James Wyatt was the brains behind the job. Westport (Cathair na Mairt), positioned on the River Carrowbeg and the shores of Clew Bay, is easily Mayo's most beautiful town and a major tourist destination for visitors to this part of the country. It's a Georgian classic, its octagonal square and tidy streets lined with trees and handsome buildings, most of which date from the late 18th century.

Follow the N84 as far as the outskirts of Galway city – about 100km (62 miles). Take the N18 south into County Clare. At Kilcolgan, turn on to the N67 and into the heart of the Burren.

## 8. The Burren

The karst landscape of the Burren is not the green Ireland of postcards. But there are wildflowers in spring, giving the 560-sq-km Burren brilliant, if ephemeral, colour amid its austere beauty. Soil may be scarce, but the small amount that gathers in the cracks and faults is well drained and nutrient-rich. This, together with the mild Atlantic climate, supports an extraordinary mix of Mediterranean, Arctic and alpine plants. Of Ireland's native wildflowers, 75% are found here.

It's 36km (22 miles) southwest to Doolin along the R460 and R476 roads, which cut through more familiar Irish landscapes. The real pleasures along here are the villages – the likes of Kilfenora and Lisdoonvarna are great for a pit stop and even a session of traditional music.

on to the N13 as far as Ballyshannon and then, as you cross into County Sligo, to Sligo town.

## 6. Sligo

An appealing overnight base, vibrant Sligo combines lively pubs and futuristic buildings with old stone bridges and a historic abbey. It also shines a spotlight on William Butler Yeats (1865–1939), Sligo's greatest literary figure and one of Ireland's premier poets.

From there it's 100km (62 miles) to Westport, across the western edge of County Clare – as you follow the N17 (and the N5 once you pass Charlestown), the landscape is flat, the road

### 9. Doolin

Doolin is renowned as a centre of Irish traditional music, but it's also known for its setting – 6km (3.7 miles) north of the Cliffs of Moher – and down near the ever-unsettled sea, the land is windblown, with huge rocks exposed by the long-vanished topsoil.

Ferries from Doolin to Inishmór take about 90 minutes to make the crossing.

### 10. Inishmór

A step (and boat- or plane-ride) beyond the desolate beauty of Connemara are the Aran Islands. Most visitors are satisfied to explore only Inishmór (Árainn) and its main attraction, Dún Aengus (Dún Aonghasa; www.heritageireland.ie/en/west/dunaonghasa/), the stunning stone fort perched perilously on the island's towering cliffs. Powerful swells pound the 60m-high cliff face. A complete lack of rails or other modern additions that would spoil this amazing ancient site means that you can not only go right up to the cliff's edge but also potentially fall to your doom below quite easily. The arid landscape west of Kilronan (Cill Rónáin), Inishmór's main settlement, is dominated by stone walls, boulders, scattered buildings and the odd patch of deep-green grass and potato plants.

Once you're back on terra firma at Doolin, it's 223km (139 miles) to Dingle via the N85 through Ennis as far as Limerick City. The N69 will take you into County Kerry as far as Tralee, beyond which it's 50km (31 miles) on the N86 to Dingle.

### 11. Dingle

Unlike the Ring of Kerry, where the cliffs tend to dominate the ocean, it's the ocean that dominates the smaller Dingle Peninsula. The opal-blue waters surrounding the promontory's multihued landscape of green hills and golden sands give rise to aquatic adventures and to fishing fleets that haul in fresh seafood that appears on the menus of some of the county's finest restaurants. Centred on charming Dingle town, there's an alternative way of life here, lived by artisans and idiosyncratic characters and found at trad sessions and folkloric festivals across Dingle's tiny settlements. The classic loop drive around Slea Head from Dingle town is 50km, (31 miles) but allow a day to take it all in.

Take the N86 as far as Annascaul and then the coastal R561 as far as Castlemaine. Then head southwest on the N70 to Killorglin and the Ring of Kerry. From Dingle, it's 53km (33 miles).

### 12. Ring of Kerry

The Ring of Kerry is the longest and the most diverse of Ireland's big circle drives, combining jaw-dropping coastal scenery with emerald pastures and villages. The 179km (111 miles) circuit usually begins in Killarney and winds past pristine beaches, the island-dotted Atlantic, medieval ruins, mountains and loughs (lakes). The coastline is at its most rugged between Waterville and Caherdaniel in the southwest of the peninsula. It can get crowded in summer, but even then the remote Skellig Ring can be uncrowded and serene – and starkly beautiful. The Ring of Kerry can easily be done as a day trip, but if you want to stretch it out, campsites are scattered along the route.

The Ring's most popular diversion is the Gap of Dunloe, an awe-inspiring mountain pass at the western edge of Killarney National Park. It's signposted off the N72 between Killarney to Killorglin. The very popular 19th-century Kate Kearney's Cottage is a pub where most visitors park their cars before walking up to the gap.

## 13. Kenmare

If you've done the Ring in an anticlockwise fashion (or cut through the Gap of Dunloe), you'll end up in Kenmare. Picturesque villages, a fine stone circle and calming coastal scenery mark the less-taken, 143km (89 miles) route from Kenmare to Cork city. When you get to Leap, turn right on to the R597 and go as far as Rosscarbery; or, even better, take twice as long (though it's only 24km/15 miles more) along narrow roads near the water the entire way.

## 14. Cork city

Ireland's second city is first in every important respect, at least according to the locals, for whom it's the 'real capital of Ireland.' The compact centre is surrounded by interesting waterways and is chock-full of great restaurants, offering the best food scene in the country.

It's only 60km (37 miles) to Ardmore, but stop in Midleton, 24km (15 miles) east of Cork along the N25 to visit the whiskey museum. Just beyond Youghal, turn right onto the R671.

## 15. Ardmore

Because it's off the main drag, Ardmore is a sleepy seaside village and one of the southeast's loveliest spots – the ideal destination for those looking for a little waterside R&R. St Declan reputedly set up shop here sometime between AD 350 and 420, which would make Ardmore the first Christian bastion in Ireland – long before St Patrick landed. The village's 12th-century round tower, one of the best examples of these structures in Ireland, is the town's most distinctive architectural feature, but you should also check out the ruins of St Declan's church and well, on a bluff above the village.

**Note:** Visiting the Giant's Causeway itself is free of charge but you pay to use the car park on a combined ticket with the Giant's Causeway Visitor Experience (028-2073 1855; www. nationaltrust.org.uk; adult/child with parking £9/4.50); parking-only tickets aren't available.

*Left, from top: The Giant's Causeway is Unesco listed; a short drive away is the beach at White Park Bay*

© Stuart Stevenson photography / Getty Images

© Jason Friend Photography Ltd / Getty Images

# Upper West Coast Highlands

The quintessential highland country of this trip, marked by single-track roads, breathtaking emptiness and a wild, fragile beauty, leaves an indelible imprint on our souls. Whether it's blazing sunshine or murky grey, the character of the land is totally unique and constantly changing.

## 1. Portree

Portree is Skye's largest and liveliest town. It has a pretty harbour lined with brightly painted houses, and there are great views of the surrounding hills. Its name (from the Gaelic for King's Harbour) commemorates James V, who came here in 1540 to pacify the local clans. MV Stardust (07798 743858; www.skyeboat-trips.co.uk) offers 1½-hour boat trips around Portree Bay, with the chance to see seals, porpoises and – if you're lucky – white-tailed sea eagles.

Coming from the south, follow the road round to the right in Portree to leave town on the A855, which after about 6 miles (10km) brings you to the Trotternish Peninsula's first sights.

## 2. Trotternish Peninsula

The Trotternish Peninsula to the north of Portree has some of Skye's most spectacular – and bizarre – scenery. Whatever the weather, it is difficult not to be blown away by the savage beauty of this place. The 50m-high, pot-bellied pinnacle of crumbling basalt known as the Old Man of Storr is prominent above the road 6 miles (10km) north of Portree. Walk up to its foot from the car park at the northern end of Loch Leathan (round trip 2 miles). Past the Old Man is a popular cliff top lookout over spectacular Kilt Rock. At the northern end of the peninsula at Kilmuir, the peat-reek of crofting life in the 18th and 19th centuries is preserved in the thatched cottages, croft houses, barns and farm implements of the evocative Skye Museum of Island Life (01470-552206;

www.skyemuseum.co.uk). Behind the museum is Kilmuir Cemetery, where a tall Celtic cross marks the grave of Jacobite heroine Flora MacDonald.

Follow the road around the peninsula, through the ferry port of Uig and on to Borge, where you take a right on to the A850 to Dunvegan. From the Old Man of Storr it's about 54 miles (87km) via this route.

## 3. Dunvegan Castle

Skye's most famous historic building, and one of its most popular tourist attractions, Dunvegan Castle (01470-521206; www.dunvegancastle.com) is the seat of the chief of Clan MacLeod. It has some interesting artefacts, including the Fairy Flag, a diaphanous silk banner that dates from sometime between the 4th and 7th centuries, and Bonnie Prince Charlie's waistcoat and a lock of his hair. The oldest parts are the 14th-century keep and dungeon but most of it dates from the 17th to 19th centuries, when it played host to Samuel Johnson, Sir Walter Scott and, most famously, Flora MacDonald. Look out for Rory Mor's Drinking Horn, a beautiful 16th-century vessel of Celtic design that could hold half a gallon of claret. Upholding the family tradition in 1956, John Macleod – the 29th chief, who died in 2007 – downed the contents in one minute and 57 seconds 'without setting down or falling down'.

It's 24 pretty miles (38km) across the heart of the island along the A863 to Sligachan, a crossroads and walkers' haven overwatched by the brooding Cuillins.

## Scotland

### 4. Cuillin Hills

The Cuillin Hills are Britain's most spectacular mountain range (the name comes from the Old Norse kjöllen, meaning 'keel-shaped'). Though small in stature (Sgurr Alasdair, the highest summit, is only 993m), the peaks are near-alpine in character, with knife-edge ridges, jagged pinnacles, scree-filled gullies and hectares of naked rock. While they are a paradise for experienced mountaineers, the higher reaches of the Cuillin are off-limits to the majority of walkers. The good news is that there are also plenty of good low-level hikes within the ability of most walkers, several leaving from Sligachan.

It's a 30-mile (48km) drive from Sligachan on the A87 along the Skye coast, past the Raasay ferry at Sconser, through Broadford and over the bridge onto the mainland at Kyle of Lochalsh. In town, take a left up the hill and follow this road to Plockton.

### 5. Plockton

Idyllic little Plockton, with its perfect cottages lining a perfect bay, looks like it was designed as a film set. And it has indeed served as just that – scenes from *The Wicker Man* were filmed here, and the village became famous as the location for the 1990s TV series *Hamish Macbeth*. It can get busy in summer, but there's no denying its appeal. The local langoustines (Plockton prawns) are deservedly famous.

Head to the A890, running northeast along Loch Carron. Turn left along the A896 along the loch's opposite side and through likeable Lochcarron village before taking a left turn to Applecross. The magnificent Bealach na Ba (Pass of the Cattle; 626m) climbs steeply and hair-raisingly via hairpin bends, then drops

© loneroc / Shutterstock

dramatically to the village with views of Skye (36 miles/58km total).

### 6. Applecross

The delightfully remote seaside village of Applecross feels like an island retreat due to its isolation and the magnificent views of Raasay and the hills of Skye that set the pulse racing, particularly at sunset. On a clear day it's an unforgettable place.

It's 25 winding miles (40km) north then east from Applecross along the coast of this peninsula to the pretty waterside village of Shieldaig, where you rejoin the A896 and head east for 7 majestic miles (11km) to Torridon, along the shore of the sea loch of the same name.

### 7. Torridon

The road running through Glen Torridon is dwarfed amid some of Britain's most beautiful scenery. Carved by ice from massive layers of

*Above, from left: Picturesque Plockton has served as the setting for TV shows and films, The Wicker Man (1973) among them; park up to admire the 50m-high Old Man of Storr on Skye*

© Jaroslav Sekeres / Shutterstock

ancient sandstone that takes its name from the region, the mountains here are steep, shapely and imposing, whether flirting with autumn mists, draped in dazzling winter snows, or reflected in the calm blue waters of Loch Torridon on a summer day. The road from lovely Shieldaig, which boasts an attractive main street of whitewashed houses right on the water, reaches the head of the sea loch at spectacularly sited Torridon village. It's a base for excursions to the Torridon peaks – serious mountains for experienced hill walkers only.

Follow the A896 northeast to Kinlochewe, then turn left along the A832, which continues to Gairloch (27 miles/43km total). The road follows the shore of beautiful Loch Maree. From a car park 1½ miles past Beinn Eighe visitor centre, there's a great way-marked 4-mile (6.4km) return walk to a plateau and cairn on the side of Beinn Eighe, offering magnificent views.

## 8. Gairloch

Gairloch is a knot of villages around the inner end of a loch of the same name. It's a good base for whale- and dolphin-watching excursions and the surrounding area has beautiful sandy beaches, good trout fishing and birdwatching. Gairloch Marine Wildlife Centre & Cruises (01445-712636; www. porpoise-gairloch. co.uk) has audiovisual and interactive displays, lots of charts, photos and knowledgeable staff. From here, cruises run three times daily (weather permitting); during the two-hour trips you may see basking sharks, porpoises and minke whales. The crew collects data on water temperature and conditions, and monitors cetacean populations, so you are subsidising important research.

It's a slow, winding, scenic 42 miles (67km) along the A832 from Gairloch north and east to the junction with the A835. Take your time and enjoy the scenic solitude.

## 9. Falls of Measach

Just west of the junction of the A835 and A832, a car park gives access to the Falls of Measach, which spill 45m into spectacularly deep and narrow Corrieshalloch Gorge. You can cross the gorge on a swaying suspension bridge, and walk west for 250m to a viewing platform that juts out dizzyingly above a sheer drop. The thundering falls and misty vapours rising from the gorge are very impressive.

From the road junction, it's 12 miles (19km) northwest on the good A835 to Ullapool.

## 10. Ullapool

This pretty port on the shores of Loch Broom is the largest settlement in Wester Ross and one of the most alluring spots in the Highlands, a

Along much of this drive you will find single-track roads that are only wide enough for one vehicle. Passing places (usually marked with a white diamond sign, or a black-and white striped pole) are used to allow oncoming traffic to get by. Remember that passing places are also for overtaking – you must pull over to let faster vehicles pass. Be wary too of lambs dashing onto the road in springtime.

Free camping is allowed almost everywhere in Scotland, and it's easy to find places to stop along this route.

wonderful destination in itself as well as a gateway to the Western Isles. Offering a row of whitewashed cottages arrayed along the harbour and special views of the loch and its flanking hills, the town has a very distinctive appeal. Housed in a converted Telford church, Ullapool Museum (www.ullapool museum.co.uk) relates the prehistoric, natural and social history of the town and Lochbroom area, with a particular focus on the emigration to Nova Scotia and other places.

It's 26 miles (42km) north along the A835 then A837 to the Skiag Bridge road junction at the heart of the Assynt region. Stop along the way to appreciate the mountainscapes and keep an eye out in the rearview mirror, as many of the best perspectives unfold behind you.

## 11. Detour: Coigach

The region west of the main A835 road from Ullapool to Ledmore Junction is known as Coigach (www.coigach.com). A lone, single-track road, off the A835 9 miles (14km) north of Ullapool, penetrates this wilderness, leading through glorious scenery to remote settlements perfect for walkers and wildlife enthusiasts. You could head back to the main road to continue your journey, or, at the western end of Loch Lurgainn, a branch road leads north to Lochinver, a scenic backroad so narrow and twisting that it's nicknamed the Wee Mad Road.

## 12. Assynt

With its otherworldly scenery of isolated peaks rising above a sea of crumpled, lochan-spattered gneiss, Assynt epitomises the northwest's wild magnificence. Glaciers have sculpted the Torridonian sandstone mountains of Assynt, including Suilven's distinctive sugarloaf

and ziggurat-like Quinag. The area is the centrepiece of the Northwest Highlands Geopark (www.nwhgeopark.com).

Half a mile south of the Skiag Bridge road junction, perched on an island at the edge of Loch Assynt, are the romantic ruins of Ardvreck Castle, a 15th-century stronghold of the MacLeods of Assynt. There are rumoured to be several ghosts at Ardvreck, including the daughter of a MacLeod chieftain sold to the devil by her father. There are wonderful summer sunsets over the castle and loch.

Head west 10 miles (16km) from Skiag Bridge along the A837 to reach Lochinver. The road runs along the northern shore of wild and moody Loch Assynt.

## 13. Lochinver

Lochinver is a sweet little fishing harbour that's a popular laid-back port of call, with good facilities and striking scenery. It's something of a gastro hub too, with several fine eateries.

Head north from Lochinver up the narrow B869 coastal route, which rewards with spectacular views and fine beaches. From the lighthouse at Point of Stoer, a one-hour cliff walk leads to the Old Man of Stoer, a spectacular sea stack. After 23 miles (37km), you join the A894 just south of Kylesku.

## 14. Kylesku & Around

Hidden away on the shores of Loch Glencoul, tiny Kylesku served as a ferry crossing until it was made redundant by beautiful Kylesku Bridge in 1984. It's a good base for walks; you can hire bikes too. Five miles (8km) southeast, in wild, remote country, lies 213m-high Eas a'Chuil Aluinn, Britain's highest waterfall. You can hike to the top of the falls from a parking area at a

*Above: Taking the two-wheel alternative to cross Kylesku Bridge; Right: A walk along the beach leads to the rock formations at Cape Wrath*

© Craig Easton / Lonely Planet

sharp bend in the main road 3 miles (5km) south of Kylesku (6 miles/10km return).

It's 10 spectacular miles (16km) up the A894 from Kylesku to Scourie. Look behind you for the best views.

### 15. Scourie & Handa Island

Scourie is a pretty crofting community with decent services, halfway between Durness and Ullapool. A few miles north lies the nature reserve of Handa Island (www. scottishwildlifetrust.org.uk). The island's western sea cliffs provide nesting sites for important breeding populations of great skuas, arctic skuas, puffins, kittiwakes, razorbills and guillemots. Reach the island from Tarbet, 6 miles (10km) north of Scourie, via a ferry (www. handa-ferry.com).

Continue 7 miles (11km) northeast from Scourie on the A894, then north 19 miles (30km) on the A838 to reach Scotland's north coast at Durness.

### 16. Durness

Scattered Durness is wonderfully set, strung out along cliffs rising from a series of pristine beaches. When the sun shines, the effects of blinding white sand, the cry of seabirds and the spring-green-coloured seas combine in a magical way. Walking around the sensational sandy coastline is a highlight, as is a visit to Cape Wrath. A walk along the beach to the north leads to Faraid Head, where you can see puffin colonies in early summer. A mile east of the centre is a path to Smoo Cave (www. smoocave.org). From the vast main chamber, you can head through to a smaller flooded cavern where a waterfall sometimes cascades from the roof. There's evidence the cave was inhabited 6000 years ago.

© Craig Easton / Lonely Planet

# Italian Grand Tour

**The gap-year journey of its day, the Grand Tour is a search for art and enlightenment, adventure and debauchery. From Turin's Savoy palaces and Leonardo's *Last Supper* to the drinking dens of Genoa and the pleasure palaces of Rome, the Grand Tour offers a chance to view some of the world's greatest masterpieces and hear Vivaldi played on 18th-century cellos. It is a rollicking trip filled with the sights, sounds and tastes that have shaped European society for centuries.**

### 1. Turin

In his travel guide, *Voyage Through Italy* (1670), travel writer and tutor Richard Lassels advocated a grand cultural tour of Europe, and in particular Italy, for young English aristocrats, during which the study of classical antiquity and the High Renaissance would ready them for future influential roles shaping the political, economic and social realities of the day.

First they travelled through France before crossing the Alps at Mt Cenis and heading to Turin (Torino), where letters of introduction admitted them to the city's agreeable Parisian-style social whirl. Turin's tree-lined boulevards still retain their elegant, French feel and many turn-of-the century cafes, such as Caffè San Carlo (Piazza San Carlo 156), still serve Torinese hot chocolate beneath their gilded chandeliers.

### 2. Detour: Milan

No Grand Tour would be complete without a detour up the A4 to Milan (Milano) to eyeball Leonardo da Vinci's iconic mural *The Last Supper* (Il Cenacolo; 02-9280 0360; www.cenacolovinciano.net). From his *Portrait of a Young Man* (c 1486) to portraits of Duke Ludovico Sforza's beautiful mistresses, *The Lady with the Ermine* (c 1489) and *La Belle Ferroniere* (c 1490), Leonardo transformed the rigid conventions of portraiture to depict highly individual images imbued with naturalism. Then he evolved concepts of idealised proportions and the depiction of internal emotional states through physical dynamism (St Jerome), all of which

cohere in the masterly Il Cenacolo.

The two-hour (170km/105 mile) drive to Genoa is all on autostrada, the final stretch twisting through the mountains. Leave Turin following signs for the A55 (towards Alessandria), which quickly merges with the A21 passing through the pretty Piedmontese countryside. Just before Alessandria turn south onto the A26 for Genoa/Livorno.

### 3. Genoa

Despite its superb location, mild microclimate and lush flora, Genoa once had a dubious reputation. Its historic centre was a warren of dark, insalubrious caruggi (alleys), stalked by prostitutes and beggars. And yet with tourists and businesspeople arriving from around the world, Genoa was, and still is, a cosmopolitan place. The Rolli Palaces, a collection of grand mansions originally meant to host visiting popes, dignitaries and royalty, made Via Balbi and Strada Nuova (now Via Giuseppe Garibaldi) two of the most famous streets in Europe. You can still visit the finest of them, the Palazzo Spinola (www.palazzospinola.beniculturali.it) and the Palazzo Reale (www.palazzorealegenova.benicul turali.it).

From here, the 365km (227 miles) drive takes most of a day, so stop for lunch in Cremona. Although the drive is on autostrada, endless fields of corn line the route. Take the A7 north out of Genoa and at Tortona exit onto the A21 around industrial Piacenza to Brescia. At Brescia, change again onto the A4 direct to Padua.

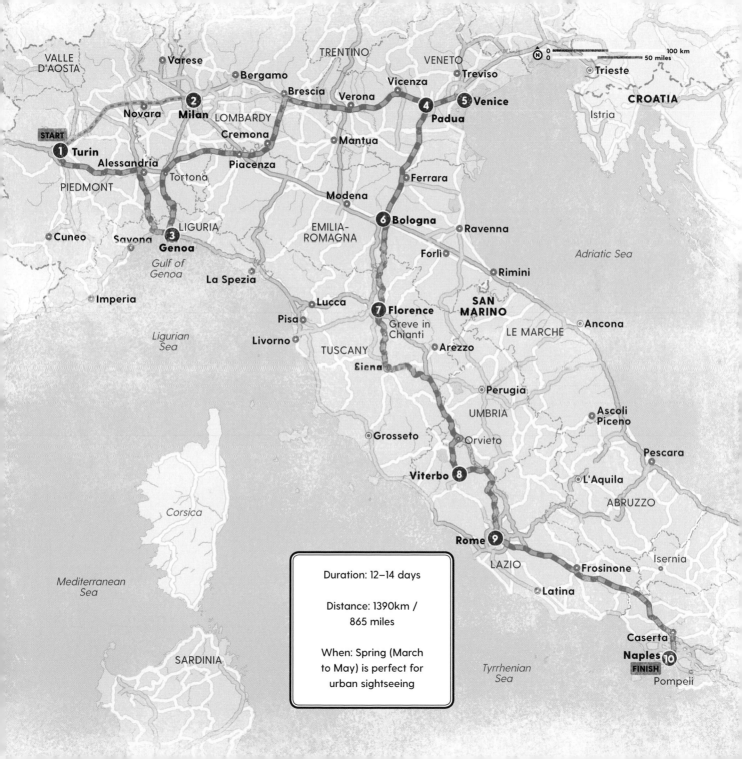

VALLE D'AOSTA

**START**

**1 Turin**

PIEDMONT

Cuneo

Novara

Varese

**2 Milan**

LOMBARDY

Cremona

Alessandria

Tortona

Piacenza

Savona

**3 Genoa**

LIGURIA

*Gulf of Genoa*

Imperia

La Spezia

*Ligurian Sea*

Bergamo

Brescia

TRENTINO

Verona

Vicenza

**4** Padua

**5 Venice**

VENETO

Treviso

**Trieste**

CROATIA

*Istria*

Mantua

Modena

Ferrara

**6 Bologna**

EMILIA-ROMAGNA

Ravenna

Forlì

Rimini

*Adriatic Sea*

Lucca

Pisa

Livorno

**7 Florence**

Greve in Chianti

TUSCANY

Siena

Arezzo

**SAN MARINO**

LE MARCHE

Ancona

Perugia

UMBRIA

Orvieto

Grosseto

**Viterbo 8**

Ascoli Piceno

Pescara

L'Aquila

ABRUZZO

Isernia

**Rome 9**

LAZIO

Frosinone

Latina

*Tyrrhenian Sea*

*Mediterranean Sea*

Corsica

SARDINIA

Caserta

**Naples 10**

**FINISH**

Pompeii

Duration: 12–14 days

Distance: 1390km / 865 miles

When: Spring (March to May) is perfect for urban sightseeing

100 km
50 miles

## 4. Padua

Bound for Venice (Venezia), Grand Tourists could hardly avoid visiting Padua (Padova), although by the 18th century international students no longer flocked to Palazzo del Bò (049 827 30 47; www.unipd.it/en/guidedtours), the Venetian Republic's radical university where Copernicus and Galileo taught classes. You can visit the university's claustrophobic, wooden anatomy theatre (the first in the world), although it's no longer de rigueur for the average tourist to witness dissections. Afterwards don't forget to pay your respects to the skulls of noble professors who donated themselves for dissection because of the difficulty involved in acquiring fresh corpses. Their skulls are lined up in the graduation hall. Giotto's spectacular frescoes are in the Cappella degli Scrovegni (Scrovegni Chapel; 049 201 00 20, www.cappelladegliscrovegni. it), where advance reservations are essential.

Barely 40km (25 miles) from Venice, the drive from Padua is through featureless areas of light industry along the A4 and then the A57.

## 5. Venice

Top of the itinerary, Venice at last! Aside from the mind-improving art in the Gallerie dell'Accademia (041 520 03 45; www. gallerieaccademia.org) and extraordinary architectural masterpieces such as the Palazzo Ducale, the Campanile, Longhena's Chiesa di Santa Maria della Salute and the glittering domes of the Basilica di San Marco (St Mark's Basilica; www.basilicasan marco.it), Venice was historically considered an exciting den of debauchery. Venetian wives were notorious for keeping handsome escorts (cicisbeo), courtesans held powerful positions at court and

much time was devoted to frequenting casinos and coffeehouses.

Retrace your steps to Padua on the A57 and A4 and navigate around the ring road in the direction of Bologna to pick up the A13 southwest for this short two-hour drive. After Padua the dual carriageway dashes through wide-open farmland and crosses the Po river, which forms the southern border of the Veneto.

## 6. Bologna

Home to Europe's oldest university (established in 1088) and once the stomping ground of Dante, Boccaccio and Petrarch, Bologna had an enviable reputation for courtesy and culture. Its historic centre, complete with 20 soaring towers, is one of the best-preserved medieval cities in the world. In the Basilica di San Petronio (www.basilicadisanpetronio. it), originally intended to dwarf St Peter's in Rome, Giovanni Cassini's sundial (1655) proved the problems with the Julian calendar giving us the leap year, while Bolognesi students advanced human knowledge in obstetrics,

**Note:** You cannot take your vehicle onto the lagoon islands of Venice, so leave it in a secure place and hop on the train to Venice Santa Lucia, where water taxis connect to all the islands.

natural science, zoology and anthropology. You can peer at their strange model waxworks and studiously labelled collections in the Palazzo Poggi (www.museopalazzopoggi. unibo.it). In art as in science, the School of Bologna gave birth to the Carracci cousins Ludovico, Agostino and Annibale, who were among the founding fathers of Italian baroque and were deeply influenced by the Counter-Reformation. See their emotionally charged blockbusters in the Pinacoteca Nazionale (www. pinacotecabologna. beniculturali.it).

Bologna sits at the intersection of the A1, A13 and A14. Navigate west out of the city, across the river Reno, onto the A1. From here it's a straight shot into Florence for 100km (62 miles), leaving the Po plains behind you and entering the low hills of Emilia-Romagna and the forested valleys of Tuscany.

## 7. Florence

From Filippo Brunelleschi's red-tiled dome atop Florence's Duomo (Cattedrale di Santa Maria del Fiore; www.operaduomo.firenze. it) to Michelangelo's and Botticelli's greatest hits, *David* and the *Birth of Venus*, in the Galleria dell'Accademia (055 29 48 83; www. firenzemusei.it) and the Galleria degli Uffizi (Uffizi Gallery; www.uffizi.beniculturali. it), Florence, according to Unesco, contains the highest number of artistic masterpieces in the world. And central Florence looks much as it did in 1550, with stone towers and cypress-lined gardens.

The next 210km (130 miles), continuing south along the A1, travels through some of Italy's most lovely scenery. Just southwest of Florence, the vineyards of Greve in Chianti harbour some great farmstays, while Arezzo is to the east. At Orvieto exit on to the SS71 and skirt Lago di Bolsena for the final 45km (28 miles) into Viterbo.

## 8. Viterbo

Stop briefly in medieval Viterbo for a quick douse in the thermal springs at the Terme dei Papi (www.termedeipapi.it), and a tour of the High Renaissance spectacle that is the Villa Lante (0761 28 80 08; Via Jacopo Barozzi 71).

Rejoin the A1 after a 28km (17 miles) drive along the rural SS675. For the next 40km (25 miles) the A1 descends into Lazio, criss-crossing the river Tevere and keeping the ridge of the Apennines to the left as it darts through tunnels. At Fiano Romano exit for Roma Nord onto the A1 for the final 20km descent into the capital.

## 9. Rome

In the 18th century Rome, even in ruins, was still thought of as the august capital of the

*Previous spread, from left: Turin's elegant urban centre; the city's Parco del Valentino; Left: dawn breaks over a Tuscan village Right, clockwise from top: the Grand Tour takes in the ruins of Pompeii; vineyards in Chianti; Bologna's medieval core*

world. Here more than anywhere the Grand Tourist was awakened to an interest in art and architecture, although the Colosseum (Colosseo; 06 3996 7700; www.coopculture.it) was still filled with debris and the Palatine Hill was covered in gardens, its excavated treasures slowly accumulating in the world's oldest national museum, the Capitoline Museums (Musei Capitolini; www.museicapitolini.org).

Arriving through the Porta del Popolo, visitors first spied the dome of St Peter's (Basilica di San Pietro; www.vatican.va) before clattering along the corso to the customs house. Once done, they headed to Piazza di Spagna, the city's principal meeting place where Keats penned his love poems and died of consumption. Although the Pantheon (www.pantheonroma.com) and Vatican Museums (Musei Vaticani; 06 6988 4676; mv.vatican.va) were a must, most travellers preferred to socialise in the grounds of the Borghese Palace (06 3 28 10; www.galleriaborghese. it).

Past Rome, the temperature becomes hotter and the landscape drier, trees give way to Mediterranean shrubbery and the grass starts to yellow. Beyond the vineyards of Frascati, just 20km (12 miles) south of Rome, the A1 heads straight to Naples (Napoli) for 225km (140 miles), a two-hour drive that often takes much longer due to heavy traffic.

## 10 Naples

Only the more adventurous Grand Tourists continued south to the salacious city of Naples. At the time Mt Vesuvius glowed menacingly, erupting six times during the 18th century and eight times in the 19th century. But Naples was the home of opera and commedia dell'arte (improvised comedic satire), and singing lessons

and seats at Teatro San Carlo (081 797 23 31; www.teatrosancarlo. it) were obligatory. Then there were the myths of Virgil and Dante to explore at Lago d'Averno and Campi Flegrei (the Phlegrean Fields). After the discovery of Pompeii (081 857 53 47; www.pompeiisites.org) in 1748, the unfolding drama of a Roman town in its death throes drew throngs of visitors. Then, as now, it was the most popular tourist sight in Italy and its priceless mosaics, frescoes and colossal sculptures filled the Museo Archeologico Nazionale (081 442 21 49; cir.campania.beniculturali. it/museoarcheologiconazionale).

*Opposite: Lago di Bolsena lies between the splendid Renaissance-strewn destinations of Florence and Viterbo; Above: a view down the River Tiber to Rome's Basilica St Peter*

# Bavaria's Romantic Road

**From the vineyards of Würzburg to the foot of the Alps, the Romantic Road (Romantische Strasse) is the most popular of Germany's touring routes. For that reason, we recommend avoiding it in the crowded summer months; try this route in winter, when the cute Bavarian towns look even prettier under a layer of snow. The well-trodden trail links some of Germany's most picturesque towns, coming to a climax at the gates of King Ludwig II's crazy castles.**

## 1. Würzburg

This scenic town in Bavaria's northeast corner straddles the Main River and is renowned for its art, architecture and delicate wines. A large student population keeps things lively, and plenty of hip nightlife pulsates through its cobbled streets. Top billing here goes to the Würzburg Residenz (www.residenz-wuerzburg.de), a vast Unesco-listed palace, built by 18th-century architect Balthasar Neumann as the home of the local prince-bishops. It's one of Germany's most important and beautiful baroque palaces. The wonderful zigzagging Treppenhaus (Staircase) is capped by what is still the world's largest fresco, a masterpiece by Giovanni Battista Tiepolo depicting allegories of the four then-known continents (Europe, Africa, America and Asia).

The 37km (23 miles) between Würzburg and the next stop, Tauberbischofsheim, is best tackled in the following way: from the centre of Würzburg take the B19 south until it joins the A3 motorway; follow this until the junction with the B81, which goes all the way to Tauberbischofsheim.

## 2. Tauberbischofsheim

The main town of the pretty Tauber Valley, this small settlement has a picturesque marketplace dominated by a neo-Gothic town hall and lined with typical half-timbered houses. Follow the remains of the medieval town walls to the Kurmainzisches Schloss, which now houses the Tauberfränkisches Landschaftsmuseum.

The 34km (21 miles) dash from Tauberbischofsheim to Weikersheim passes through Lauda-Königshofen, a pretty stop in the Tauber Valley.

## 3. Weikersheim

Undervisited Weikersheim is home to the magnificent Schloss Weikersheim (www.schloss-weikersheim.de), the finest palace on the entire Romantic Road. Renaissance to the core, it's surrounded by beautiful formal gardens inspired by Versailles.

The short 28km (17 miles) journey between Weikersheim and Rothenburg ob der Tauber follows minor country roads all the way, with the route passing through a rolling patchwork of fields. You could also detour via Creglingen, a minor stop on the Romantic Road.

## 4. Rothenburg ob der Tauber

A well-preserved historical town, Rothenburg ob der Tauber is the most popular stop on the Romantic Road. But when you're finished with the main sights, there are a couple of less obvious attractions here. Hidden down a little alley is the Alt-Rothenburger Handwerkerhaus, where numerous artisans – including coopers, weavers, cobblers and potters – have their workshops today, and mostly have had for the house's 700-plus-years existence. It's half museum, half active workplace and you can easily spend an hour or so watching the craftsmen at work.

The quickest and simplest way between Rothenburg ob

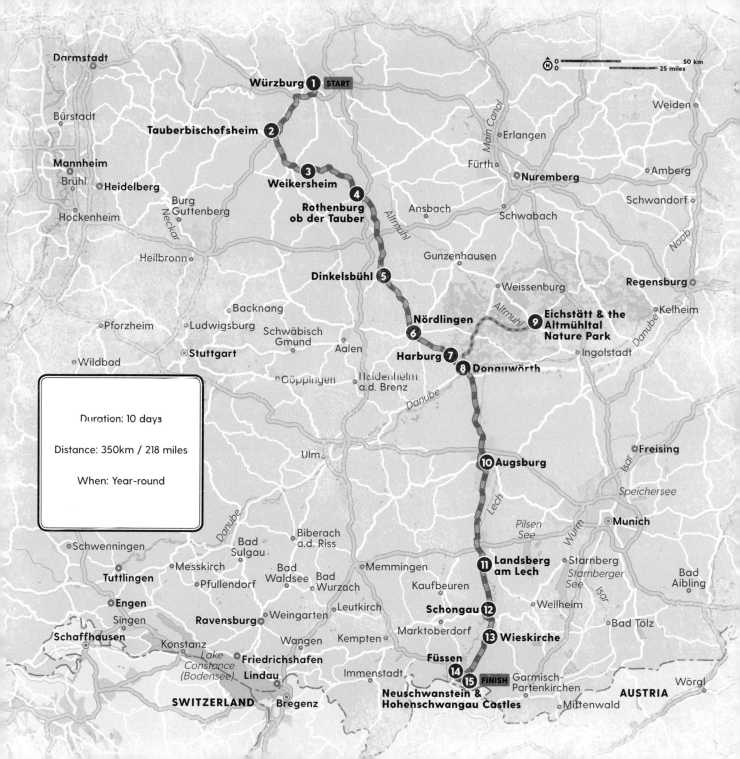

Darmstadt

Bürstadt

Mannheim
Brühl  Heidelberg

Hockenheim

Burg
Guttenberg

Heilbronn

Wildbad

Pforzheim

Stuttgart

Backnang

Ludwigsburg
Schwäbisch
Gmünd

Aalen

Göppingen
Heidenheim
a.d. Brenz

Ulm

Schwenningen

Bad
Sulgau

Biberach
a.d. Riss

Messkirch
Pfullendorf

Bad
Waldsee
Bad
Wurzach

Memmingen

Tuttlingen

Engen

Ravensburg
Weingarten
Wangen

Leutkirch

Kempten

Kaufbeuren

Singen

Schaffhausen

Konstanz

Lake
Constance
(Bodensee)
Friedrichshafen
Lindau

Immenstadt

SWITZERLAND
Bregenz

Würzburg ① START

Tauberbischofsheim ②

③
Weikersheim

④
Rothenburg
ob der Tauber

Dinkelsbühl ⑤

Nördlingen
⑥

Harburg ⑦
⑧ Donauwörth

Altmühl

Ansbach

Gunzenhausen

Main Canal

Erlangen

Fürth

NUREMBERG

Schwabach

Weissenburg

Altmühl

⑨ Eichstätt & the
Altmühltal
Nature Park

Ingolstadt

Weiden

Amberg

Schwandorf

Regensburg

Kelheim

Danube

Naab

Danube

⑩ Augsburg

Lech

Pilsen
See

Freising

Isar

Speichersee

Munich

Wurm

Starnberg
Starnberger
See

Weilheim

Isar

Bad
Aibling

⑪ Landsberg
am Lech

Schongau ⑫

⑬ Wieskirche

Marktoberdorf

Füssen
⑭

⑮ FINISH

Neuschwanstein &
Hohenschwangau Castles

Bad Tölz

Garmisch-
Partenkirchen

Mittenwald

Wörgl

AUSTRIA

Duration: 10 days

Distance: 350km / 218 miles

When: Year-round

# Germany

der Tauber and Dinkelsbühl is along the A7 motorway (50km/31 miles). For a gentler but slower and longer experience, follow the official Romantic Road route, which tacks along country roads via Schillingsfürst, another quaint halt.

## 5. Dinkelsbühl

Immaculately preserved Dinkelsbühl is arguably the Romantic Road's quaintest and most authentically medieval halt. Just like Rothenburg it is ringed by medieval walls, which boast 18 towers and four gates. The joy of Dinkelsbühl is aimless wandering through the crooked lanes, but for a lowdown on the town's history visit the Haus der Geschichte, in the same building as the tourist office.

Just 32km (20 miles) separate Dinkelsbühl from Nördlingen along the B25; drivers are accompanied by the Wörnitz River for the first part of the journey. Just a few kilometres short of Nördlingen is Wallerstein, a small market town with the beautiful parish church of St Alban, also a Romantic Road stop.

## 6. Nördlingen

Charmingly medieval, Nördlingen lies within the Ries Basin, a massive impact crater gouged out by a meteorite more than 15 million years ago. The crater – some 25km in diameter – is one of the best-preserved on earth, and has been declared a special 'geopark'. Nördlingen's 14th-century walls, all original, mimic the crater's rim and are almost perfectly circular. The Rieskrater Museum tells the story.

The 19km (12 mile) drive from Nördlingen to Harburg is a simple affair along the arrow-straight B25 all the way. The road crosses the flatlands created by the Ries meteorite, now fertile agricultural land.

© JAM WORLD IMAGES / Alamy Stock Photo

## 7. Harburg

Looming over the Wörnitz River, the medieval covered parapets, towers, turrets, keep and red-tiled roofs of the 12th-century Schloss Harburg (www.burg-harburg.de) are so perfectly preserved they almost seem like part of a film set. From the castle, the walk to Harburg's cute, half-timbered Altstadt (old town) takes around 10 minutes, slightly

*Clockwise from above: It's called the Romantic Road for good reason – pretty Harburg on the Wörnitz River; Bavaria's Pfaffenwinkel foothills; the historical houses on Rothenburg ob der Tauber's cobbles streets*

Donauwörth had its heyday as a Free Imperial City in the 14th century. WWII destroyed 75% of the medieval old town but three gates and five town-wall towers still guard it today. The main street is Reichstrasse, which is where you'll discover the Liebfraukirche (Reichstrasse), a 15th-century Gothic church with original frescos and a curiously sloping floor that drops 120cm. Swabia's largest church bell (6550kg) swings in the belfry.

Augsburg is 47km (29 miles) away via the B2 and the A8 motorway. The scenic route via backroads east of the A8 passes close to the pretty town of Rain, another minor halt on the Romantic Road.

## 9. Detour: Eichstätt & the Altmühltal Nature Park

A short 55km (34 miles) off the Romantic Road from Donauwörth lies the town of Eichstatt, the main jumping-off point for the serenely picturesque 2900-sq-km Altmühltal Nature Park, which follows the wooded valley of the Altmühl River. Canoeing the river is a top activity here, as are cycling and camping.

## 10. Augsburg

Augsburg is the Romantic Road's largest city and one of Germany's oldest, founded by the stepchildren of Roman emperor Augustus over 2000 years ago. This attractive city of spires and cobbles is an engaging stop, though one with a less quaint atmosphere than others along the route. Augsburg's top sight is the Fuggerei (www.fugger.de), Europe's oldest Catholic welfare settlement, founded by banker and merchant Jakob Fugger in 1521.

Two famous Germans have close associations with Augsburg. The Protestant Reformation

more the other way as you're heading uphill.

A mere 12km (7 miles) separate tiny Harburg with its bigger neighbour Donauwörth. The route follows the B25 all the way across undulating farmland.

## 8. Donauwörth

Sitting pretty at the confluence of the Danube and Wörnitz Rivers, the small town of

leader Martin Luther stayed here in 1518 – his story is told at the St Anna Kirche (Im Annahof 2, off Annastrasse). The birthplace of the poet and playwright Bertolt Brecht is now a museum called the Bertolt-Brecht-Haus (0821-324 2779).

The 41km (25 mile) drive from Augsburg to Landsberg am Lech is a simple affair along the B17. The route mostly follows the valley of the Lech River, which links the two towns. Look out for signs to the amusingly named town of Kissing!

## 11. Landsberg am Lech

A walled town on the River Lech, Landsberg has a less commercial ambience than others on the route. Just like the Wieskirche further south, the small baroque Johanniskirche (Vorderer Anger) is a creation by the baroque architect Dominikus Zimmermann, who lived in Landsberg and served as its mayor. The town's Neues Stadtmuseum (www.museum-landsberg. de) tells Landsberg's tale from prehistory to the 20th century.

© roberthardling / Alamy Stock Photolanet

Still tracing the valley of the River Lech, the 28km (17 mile) drive along the B17 between Landsberg am Lech and Schongau shouldn't take more than 30 minutes. En route you pass through Hohenfurch, a pretty little town regarded as the gateway to the Pfaffenwinkel, a foothill region of the Alps.

## 12. Schongau

One of the lesser-visited stops on the Romantic Road, the attractive town of Schongau is known for its largely intact medieval defences. The Gothic Ballenhaus (Marienplatz 2) served as the town hall until 1902 and has a distinctive stepped gable. It now houses a cafe. Other attractions include the Church of Maria Himmelfahrt (Kirchenstrasse 23), which sports a choir by Dominikus Zimmermann.

There's a convenient overnight stop in town; look for signs to the RV park (Stellplatze) Lechuferstrasse (08861 214-181).

Take the B17 south until you reach Steingaden. From there country roads lead east and then south to Wies. This is where Bavaria starts to take on the look of the Alps, with flower-filled meadows in summer and views of the high peaks when the weather is clear.

## 13. Wieskirche

Located in the village of Wies, the Wieskirche (08862-932 930; www. wieskirche.de) is one of Bavaria's best-known baroque churches and a Unesco-listed site, all of it the monumental work of the legendary artist-brothers Dominikus and Johann Baptist Zimmermann. In 1730 a farmer in Steingaden claimed he'd witnessed the miracle of his Christ statue shedding tears. Pilgrims poured into the town in such numbers over the next

*Left: The Unesco-listed baroque-era Wieskirche Right: Neuschwanstein is fairy-tale made real Following spread, from left: Ludwig II's Schloss Hohenschwangau; Lake Bannwaldsee, nearby*

© Rudy Balasko / Shutterstock

decade that the local abbot commissioned a new church to house the weepy work.

From the Wieskirche, the best way to reach the next stop at Füssen is to backtrack to Steingaden and rejoin the B17 there. The entire journey is 27km (16 miles) through the increasingly undulating foothills of the Alps, with some gorgeous views of the ever-nearing peaks along the way.

## 14. Füssen

Nestled at the foot of the Alps, tourist-busy Füssen is all about the nearby castles of Neuschwanstein and Hohenschwangau, but there are other reasons to linger longer in the area. The town's historical centre is worth half a day's exploration and, from here, you can easily escape from the crowds into a landscape of gentle hiking trails and Alpine vistas. When you've had your fill of these, take an hour or two to drop by Füssen's very own castle, the Hohes Schloss (Magnusplatz 10), today home to an art gallery.

To drive to King Ludwig II's castles, take the B17 across the river until you see the signs for Hohenschwangau. Parking is at a premium in summer. However, as the castles are a mere 4km (2.5 miles) from the centre of Füssen it's simpler to take public transport. RVO buses 78 and 73 (www.rvo-bus.de) run there from Füssen Bahnhof.

## 15. Neuschwanstein & Hohenschwangau Castles

The undisputed highlights of any trip to Bavaria, these two castles make a fitting climax to the Romantic Road.

Schloss Neuschwanstein (tickets 08362-930 830; www.neuschwanstein. de) was a model for Disney's Sleeping Beauty castle. King

**Note:** The castles can only be visited on guided tours (35 minutes). Buy timed tickets from the Ticket Centre (08362-930 830; www.hohenschwangau.de; Alpenseestrasse 12; 8am-5.30pm Apr–mid-Oct, 9am-3.30pm mid-Oct–Mar) at the foot of the castles. In summer, arrive as early as 8am to ensure you get in that day.

Ludwig II planned this fairy-tale pile himself, with the help of a stage designer rather than an architect. He envisioned it as a giant stage on which to recreate the world of Germanic mythology, inspired by the operatic works of his friend Richard Wagner.

It was at nearby Schloss Hohenschwangau (08362-930 830; www.hohenschwangau.de) that King Ludwig II grew up and later enjoyed summers until his death in 1886. His father, Maximilian II, built this palace in a neo-Gothic style atop 12th-century ruins. Less showy than Neuschwanstein, Hohenschwangau has a distinctly lived-in feel, where every piece of furniture is a used original. It was at Hohenschwangau where Ludwig first met Wagner.

# Patagonia's Carretera Austral

At 1239km (770 miles), the Carretera Austral (Southern Highway, aka Route 7) is Chile's most challenging road trip, but one that rewards those willing to brave the often-rough road. The route bisects Patagonia, home to a handful of pioneers who've managed to tame the land just enough to make a living in the small settlements that dot the route, and the remote land of mountains, lakes, forests, fjords and tiny settlements is epic in every sense.

### 1. Puerto Montt
From the Chilean Lake District's busy port town of Puerto Montt, hop onto Route 7, the Carretera Austral, heading south, to catch the first of many ferries at Caleta La Arena. The ferry deposits you at Caleta Puelche, from where the Carretera continues alongside the water toward Contao before turning inland. At Hornopiren there's another ferry that takes you down to Leptepu, then a third short hop to Caleta Gonzalo, the start of the long drive south.

### 2. Parque Pumalín
Caleta Puelche is the gateway to the southern half of Parque Pumalín, a 750,000-acre protected area that is part of the legacy of US conservationist Doug Tompkins. Well-kept trails branch off from either side of the gravel road, where you can stretch your legs along a short trail that loops through a grove of millennia-old alerce (Patagonian cypress) trees. Enjoy the feeling of being dwarfed by these giants and the enormous nalca (Chilean rhubarb) leaves that erupt from the dripping vegetation all around. There's camping all through the park, including at Camping Rio Gonzalo (reservas@parquepumalin.cl). From here, continue south on Route 7 to Chaitén.

### 3. Chaitén
The Chaitén volcano erupted in 2008, burying half the town in a cocktail of mud and ash. Essential services have long been restored, but those abandoned, dilapidated houses are a stark contrast to the sunny little rodeo town from before the eruption. You'll find supermarkets, banks and gas stations here – a good time to replenish your supplies.

### 4. El Amarillo
Route 7 heads inland again here. A beautifully paved section of the road sweeps southeast through a valley, then passes through the village of El Amarillo, the jumping off point for Parque Pumalín's southernmost section.

Hikers should seek out the Ventisquero El Amarillo trail, a stunning hike to the base of Michinmahuida glacier from what is possibly the world's prettiest campsite (mountain-ringed Ventisquero Campground, an hour's hike in from the road). There are many other places to camp along this section of road.

### 5. Futaleufu
Continue onward to where the Carretera Austral forks at the village of Villa Santa Lucia, then take a detour towards the Argentinian border, skirting the glacial Yelcho Lake and following the Futaleufu river upstream to its eponymous picture-perfect village. The aquamarine Futaleufu is one of the world's top white-water rafting rivers; it's worth lingering long enough to hire a guide and test the waters. There are lots of campgrounds along this stretch (as well as a few places to discreetly pull off to the side of the road for the night).

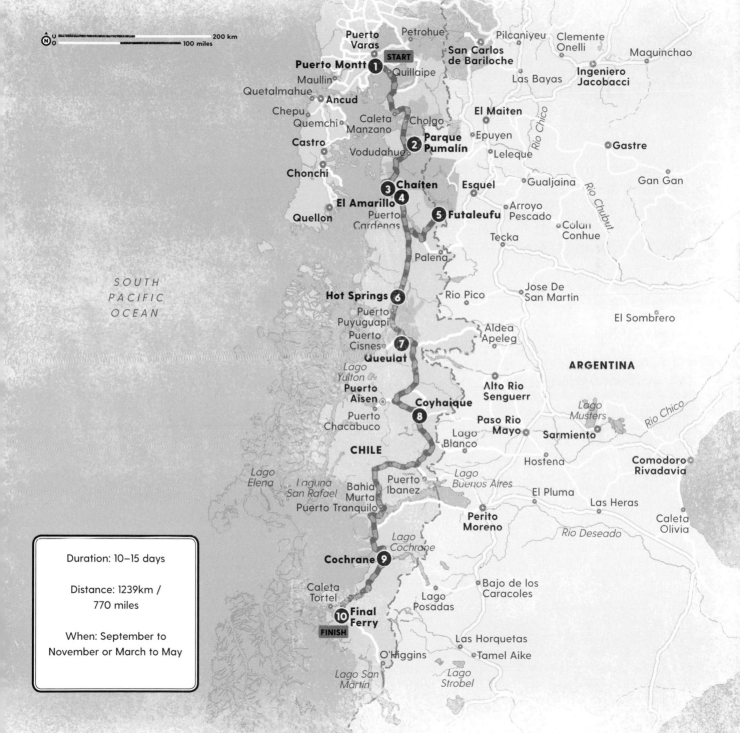

© Juan Carlos Ruiz / 500px

# Chile

## 6. Hot Springs

After a day or two of whitewater, the drive back to the southern highway will seem tranquil by comparison. Head back to Route 7 and south once more, past La Junta, a former estancia (ranch) turned market town with a monument to Pinochet. This is another good place to refuel and re-stock. Heading downhill through a dense forest, the road then emerges by Puyuhuapi on the Ventisquero Sound. This town was settled by enterprising Germans in the 1930s – they set up a textiles factory, which still flourishes. The area is particularly well known for its hot springs – including the basic Termas del Ventisquero, further south beside the road.

## 7. Queulat

The next day's drive is along a potholed, narrow, bumpy stretch of road that skirts the edge of the fjord, passing through the mist-shrouded Parque Nacional Queulat, wedged between craggy mountains. From the visitor centre, a short distance off the road, there is a good short hike to the lookout that takes in the Ventisquero Colgante, the park's hanging glacier. You'll pass secluded, high-end fishing lodges before turning inland and climbing to Queulat Pass. The road's narrow, serpentine curves are liberally strewn with jutting rocks, crisscrossed by shallow streams and cratered with enormous potholes. In spite of that, this is among the most beautiful parts of the Carretera Austral: the narrow road is hemmed in by unruly vegetation, and glacier-fringed mountains rise up ahead, glistening with ribbons of waterfalls.

## 8. Coyhaique

The potholes turn into a stretch of paving and the land is immediately less remote, as

**Note:** This drive is best done from October to April. While parts of the road are paved (watch out for potholes), construction is ongoing and around 70 percent of the highway is still dirt and gravel, prone to landslides in places. Avoid driving at night, and give yourself plenty of extra time in general, as certain sections of the road are susceptible to landslides that will cause traffic delays. You won't need a 4WD, but a vehicle with high clearance is essential. There are petrol stations in most towns, but reliable ATMs are scarce, so bring plenty of cash. Make advance reservations for ferries if travelling in peak season.

craggy peaks give way to rolling farmland and, finally, the Southern Highway's metropolis: the pioneer town of Coyhaique, where a web of streets radiate from the pentagonal main square. It's worth a brief detour to coastal Puerto Chacabuco: from here you can take a day trip with Catamaranes del Sur (www.catamaranesdelsur.cl) in a high-speed catamaran to the San Valentín glacier. Zodiac boats make their ponderous way through a sea filled with enormous chunks of ice to the glacier's 60m face.

South of Coyhaique, a good gravel road traverses wide valleys overlooked by snow-tipped peaks in pioneer country, with occasional sightings of sheep-herding huasos (cowboys) on horseback. South of Lago General Carrera – Chile's great inland sea – you'll see the turnoff for Patagonia Park, the region's newest protected area. There are three official campgrounds inside the park, all first-come, first-served; stop by the headquarters building to register.

## 9. Cochrane

Past the park, the former ranching town of Cochrane is the last chance to fuel up and eat a good steak before the last long, lonely stretch to Villa O'Higgins, at the very end of the road. But before you reach Cochrane, take a one-hour detour just north at the turnoff to Valle Chacabuco – a national park project that's part of the Tompkins legacy, with a fancy lodge, regenerated wilderness and a re-established wildlife corridor for guanacos, foxes and huemul – Chile's endangered deer.

As you continue south from Cochrane, don't neglect a visit to Caleta Tortel, a unique fishing village beautifully positioned between two ice fields, its cypress-wood houses connected by creaky boardwalks and water taxis rather than roads. It's the last turnoff south of Cochrane.

## 10. Final Ferry

Back on the Carretera Austral, a final, short ferry crossing awaits at Puerto Yungay. The road that follows is genuinely hair-raising: a bumpy washboard with narrow hairpin bends and a sheer drop to one side. It promises the untimely demise of any driver showing less than constant vigilance. Then the land flattens out and you reach your destination: a neat grid of streets huddling against towering mountains, the isolated little pioneer outpost of O'Higgins. (It's named for founding father Bernardo O'Higgins, a hero of Spanish-Irish heritage who led the Chilean fight for independence from Spain.) Your reward for making it this far? A big plate of the local speciality, cordero al palo – delicious Patagonian lamb barbecued over a wood fire.

*Previous spread: Petrohué Cascades in the Chilean Lake District; Opposite: the Río Simpson Valley, just off the road to Coyhaique; Below: a detour from the Carretera Austral takes drivers across a rickety bridge over the Río Baker – just don't do it in your van!*

# Argentina's Calchaquí Valleys

**This short yet scintillating route involves three days of winding along the windswept Valles Calchaquíes of the Andean foothills, crossing three vastly different ravines and passing by vineyards and desert before looping back to the starting point at vibrant Salta.**

### 1. Salta

When adobe walls vibrate to the sound of trembling guitars, the air smells of sizzling steaks and your tongue tastes of greasy empanadas and jammy Malbec, you'll know you've finally made it to a peña. These music halls, famed for their zamba folk singers and meaty comfort foods, are the big draw luring local Argentines to Salta, a city in the northwestern corner of this triangular nation where it bumps up against the dusty frontiers of Chile and Bolivia.

Salta means 'the beautiful one' in the language of the indigenous Aymara people. Spanish-speaking Argentines call it 'Salta la Linda,' or 'Salta the beautiful.' With its bubblegum-pink cathedral, soaring neoclassical architecture and lively curb-side cafes, it's not hard to see why. This time capsule of a city sprang up on the outer fringes of the Incan Empire during the height of the Spanish conquest and would go on to become a vital cog of commerce nearly halfway between Lima and Buenos Aires. Spend some time exploring Salta's storied institutions on Plaza 9 do Julio, including a treasure-filled archaeology museum, before moving on.

### 2. Quebrada de Escoipe

The real adventure begins on the pock-marked roads leading out of town and into the sun-baked nether regions of greater Salta Province. The first of the three ravines, Quebrada de Escoipe, is surely the work of Mother Nature's abstract expressionist friend; its mountains are multicoloured thanks to the oxidation of minerals such as sulphur (yellow), iron (red) and copper (green) over thousands of years. After

crossing this surreal landscape, zigzag your way to the top of Bishop's Slope, a 3400m-high overlook where visitors seek the blessing of Archangel Raphael (patron saint of travellers) at a chapel built in his honor. Pick up some road snacks such as llama sausage and goat's cheese at the kiosk by the chapel before continuing on.

### 3. Parque Nacional los Cardones

This reserve is a photographer's dream: amid the rust-red hills, cartoonish cacti appear on the horizon like an army of green ghosts wandering through a desert plain. The adobe homes and time-forgotten streets of Cachi invite a stroll through the village to the banana-yellow church, whose roof was hewn with cactus wood.

### 4. Quebrada de las Flechas

Returning to the open air of the Andean foothills, forge onward past the archaeological ruins of a pre-Inca city called La Paya into the Quebrada de las Flechas (Ravine of Arrows). It's a landscape not unlike the badlands of North America, its beguiling formations making you wonder whether the Earth hasn't tilted just a little bit off its axis.

With massive condors soaring up above and hiking trails snaking off into the distance, it's a place one could linger for hours. But on the far side of this spectacular geological rift lies an even more appetising treat: the vineyards of Cafayate.

### 5. Cafayate

Cafayate is Argentina's second wine centre after Mendoza, but it's much more down to earth and approachable than its

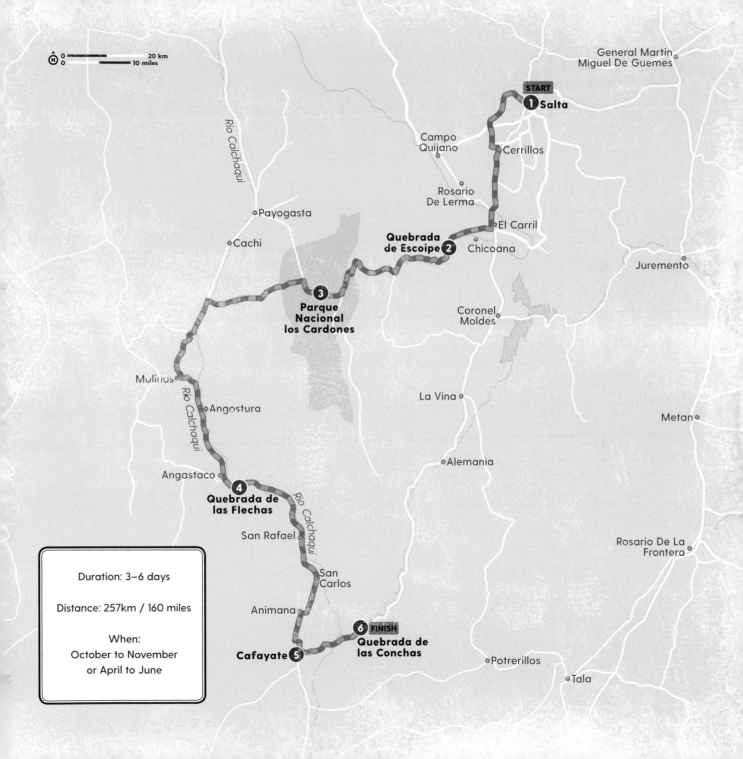

**START**
**1 Salta**

**2 Quebrada de Escoipe**

**3 Parque Nacional los Cardones**

**4 Quebrada de las Flechas**

**5 Cafayate**

**6 Quebrada de las Conchas** **FINISH**

General Martin Miguel De Guemes

Campo Quijano

Cerrillos

Rosario De Lerma

El Carril

Chicoana

Juremento

Coronel Moldes

Payogasta

Cachi

La Vina

Metan

Molinos

Angostura

Alemania

Angastaco

San Rafael

San Carlos

Rosario De La Frontera

Animana

Potrerillos

Tala

*Rio Calchaqui*

0 — 20 km
0 — 10 miles

Duration: 3–6 days

Distance: 257km / 160 miles

When:
October to November
or April to June

# Argentina

ritzier neighbour to the south. While Mendoza prizes big bold bottles of Malbec, Cafayate is a region dominated by the more demure torrontes, a white wine grape that grows exceptionally well in these cold, windswept valleys. Torrontes has a deceptively sweet nose (like a Riesling) that belies its dry finish. As such, it goes down like grape juice when you're basking in Cafayate's afternoon sun.

Cafayate is home to some of the highest altitude vineyards in the world, so to sip and swirl your way through this quite literally breathtaking landscape of soaring mountains and emerald vines is a rare experience. The town itself – with its Andean handicraft markets and family-run bodegas – has a refreshing authenticity.

## 6. Quebrada de las Conchas

Leave the rolling vines behind and enter yet another magnificent landscape: the fossil-rich Quebrada de las Conchas (Ravine of the Shells). This remnant of an ancient lakebed is rife with otherworldly rock formations such as the Garganta del Diablo (Devil's Throat) and Anfiteatro (Amphitheatre). The latter is the site of a prehistoric waterfall with solid rock that now takes on blanket-like folds and improbable swirls. Its walls too are riddled with holes – the homes of burrowing parrots.

The final leg of the drive skirts past a ghost town called Alemania and an artificial lake, Cabra Corral, that's become a popular weekend retreat for Saltenos. Green fields of tobacco then give way to a smattering of increasingly substantial villages. Soon the adobe walls are vibrating once again, the air is thick with sizzling steaks and you know you've made it back to the city of Salta.

Clockwise from far left: National route 40, quebrada de las Flechas, broken arrows, Salta, Cafayate, Argentina; Zamba folk singers in a music hall in Salta, the starting point for the drive through the Calchaquí Valleys; the city's Iglesia San Francisco de Asis

Tips: Night-time temperatures can dip to near freezing in the dry winter months (Jun-Aug), while summer (Dec-Mar) is rainier and hotter. Heavy summer rains can cause flooding and make some roads impassable.
Don't have your own campervan? There are several places in and around Buenos Aires to rent one, including: www.andeanroads.com/en/ and www.campanda.com/rv/argentina.

# Four Corners Cruise

**Everything about this trip demands superlatives – from the Grand Canyon to Vegas, Zion and beyond, it's a procession of some of the biggest, boldest items on many a bucket list.**

### 1. Las Vegas

Familiarise yourself with the strip via a car cruise by all means, but explore the underbelly of Sin City's synthetic charms on a morning walk past the iconic casinos and hotels of the Strip, then end the night with an illuminated stroll at the Neon Museum (702-387-6366; www.neonmuseum. org).

Follow I-15 north for 34 miles (55km), then take exit 75. From here, Hwy 169/Valley of Fire Hwy travels 18 miles (29km) to Valley of Fire State Park, a masterwork of desert scenery. The Valley of Fire Hwy and Hwy 169 run through the park (www.parks.nv.gov/parks/valley-of-fire). Spring and autumn are the best times to visit; avoid summer when temperatures typically exceed 100°F (37°C).

Return to I-15 north, cruising through Arizona into Utah. Leave the highway at exit 16 and follow Hwy 9 east for 32 miles (51 km).

### 2. Zion National Park

The climb up Angels Landing in Zion National Park (www. nps.gov/zion) may be the best day hike in North America. From Grotto Trailhead, the 5.4-mile (8.6km) round-trip crosses the Virgin River, hugs a towering cliff side, squeezes through a narrow canyon, snakes up Walters Wiggles, then traverses a razor-thin ridge where steel chains and the encouraging words of strangers are your only safety net. Your reward after the final scramble to the 5790ft summit? A bird's-eye view of Zion Canyon.

Twist out of the park on Hwy 9 east, driving almost 25 miles (40km) to Hwy 89. Follow Hwy 89 south to the vast open-air movie set that is Kanab.

### 3. Kanab

Sitting between Zion, Grand Staircase–Escalante and the Grand Canyon North Rim, Kanab is a good spot for a base camp. Hundreds of Western movies were filmed here – John Wayne and other gunslingin' celebs really put the town on the map. Today, animal lovers know that the town is home to the Best Friends Animal Sanctuary (435-644-2001; www.bestfriends.org), the country's largest no-kill animal shelter. Tours are free, but call ahead to make a reservation.

Continue into Arizona – now on Hwy 89A – and climb the Kaibab Plateau. Turn south onto Hwy 67 at Jacob Lake and drive 44 miles (71km) to Grand Canyon Lodge.

### 4. Grand Canyon National Park North Rim

While driving through the ponderosa forest that opens onto rolling meadows in Kaibab National Forest, keep an eye out for mule deer as you approach the entrance to the park (www.nps.gov/grca). Stop by the North Rim Visitor Center, beside Grand Canyon Lodge), for information and to join ranger-led nature walks and nighttime programmes.

For an easy scenic half-day hike, follow the 4-mile (6.4km) Cape Final Trail (round-trip) through ponderosa pine forests with great canyon views. The diffcult 14-mile (23km) North Kaibab Trail is the only maintained rim-to-river trail and connects with trails to the South Rim near Phantom Ranch. The trailhead is 2 miles (3.2km) north of Grand Canyon Lodge.

Track back to Jacob Lake, then head east on Hwy 89A, down the Kaibab Plateau, past blink-and-miss-it Marble Canyon and to the junction with Hwy 89. Turn left and drive 26 miles (42km) north to Page.

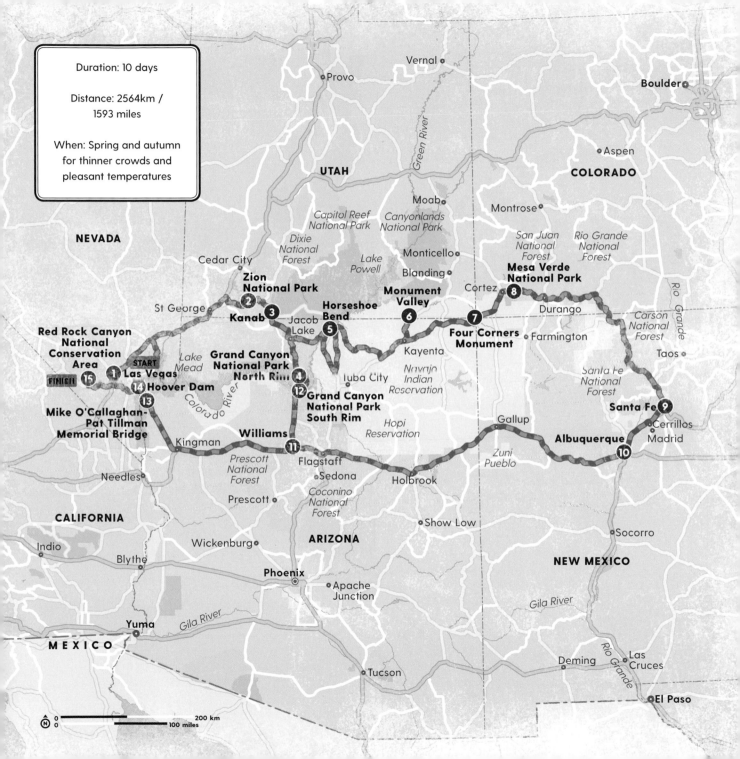

## 5. Horseshoe Bend

The clifftop view at Horseshoe Bend will sear itself onto your memory. One thousand feet below, the seemingly placid, glistening water of the Colorado River carves a perfect U through a colossal thickness of Navajo sandstone. It's simultaneously beautiful and terrifying, particularly as you approach the cliff's edge. There are no railings – it's just you, a sheer drop and dozens of people taking selfies. Free-range toddlers are not a good idea. From the parking lot it's a 0.75-mile (1.2km) one-way hike to the rim. The trailhead is on Hwy 89, south of Page and just south of mile marker 541.

Rejoin Hwy 89 and drive north a short distance to Hwy 98. Turn right and follow 98 southeast to Hwy 160. Turn left and drive 34 miles (55km) north, passing the entrance to Navajo National Monument. In Kayenta, turn left onto Hwy 163 North and drive almost 22 miles (35km) to Monument Valley, on the Arizona–Utah border.

## 6. Monument Valley

Beauty comes in many forms on this drive, but Monument Valley's majestic array of rugged buttes and wind-worn mesas must be its most sensational. For up-close views of the formations, drive into the Monument Valley Navajo Tribal Park (435-727-5870; www.navajo nationparks.org) and follow the unpaved 17-mile (27km) scenic loop passing some of the park's most dramatic formations, such as the East and West Mitten Buttes and the Three Sisters.

Follow Hwy 163 back to Kayenta. Turn left and take Hwy 160 east about 73 miles (117km) to tiny Tee Noc Pos. Take a sharp left to stay on Hwy 160 and drive 6 miles (10km) to Four Corners Rd and the Monument.

## 7. Four Corners Monument

It's seriously remote, but you can't skip the Four Corners Monument (928-871-6647; www. navajonationparks.org) on a road trip through the centre of the southwest. Once you arrive, put one foot into Arizona and the other in New Mexico. Slap one hand in Utah and the other in Colorado. Smile for the camera. It makes a good photo, even if it's not accurate – government surveyors have admitted the marker is almost 2000ft east of where it should be (though it remains a legally recognized border point).

the Chapin Mesa Museum and walk through the Spruce Tree House, where you can climb down a wooden ladder into a kiva. Mesa Verde rewards travellers who set aside a day or more to take the ranger-led tours of Cliff Palace and Balcony House, explore Wetherill Mesa (the quieter side of canyon), linger around the museum, or participate in one of the campfire programmes at Morefield Campground (970-529-4465; www. visitmesaverde.com).

Hop back onto US 160 for 36 miles (58km) east to Durango, and then another 61 miles (98km) to join US 84 south for the 151-mile (243km) run to Santa Fe. You'll pass through Abiquiú, home of Georgia O'Keeffe from 1949 until her death in 1986. Continue toward Santa Fe, exiting onto N Guadalupe St to head toward the Plaza.

### 9. Santa Fe

This 400-year-old city is pretty darn inviting. You've got the juxtaposition of art and landscape, with cow skulls hanging from sky-blue walls and slender crosses topping centuries-old missions. And then there's the comfortable mingling of American Indian, Hispanic and Anglo cultures, with ancient pueblos, 300-year-old haciendas and stylish modern buildings standing in easy proximity. The city is anchored by the Plaza, which was the end of the Santa Fe Trail between 1822 and 1880. The beauty of the region was captured by New Mexico's most famous artist, Georgia O'Keeffe; the Georgia O'Keeffe Museum (505-946-1000; www.okeeffemuseum.org) showcases her work.

The historic route to Albuquerque is the Turquoise Trail, which follows Hwy 14 south for 50 miles (80km) through Los Cerrillos and Madrid. If you're in a hurry, take I-25 south.

© Putt Sakdhnagool / 500px

© Alexander Howard / Lonely Planet

Return to Hwy 160 and turn left. It's a 50-mile (80km) drive across the northwestern tip of New Mexico and through Colorado to Mesa Verde. Hwy 160 becomes Hwy 491 for around 20 miles (32km) of this journey.

### 8. Mesa Verde National Park

Ancestral Puebloan sites are found throughout the canyons and mesas of Mesa Verde (970 529 4465; www.nps.gov/meve), perched on a high plateau south of Cortez and Mancos. If you only have time for a short visit, check out

## 10. Albuquerque

Most of Albuquerque's top sites are concentrated in Old Town. Take the extravagant route to the top of 10,378ft Sandia Crest via the Sandia Peak Tramway (505-856-7325; www.sandiapeak.com; 3). The 2.7-mile tram ride starts in the desert realm of cholla cactus and soars to the pine-topped summit. For exercise, take the beautiful 8-mile (one-way) La Luz Trail back down. It gets hot, so start early.

From Albuquerque to Williams, in Arizona, I-40 overlaps or parallels Route 66. It's 359 miles (578km) to Williams.

## 11. Williams

Train buffs, Route 66 enthusiasts and Grand Canyon-bound vacationers all cross paths in Williams, an inviting small town with all the charm and authenticity of 'Main Street

© aprilpix / 500px

America.' On Route 66 the divey World Famous Sultana Bar (928-635-2021; 301 W Route 66), which once housed a speakeasy, is a great place to sink some suds beneath a menagerie of stuffed wildlife.

## 12. Grand Canyon National Park South Rim

A walk along the Rim Trail (www.nps.gov/grca) in Grand Canyon Village brings stunning views of the iconic canyon, as well as historic buildings, American Indian crafts and geological displays. Starting from the plaza at Bright Angel Trail, walk east on the Rim Trail to Kolb Studio (928-638-2771; www.nps.gov/grca), which holds a small bookstore and an art gallery. Next door is Lookout Studio (www.nps.gov/grca), designed by noted architect Mary Jane Colter to look like the stone dwellings of the Southwest's

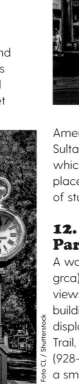

© Professional Foto CL / Shutterstock

*Previous spread, from top: Monument Valley, Utah; Hwy 169 in Valley of Fire State Park; From left: four-century-old Santa Fe; Fremont St, Las Vegas; the Hoover Dam and Bridge*

© MedFaiFotograf / Shutterstock

# USA / Four Corners

Puebloans. The Hopi House (www.nps.gov/grca), another Colter-designed structure, has sold high-quality American Indian jewellery and other crafts since 1904. Just east, the Trail of Time (www.nps.gov/grca) interpretative display traces the history of the canyon's formation. End with the intriguing exhibits and gorgeous views of the Yavapai Geology Museum (928-638-7890; www.nps.gov/grca).

Back in Williams, take the I-40 113 miles (182km) west to Kingman, then join US 93 north. Head north for 75 miles (121km), crossing into Nevada, where exit 2 leads on to Hwy 172 and the Hoover Dam.

## 13. Mike O'Callaghan–Pat Tillman Memorial Bridge

This graceful span, dedicated in 2010, was named for Mike O'Callaghan, governor of Nevada from 1971 to 1979, and for NFL star Pat Tillman, who was a safety for the Arizona Cardinals when he enlisted as a US Army Ranger after September 11. Tillman was killed by friendly fire during a battle in Afghanistan in 2004. Open to pedestrians along a walkway separated from traffic on Hwy 93, the bridge sits 900ft above the Colorado River. It's the second-highest bridge in the US, and provides a bird's-eye eye view of the Hoover Dam and Lake Mead behind it.

Turn right onto the access road and drive a short distance down to Hoover Dam.

## 14. Hoover Dam

A statue of bronze winged figures stands atop Hoover Dam (702-494-2517; www.usbr.gov/lc/hooverdam), memorialising those who built the massive 726ft concrete structure, one of the world's tallest dams. This New Deal public

*Left: The unbeatable hiking trails of Utah's Zion National Park can be accessed by heading east on Hwy 9*

works project, completed ahead of schedule and under budget in 1936, was the first major dam of the Colorado River. Thousands of men and their families, eager for work in the height of the Depression, came to Black Canyon and worked in excruciating conditions – dangling hundreds of feet above the canyon in desert heat of up to 120°F (49°C). Over 100 lost their lives. Guided tours begin at the visitor centre.

Return to US 93, following it west then north as it joins I-515. Take exit 61 for I-215 north. After 11 miles (18km) I-215 becomes Clark County 215. Follow it just over 13 miles (21km) to Charleston Blvd/Hwy 159 at exit 26 and follow it west

## 15. Red Rock Canyon National Conservation Area

Evidence of awesome natural forces is everywhere in this national conservation area (702-515-5350; www. redrockcanyonlv.org). Created about 65 million years ago, the canyon is more like a valley, with a steep, rugged red rock escarpment rising 3000ft on its western edge, dramatic evidence of tectonic-plate collisions. The 13-mile (21km), one-way scenic drive passes some of the canyon's most striking features, where you can access hiking trails and rock-climbing routes. The 2.5-mile (4km) round-trip hike to Calico Tanks climbs through the sandstone and ends atop rocks offering a grand view of the desert and mountains, with Vegas thrown in for sizzle. National Park passes are accepted for admission.

231

# Florida's Scenic Highway 1

**Glittering Miami provides a spectacular finale to an epic coastal road trip featuring fascinating historical sights. Drive the length of Florida all the way down the coast and you'll get a sampling of everything we love about the Sunshine State...the oldest permanent settlement in the US, family-friendly attractions, Latin flavour, the pretty-as-a-picture pastel Art Deco architecture of Miami and – oh, yeah – miles and miles of beautiful beaches right beside you.**

### 1. Amelia Island

Start your drive just 13 miles (21km) south of the Georgia border on Amelia Island, a glorious barrier island with the moss-draped charm of the Deep South. Vacationers have been flocking here since the 1890s, when Henry Flagler's railroad converted the area into a playground for the rich. The legacy of that golden era remains visible today in Amelia's central town of Fernandina Beach, with 50 blocks of historic buildings, Victorian B&Bs and restaurants housed in converted fishing cottages.

Meander down Hwy 1A for about half an hour, passing both Big and Little Talbot Island State Parks. After you enter Fort George Island, take the right fork in the road to get to the Ribault Club.

### 2. Fort George Island

History runs deep at Fort George Island Cultural State Park (904-2512320; www.floridastateparks. org/fortgeorgeisland). Enormous shell middens date the island's habitation by Native Americans to more than 5000 years ago. In 1736 British general James Oglethorpe erected a fort in the area, though it's long since vanished and its exact location is uncertain. In the 1920s flappers flocked to the ritzy Ribault Club (904-251-2802; www.nps. gov/timu) for Gatsby-esque bashes with lawn bowling and yachting. Today it houses the island's visitor centre, which can provide you with a CD tour of the area. Perhaps most fascinating – certainly most sobering – is Kingsley Plantation (904-2513537; www.nps.gov/timu),

Florida's oldest plantation house, built in 1798. Because of its remote location, it's not a grand Southern mansion, but it does provide a fairly unflinching look at slavery through exhibits and the remains of 23 slave cabins.

Follow Hwy 105 inland 15 miles (24km) to I-95, then shoot straight south into Jacksonville, some 24 miles (39km) away.

### 3. Jacksonville

With its high-rises, freeways and chain hotels, Jacksonville is a bit of a departure from our coastal theme, but it offers lots of dining options, and its restored historic districts are worth a wander. Check out the Five Points and San Marco neighbourhoods; both are charming, walkable areas lined with bistros, boutiques and bars. It's also a good chance to work in a little culture at the Cummer Museum of Art (www. cummer.org), which has a genuinely excellent collection of American and European paintings, Asian decorative art and antiquities; or the Museum of Modern Art Jacksonville (MOCA; 904-366-6911; www.mocajacksonville. org), which houses contemporary paintings, sculptures, prints, photography and film.

Take Hwy 1 southwest for an hour straight into St Augustine, where it becomes Ponce de Leon Blvd.

### 4. St Augustine

Founded by the Spanish in 1565, St Augustine is the oldest permanent settlement in the US. Tourists flock here to stroll the ancient streets, and horse-drawn carriages clip-clop

GEORGIA

Tallahassee

START ① Amelia Island

② Fort George Island

Jacksonville ③

④ St Augustine

⑤ Fort Matanzas National Monument

Lake City

Green Cove Springs

Cross City

Gainesville

Palatka

Cedar Key

Ocala

⑥ Daytona Beach

⑦ Ponce Inlet

ATLANTIC OCEAN

⑧ Canaveral National Seashore

Orlando

Titusville

⑨ Space Coast

Cape Canaveral

Melbourne

Tampa

Lakeland

St Petersburg

FLORIDA

Bradenton

Sarasota

Okeechobee

Fort Pierce

Hobe Sound

Lake Okeechobee

Gulf of Mexico

La Belle

Belle Glade

West Palm Beach ⑪ ⑩ Palm Beach

Fort Myers

Delray Beach

Fort Myers Beach

Naples

Big Cypress National Preserve

⑫ Fort Lauderdale

Hollywood

Miami ⑬ ⑭ Miami Beach

FINISH

Everglades National Park

Biscayne National Park

0     100 km

0     50 miles

N

Duration: 6 days

Distance: 764km / 475 miles

When:
November to April,
when it's
warm but not hot

past townsfolk dressed in period costume. It's definitely touristy, with tons of museums, tours and attractions vying for your attention. Start with the Colonial Quarter (904-342-2857; www.colonialquarter. com), a re-creation of 18th-century St Augustine complete with craftspeople demonstrating blacksmithing, leather working and other trades. Stop by the Visitor Information Center (904-825-1000; www. floridashistoriccoast.com) to find out about your other options, including ghost tours, the Pirate and Treasure Museum, Castillo de San Marcos National Monument, and the Fountain of Youth, a goofy tourist attraction disguised as an archaeological park that is purportedly the very spot where Ponce de Leon landed.

Take the Bridge of Lions toward the beach then follow Hwy 1A south for 13 miles (21km) to Fort Matanzas.

## 5. Fort Matanzas National Monument

By now you've seen first-hand that the Florida coast isn't all about fun in the sun; it also has a rich history that goes back hundreds of years. History buffs will enjoy a visit to this tiny Spanish fort (904-471-0116; www.nps.gov/foma) built in 1742. Its purpose? To guard Matanzas Inlet – a waterway leading straight up to St Augustine – from British invasion. On the lovely (and free) boat ride over, park rangers narrate the fort's history and explain the gruesome origins of the name. ('Matanzas' means 'slaughters' in Spanish; let's just say things went badly for a couple of hundred French Huguenot

*Above, from left: Canaveral National Seashore provides 24 miles of natural beach; simply follow the signs...*

© Dennis MacDonald / Alamy Stock Photo

soldiers back in 1565.)

Hopping over to I-95 will only shave a little bit off the hour-long trip; you might as well enjoy putting along Hwy 1A to Daytona Beach, 40 miles (64km) south.

## 6. Daytona Beach

With typical Floridian hype, Daytona Beach bills itself as 'The World's Most Famous Beach.' But its fame is less about quality – the beach is actually mediocre – than the size of the parties this expansive beach has witnessed during spring break, Speed Weeks and motorcycle events when half a million bikers roar into town. One Daytona title no one disputes is 'Birthplace of NASCAR' – it started here in 1947. Its origins go back as far as 1902 to drag races held on the beach's hard-packed sands. Catch a race at the Daytona International Speedway (800-748-7467; www.daytonainternational speedway. com). When there's no race, you can wander the massive stands for free or take a tram tour of the track and pit area. Race-car fanatics can indulge in the Richard Petty Driving Experience (800-2373889; www.drivepetty. com) and feel the thrill of riding shotgun or even taking the wheel themselves.

Take South Atlantic Ave 10 miles (16km) south along the coast to get to Ponce Inlet.

## 7. Ponce Inlet

What's a beach road trip without a good lighthouse? About 6 miles (10km) south of Daytona Beach is the Ponce de Leon Inlet Lighthouse & Museum (386-761-1821; www. ponceinlet.org). Stop by for a photo op with the handsome red-brick tower built in 1887, then climb the 203 steps to the top for great views of the surrounding beaches.

Backtrack up Atlantic, then cut over to Hwy 1/ FL 5 and head south for 20 minutes. Pre-planning pays here, because your route depends on where you're heading. One road goes 6 miles south from New Smyrna Beach, and another 6 miles north from the wildlife refuge. Both dead-end, leaving 16 (26km) miles of beach between them.

## 8. Canaveral National Seashore

These 24 miles (39km) of pristine, windswept beaches comprise the longest stretch of undeveloped beach on Florida's east coast. On the north end is family-friendly Apollo Beach, which shines in a class of its own with gentle surf and miles of solitude. On the south end, Playalinda Beach is surfer central. Just west of (and including) the beach, the 140,000-acre Merritt Island National Wildlife Refuge (321-861-5601; www.fws.gov/merrittisland) is an unspoiled oasis for birds and wildlife. It's one of the country's best birding spots, especially from October to May, and more endangered and threatened species of wildlife inhabit the swamps, marshes and hardwood hammocks here than at any other site in the continental US. An easy quarter-mile boardwalk will whet your appetite for everything the refuge has to offer. Other highlights include the Manatee Observation Deck, the 7-mile (11km) Black Point Wildlife Drive, and a variety of hiking trails.

Although Kennedy Space Center is just south of the Merritt Island Refuge, you have to go back into Titusville, travel south 5 miles (8km) on Hwy 1/FL 5, then take the Nasa Causeway back over to get there.

## 9. Space Coast

The Space Coast's main claim to fame (other than being the setting for the iconic 1960s TV series *I Dream of Jeannie*) is being the real-life home to the Kennedy Space Center (866-737-5235; www.kennedyspacecenter.com) and its massive visitor complex. Once a working spaceflight facility, Kennedy Space Center is shifting from a living museum to a historical one since the end of NASA's space shuttle program in 2011.

Hop back onto the freeway (I-95) for the 2½hour drive south to Palm Beach.

## 10. Palm Beach

History and nature give way to money and culture as you reach the southern part of the coast, and Palm Beach looks every inch the playground for the rich and famous that it is. But fear not: the 99% can stroll along the beach – kept pleasantly seaweed-free by the town – ogle the massive gated compounds on A1A or window-shop in uber-ritzy Worth Ave, all for free. The best reason to stop here is Flagler Museum (561-655-2833; www.flaglermuseum.us), housed in the spectacular, beaux-art-styled Whitehall Mansion built by Henry Flagler in 1902.

When you're ready to mix once more with the commoners, head back inland. West Palm Beach is just a causeway away.

## 11. West Palm Beach

While Palm Beach has the money, West Palm Beach has the largest art museum in Florida, the Norton Museum of Art (561-832-5196; www.norton.org). The Nessel Wing features a colourful crowdpleaser: a ceiling made from nearly 700 pieces of handblown glass by Dale Chihuly. Come evening, if you're not sure what you're in the mood for, head to CityPlace (561-366-1000; www.cityplace.com), a massive outdoor shopping and entertainment centre. There you'll find a slew of stores, about a dozen

restaurants, a 20-screen movie theatre and the Harriet Himmel Theater – not to mention free concerts in the outdoor plaza.

Fort Lauderdale is a straight shot down I-95, 45 miles (72km) south of Palm Beach. Taking Hwy 1A will add half an hour to your trip.

## 12. Fort Lauderdale

Fort Lauderdale Beach isn't the spring-break destination it once was, although you can still find outposts of beach-bummin' bars and motels in between the swanky boutique hotels and multimillion-dollar yachts. Few visitors venture far inland except maybe to dine and shop along Las Olas Blvd; most spend the bulk of their time on the coast, frolicking at water's edge. The promenade – a wide, brick, palm-tree-dotted pathway swooping along the beach – is a magnet for runners, in-line skaters, walkers and cyclists. The white-sand beach, meanwhile, is one of the nation's cleanest and best.

Things are heating up. Miami is just half an hour south of Fort Lauderdale down I-95.

*Clockwise from top: A boardwalk over the dunes on Amelia Island; a lifeguard at their post on South Beach, Miami; art deco architecture on the city's Ocean Dr*

© Olga Yudina / Shutterstock

## 13. Miami

Miami moves to a different rhythm from anywhere else in the USA, with pastel-hued, subtropical beauty and Latin sexiness at every turn. Just west of downtown on Calle Ocho (8th St), you'll find Little Havana, the most prominent community of Cuban Americans in the US. One of the best times to come is the last Friday of the month during Viernes Culturales (Cultural Fridays; www.viernes culturales.org), a street fair showcasing Latino artists and musicians. Or catch the vibe at Máximo Gómez Park, where old-timers gather to play dominoes to the strains of Latin music.

Wynwood and the Design District are Miami's official arts neighborhoods; don't miss the murals at Wynwood Walls (www.thewynwood walls.com), where blocks of murals form a drive-through art gallery.

We've saved the best for last. Cross over the Julia Tuttle Causeway or the MacArthur Causeway to find yourself in Art-Deco-laden Miami Beach.

## 14. Miami Beach

Miami Beach has some of the best beaches in the country, with white sand and warm turquoise water, but it also has the largest concentration of Art Deco anywhere in the world, with some 1200 buildings lining the streets around Ocean Dr and Collins Ave. Arrange a tour at the Art Deco Welcome Center (305-672-2014; www.mdpl.org) or pick up a walking-tour map in the gift shop. Fronting the beach, Ocean Ave is lined with cafes that spill out onto the sidewalk; stroll along until you find one that suits your cravings. Another highly strollable area is Lincoln Road Mall, a pedestrian promenade that's lined with stores, restaurants and bars.

About an hour's drive south of Miami Beach, Biscayne National Park (305-230-1144; www.nps.gov/bisc) is a protected marine sanctuary harbouring amazing tropical coral reef systems, most within sight of Miami's skyline. It's only accessible by water: you can take a glassbottomed-boat tour, snorkel or scuba dive, or rent a canoe or kayak to lose yourself in this 300-sq-mile system of islands, underwater shipwrecks and mangrove forests.

© littlenySTOCK / Shutterstock

# Minnesota's Highway 61

Celebrated in Bob Dylan's 1965 album *Highway 61 Revisited*, this North Shore road has charms all of its own. It's a journey dominated by water, where ore-toting freighters ply the ports, little fishing fleets haul in the day's catch, and wave-bashed cliffs along Lake Superior are the reward of those willing to trek in the Nobel Laureate's footsteps.

### 1. Duluth

Dramatically spliced into a cliff that tumbles down to Lake Superior, Duluth is one of the busiest ports in the nation. Canal Park downtown is a good spot to see the action. Start at the Aerial Lift Bridge, Duluth's landmark that raises its mighty arm to let horn-bellowing ships into port. About 1000 freighters a year glide through. The screens outside the Maritime Visitor Center (218-720-5260; www.lsmma.com) announce when the big boats come and go; inside holds first-rate exhibitions on Great Lakes shipping and shipwrecks.

Duluth is also the birthplace of Bob Dylan, though the town is pretty laid-back about its famous son. You're on your own to find Dylan's childhood home (519 N 3rd Ave E), up a hill a few blocks northeast of downtown. Dylan lived on the top floor until age six, when his family moved inland to Hibbing. It's a private, unmarked residence, so all you can do is check it out from the street.

Take London Rd, aka Hwy 61, heading northeast out of town. Follow the signs for the North Shore Scenic Dr (also called Scenic 61 or Old Hwy 61). There's a Hwy 61 expressway that also covers the next 20 miles (32km), but steer clear and dawdle on the original, curvy, two-lane route instead.

### 2. Knife River

Unspoiled shoreline and fisherfolk casting at river mouths are your companions along the way until you reach Russ Kendall's Smoke House (218-834-5995; 149 Scenic Dr) in Knife River. A groovy neon sign beckons you in. Four generations of Kendall folk have cooked up the locally plucked trout and line-caught Alaskan salmon. Buy a brown-sugar-cured slab; staff will wrap it in newspaper, and you'll be set for picnics for miles to come.

Continue northeast on Hwy 61 to Two Harbors, a couple of miles up the road.

### 3. Two Harbors

Minnesota's only operating lighthouse (www.lake countyhistoricalsociety.org) rises up over Agate Bay. The 1892 fog-buster sticks to a rhythm – 0.4-second flash, 4.6 seconds of darkness, 0.4-second flash, 14.6 seconds of darkness. That's how it goes all day, every day; check it out. Hiking buffs should stop in the Superior Hiking Trail Headquarters (218-834-2700; www.shta. org). The awesome 290-mile (467km) footpath follows the lake-hugging ridgeline between Duluth and the Canadian border. Trailheads with parking lots pop up every 5 to 10 miles (8-16km), making it ideal for day hikes. The headquarters has maps and information.

Motor onward on Hwy 61, past the hamlet of Castle Danger (named for a boat that ran aground nearby) to Gooseberry Falls State Park, a 13-mile (21km) drive.

### 4. Gooseberry Falls State Park

The five cascades, scenic gorge and easy trails draw carloads of visitors to Gooseberry Falls State Park (218-8343855; www.dnr.state.mn.us). Several cool stone and log buildings, built by Civilian Conservation Corps in the

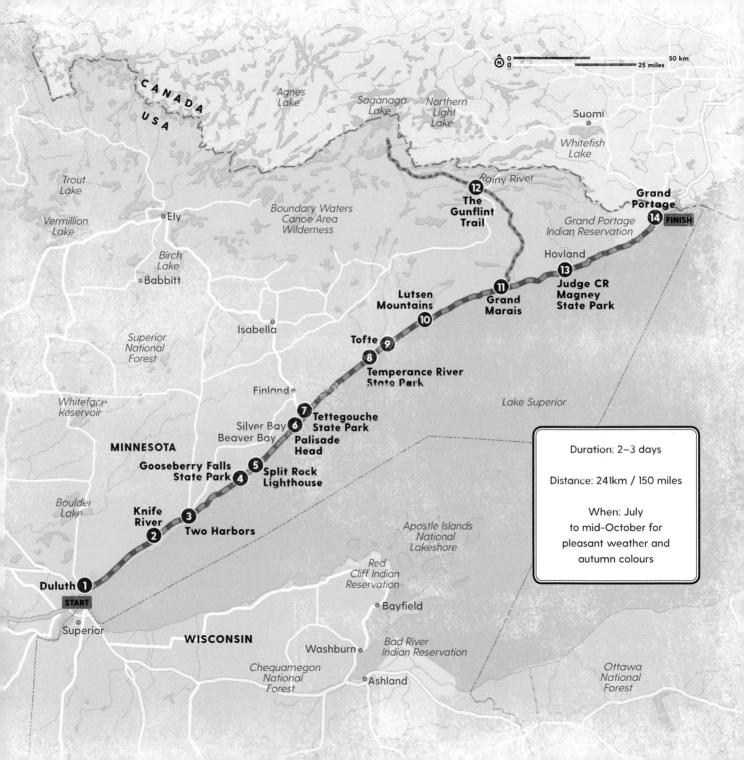

1930s, dot the premises and hold exhibits and concessions. The Lower and Middle Falls offer the quickest access via a 0.6-mile (1km) paved walkway. Hardier types can trek the 2-mile (3.2km) Gooseberry River Loop, which is part of the Superior Hiking Trail. To embark, leave your car at the visitor centre lot (at Mile 38.9). Follow the trail to the Upper Falls, then continue upstream on the Fifth Falls Trail. Cross the bridge at Fifth Falls, then return on the river's other side to where you started. Voila! It's one of the simplest Superior trail jaunts you'll find.

Yep, it's back to Hwy 61 heading northeast, this time for 6 miles (10km).

## 5. Split Rock Lighthouse

The most visited spot on the entire North Shore is Split Rock Lighthouse State Park (218-5957625; www.dnr. state.mn.us). The shiner itself is a state historic site with a separate admission fee. Guided tours are available (they depart hourly), or you can explore on your own. If you don't mind stairs, say 170 or so each way, tramp down the cliff to the beach for incredible views of the lighthouse and surrounding shore. The lighthouse was built after a whopping storm in November 1905 battered 29 ships in the area. Modern navigation equipment rendered it obsolete by 1969. No matter. It remains one of the most picture-perfect structures you'll come across.

Onward on Hwy 61 for 10 miles (16km). Not long after cruising by taconite-crazed Silver Bay, watch for the sign to Palisade Head.

## 6. Palisade Head

Palisade Head is an old lava flow that morphed into some awesomely sheer, rust-red cliffs. A narrow road winds around to the top, where there's a small parking lot. The view that unfurls

is tremendous. On a clear day you can see Wisconsin's Apostle Islands. Rock climbers love the Head, and you'll probably see a lot of them hanging around.

Return to Hwy 61. Palisade Head is actually part of Tettegouche State Park, though it's not contiguous. The park's main span begins 2 miles (3.2km) up the road.

## 7. Tettegouche State Park

Like most of the parks dotting the North Shore, Tettegouche State Park (218-353-8800; www.dnr.state.mn.us) offers fishing, camping, paddling, and hiking trails to waterfalls and little lakes, plus skiing and snowshoe trails in winter. There are two unique to-do's, both accessed near the park entrance (Mile 58.5). Leave your car in the parking lot by the visitor centre, then hit the trail to Shovel Point. It's a 1.5-mile (2.4km) round-trip jaunt over lots of steps and boardwalks. It pays off with sublime views of the rugged landscape from the point's tip. Watch the lake's awesome power as waves smash below. And keep an eye out for peregrine falcons that nest in the area. Tettegouche's other cool feature is the idyllic swimming hole at the Baptism River's mouth. Walk along the picnic area by the visitor center and you'll run into it.

Hwy 61 rolls by more birch trees, parks and cloud-flecked skies for the next 22 miles (35km). Not far past Taconite Harbor (now used to load and unload coal for the adjacent power plant), you'll come to Temperance River.

## 8. Temperance River State Park

Get ready for another gorgeous, falls-filled landscape. The eponymous waterway at

Temperance River State Park (218-663-3100; www.dnr. state.mn.us) belies its moderate name and roars through a narrow, twisting gorge. The scene is easy to get to, with highway-side parking. Then hike over footbridges and around rock pools to see the action.

It's a quick 2 miles (3.2km) up Hwy 61 to Tofte.

## 9. Tofte

The teeny town of Tofte is worth a stop to browse the North Shore Commercial Fishing Museum. The twin-gabled red building holds fishing nets, a fishing boat and other tools of the trade, as well as intriguing photos, most of them from the original Norwegian families who settled and fished here in the late 1800s. Nearby Sawtooth Outfitters (218-663-7643; www. sawtoothoutfi tters.com) offers guided kayaking tours for all levels of paddling. It has trips on the Temperance River and out on Lake Superior, as well as easier jaunts on wildlife-rich inland lakes. Sawtooth also rents mountain bikes to pedal over the many trails in the area, including the popular Gitchi Gami State Bike Trail.

Get back on Hwy 61 and head 7 piney miles (11km) northeast.

## 10. Lutsen Mountains

Lutsen (218-406-1320; www .lutsen.com) is a ski resort – the biggest alpine ski area in the

*Above, from left: Temperance River State Park on the north shore of Lake Superior; take the winding road to the car park at Palisade Head with its view of Shovel Point*

## USA / Minnesota

Midwest, in fact. So it bustles in winter when skiers and snowboarders pile in for the 95 runs on four mountains. In summer, visitors come for the aerial gondola to the top of Moose Mountain. The red cars glide at treetop level into the valley and over the Poplar River before reaching the mountain top 1000ft later. Gape at the view from the chalet and hike the paths. The Superior Hiking Trail cuts through and you can take it plus a spur for the 4.5-mile (7km) trek back down the mountain. Kids go crazy for the alpine slide on Eagle Mountain; it's accessed by chairlift. The resort also arranges family-friendly canoe trips in voyageur-style vessels on the Poplar River.

Back to Hwy 61, past maple- and birch-rich Cascade River State Park (particularly pretty in autumn), for 20 miles (32km) to Grand Marais.

### 11. Grand Marais

Artsy little Grand Marais makes an excellent base to explore the region. Stroll the waterfront, watch the small fishing fleet head out, and take advantage of the characterful local eateries. DIY enthusiasts can learn to build boats, tie flies or harvest wild rice at the North House Folk School (218-3879762; www.northhouse.org). The course list, which strives to preserve local traditions, is phenomenal – as is the school's two-hour sailing trip aboard the Vikingesque schooner Hjordis.

### 12. Detour: The Gunfint Trail

Aka Hwy 12, the Gunflint Trail (www.gunflint-trail.com) slices inland from Grand Marais and ends near Saganaga Lake. The paved, 57-mile-long (92km) byway dips into the Boundary Waters Canoe Area Wilderness (www.fs.usda. gov/attmain/superior/specialplaces), the

legendarily remote paddlers' paradise. For Boundary permits and information, visit the Gunflint Ranger Station (218-387-1750; 2020 Hwy 61), a stone's throw southwest of Grand Marais on Hwy 61. Even if you're not canoeing, the road has excellent hiking, picnicking and moose-viewing. Look for the big antlered guys and gals around dawn or dusk in wet, swampy areas. It takes 1½ hours to drive the Gunflint Trail one way, but you'll want longer for hiking, ziplining and moose stops.

Beyond Grand Marais Hwy 61 widens, you see fewer people, and the lake reveals more of

© Dennis O'Hara / Shutterstock

*Above, clockwise from left: Split Rock Lighthouse, built in 1910; battle re-enactors call a truce at Grand Portage; the Gunflint Trail is a worthwhile detour from Hwy 61*

but the other half disappears down a huge hole and flows underground. Where it goes is a mystery – scientists have never been able to determine the water's outlet. It's a moderately breath-sapping 1.1-mile (1.8km) walk each way. Across the road from the park is Naniboujou Lodge. Built in the 1920s, the property was once a private club for Babe Ruth and his contemporaries, who smoked cigars in the Great Hall, warmed by the 20ft-high stone fireplace. The pièce de résistance is the hall's massive domed ceiling painted with mind-blowing, psychedelic-colored Cree Indian designs. The hall is now the lodge's dining room, and you're welcome to take a peek (or meal).

The final 26-mile (42km) stretch passes through the Grand Portage Indian Reservation to Grand Portage National Monument.

## 14. Grand Portage

Named for the voyagers who had to carry their canoes around the Pigeon River rapids, Grand Portage National Monument (218-475-0123; www.nps.gov/grpo) was the centre of a farflung fur-trading empire, and the reconstructed 1788 trading post and Ojibwe village show how the community lived in the harsh environment. Learn how the original inhabitants prepared wild rice and pressed beaver pelts as you wander through the Great Hall, kitchen, canoe warehouse and other buildings.

The half-mile paved path that goes to Mt Rose rewards with killer views. Or make like a voyageur and walk the 17-mile (27km) round-trip Grand Portage Trail that traces the early fur-men's route. Grand Portage is impressively lonely and windblown – fitting for the end of the road. Because with that, Hwy 61 stops cold at the Canadian border.

itself. After 14 miles (23km), you'll arrive at Judge CR Magney State Park.

## 13. Judge CR Magney State Park

The namesake of the park (218-387-6300; www. dnr.state.mn.us) was a former mayor of Duluth and Minnesota Supreme Court justice who helped preserve the area. His own patch of land is a beauty. Hiking to Devil's Kettle, the famous falls where the Brule River splits around a huge rock, is a must. Half of the flow drops 50ft in a typically gorgeous North Shore gush,

# Pacific Coastal Route

Bewitching ribbons of Hwy 1 and Hwy 101 await all along this route up the West Coast, from California into Oregon and Washington. Uncover beaches, seafood shacks and piers for catching sunsets over boundless ocean horizons – better yet, your odds of finding an overnight spot with an ocean view along this route are excellent.

### 1. San Francisco

There will be gridlock, but don't despair. Hwy 1 runs straight through the city's biggest, most breathable greenspace: Golden Gate Park, a conservatory of flowers, arboretum and botanical gardens.

Follow Hwy 1 north over the Golden Gate Bridge. Guarding the entry to San Francisco Bay, this iconic bridge is named after the straits it spans, not for its 'International Orange' paint job. Park in the lot on the bridge's south or north side, then traipse out onto the pedestrian walkway for a photo.

Slow-moving, wonderfully twisted Hwy 1 runs along the Marin County coast, passing nearby Point Reyes. Over the next 100 miles (161km) from Bodega Bay to Mendocino, revel in a remarkably uninterrupted stretch of coastal highway. More than halfway along, watch for the lighthouse road turnoff north of Point Arena town.

### 2. Around Point Arena

The fishing fleets of Bodega Bay and Jenner's harbour-seal colony are the last things you'll see before the highway dives into California's great rural northlands. Hwy 1 twists and turns past the Sonoma Coast's state parks packed with hiking trails, sand dunes and beaches, as well as underwater marine reserves, rhododendron groves and a 19th-century Russian fur-trading fort. At Sea Ranch, don't let exclusive-looking vacation homes prevent you from following public-access trailhead signs and stairways to empty beaches.

Further north, guarding an unbelievably windy point since 1908, Point Arena Lighthouse is the only lighthouse in California where you can actually climb to the top.

It's an hour-long, 35-mile (56km) drive north along Hwy 1 from the Point Arena Lighthouse turnoff to Mendocino, crossing the Navarro, Little and Big Rivers. Stop and stretch (or stop for the night) at one of the wind-tossed state beaches or parklands along the way.

### 3. Mendocino & Fort Bragg

Looking more like Cape Cod than California, the quaint maritime town of Mendocino has white picket fences surrounding New England–style cottages with blooming gardens and redwood-built water towers. Its dramatic headlands jutting into the Pacific, this yesteryear timber town and shipping port was 'discovered' by artists and bohemians in the 1950s and has served as a scenic backdrop in over 50 movies. Once you've browsed the souvenir shops and art galleries selling everything from driftwood carvings to homemade fruit jams, escape north to workaday Fort Bragg, with its simple fishing harbour and craft brew pub.

About 25 miles (40km) north of Mendocino, Westport is the last hamlet along this rugged stretch of Hwy 1. Rejoin Hwy 101 northbound at Leggett for another 90 miles (145km) to Eureka, detouring along the Avenue of the Giants and, if you have more time to spare, to the Lost Coast.

### 4. Eureka

Hwy 101 trundles alongside Humboldt Bay National Wildlife Refuge (707-733-5406; www.fws. gov/refuge/humboldt_bay), a stopover for migratory birds on the Pacific Flyway.

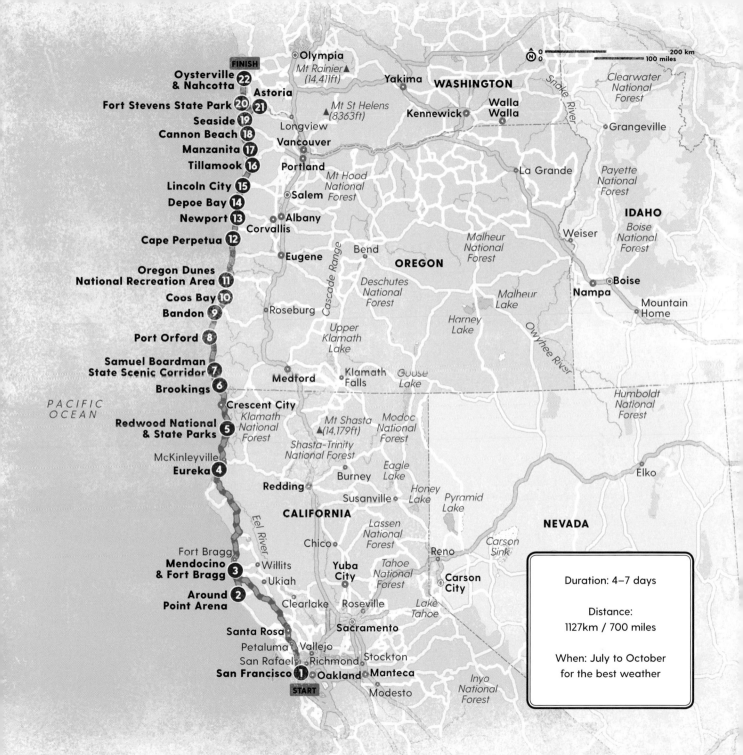

**FINISH**

Oysterville & Nahcotta — 22

Astoria

Fort Stevens State Park — 20 — 21

Seaside — 19

Cannon Beach — 18

Manzanita — 17

Tillamook — 16

Lincoln City — 15

Depoe Bay — 14

Newport — 13

Cape Perpetua — 12

Oregon Dunes National Recreation Area — 11

Coos Bay — 10

Bandon — 9

Port Orford — 8

Samuel Boardman State Scenic Corridor — 7

Brookings — 6

Crescent City

Redwood National & State Parks — 5

McKinleyville

Eureka — 4

Fort Bragg

Mendocino & Fort Bragg — 3

Around Point Arena — 2

Santa Rosa

Petaluma
San Rafael

**San Francisco** — 1

**START**

*PACIFIC OCEAN*

WASHINGTON

Olympia
Mt Rainier (14,411ft)
Yakima
Mt St Helens (8363ft)
Kennewick
Walla Walla
Longview
Vancouver
Portland
Mt Hood National Forest
Salem
Albany
Corvallis
Eugene
Bend
OREGON
Roseburg
Upper Klamath Lake
Medford
Klamath Falls
Goose Lake
Crescent City
Klamath National Forest
Mt Shasta (14,179ft)
Modoc National Forest
Shasta-Trinity National Forest
Eagle Lake
Burney
Redding
Honey Lake
Susanville
Pyramid Lake
CALIFORNIA
Chico
Lassen National Forest
Reno
Willits
Ukiah
Yuba City
Tahoe National Forest
Carson City
Clearlake
Roseville
Lake Tahoe
Sacramento
Vallejo
Richmond
Stockton
Oakland
Manteca
Modesto
Inyo National Forest

Clearwater National Forest
Grangeville
La Grande
Payette National Forest
IDAHO
Boise National Forest
Weiser
Boise
Nampa
Mountain Home
Humboldt National Forest
Elko
NEVADA
Carson Sink

*Snake River*
*Owyhee River*
*Eel River*
*Cascade Range*
*Malheur National Forest*
*Deschutes National Forest*
*Malheur Lake*
*Harney Lake*

N

200 km
100 miles

Duration: 4–7 days

Distance:
1127km / 700 miles

When: July to October
for the best weather

Next comes the sleepy railroad town of Eureka.

Follow Hwy 101 north past the Rastafarian-hippie college town of Arcata and turnoffs for Trinidad State Beach and Patrick's Point State Park (which has three campgrounds; www.parks.ca.gov/?page_id=417). Hwy 101 drops out of the trees beside marshy Humboldt Lagoons State Park, rolling north towards Orick, just over 40 miles (64km) from Eureka.

## 5. Redwood National & State Parks

At last, you'll reach Redwood National Park (707-465-7335; www.nps. gov/redw). Commune with the coastal giants inside Lady Bird Johnson Grove or the majestic Tall Trees Grove (free drive-and-hike permit required). For more untouched redwood forests, wind along the 8-mile (13km) Newton B Drury Scenic Parkway in Prairie Creek Redwoods State Park (707-488-2039; www.parks.ca.gov), passing grassy meadows where Roosevelt elk roam. Then follow Hwy 101 north to Crescent City, the last pit-stop before the Oregon border.

## 6. Brookings, Oregon

Your first stop on the Oregon coast, Brookings has some of the warmest temperatures on the coast, and is a leader in Easter lily-bulb production; in July, fields south of town are filled with bright colours and a heavy scent. In May and June you'll also find magnificent floral displays at the hilly, 30-acre Azalea Park.

## 7. Samuel Boardman State Scenic Corridor

This 12-mile (19km) stretch of coastal splendor features giant stands of Sitka spruce, natural rock bridges, tide pools and loads of hiking trails. Along the highway are well over a dozen roadside stops and picnic areas, most of which allow you to stay for 12 hours – so they make excellent dry camping spots, and you'll wake to an Instagrammable ocean view.

The viewing platform at Natural Bridge Viewpoint (Mile 346, Hwy 101) offers a glorious photo op of rock arches – the remnants of collapsed sea caves – after which you can decide whether you want to commit to the hike down to China Beach.

## 8. Port Orford

Perched on a grassy headland, the hamlet of Port Orford is located in one of the most scenic stretches of coastal highway, and there are stellar views even from the centre of town. If you're feeling ambitious, take the 3-mile (4.8km) trail up Humbug Mountain, which takes you up, up, up past streams and through prehistoric-looking landscapes to the top, where you'll be treated to dramatic views of Cape Sebastian and the Pacific. If it's time to stop for the night, a parking lot atop the hill at the end of Harbor Rd charges a nominal fee for overnight camping (and restrooms at the visitor centre nearby).

## 9. Bandon

Optimistically touted as Bandon-by-the-Sea, this little town sits happily at the bay of the Coquille River, with an Old Town district that's been gentrified into a picturesque harbourside shopping location. Along the beach, ledges of stone rise out of the surf to provide shelter for seals, sea lions and myriad forms of life in tide pools. One of the coast's most interesting rock formations is the much-photographed Face Rock, a huge monolith with some uncanny facial features that does indeed look like a woman with her head thrown back – giving rise to a requisite Native American legend.

## 10. Coos Bay

The no-nonsense city of Coos Bay and its modest neighbour North Bend make up the largest urban area on the Oregon coast. Coos Bay was once the largest timber port in the world. The logs are long gone, but tourists are slowly taking their place.

Cape Arago Hwy leads 14 miles (22.5km) southwest of town to Cape Arago State Park (800-551-6949; www.oregonstateparks.org), where grassy picnic grounds make for great perches over a pounding sea. The park protects some of the best tide pools on the Oregon coast and is well worth the short detour.

## 11. Oregon Dunes National Recreation Area

This stretch of coast offers something altogether different in the landscape: sand. Lots of it. Stretching 50 miles (80km), the Oregon Dunes are the largest expanse of oceanfront sand dunes in the US. Sometimes topping heights of 500ft, these mountains of sand undulate inland up to 3 miles (5km). Hikers and birdwatchers stick to the peaceful northern half of the dunes, and the southern half is dominated by dune buggies and dirt bikes. At Mile 200.8, the Oregon Dunes Overlook is the easiest place to take a gander.

In Reedsport, the Umpqua Lighthouse State Park offers summer tours of the 1894 lighthouse (541-271-4631).

## 12. Cape Perpetua

Whatever you do, don't miss the spectacular scenery of the Cape Perpetua Scenic Area, 3

© Mark Read / Lonely Planet

miles (5km) south of Yachats. You could easily spend a day or two exploring trails that take you through moss-laden, old-growth forests to rocky beaches, tide pools and blasting marine geysers. At the very least, drive up to the Cape Perpetua Overlook for a colossal coastal view from 800ft above sea level – the highest point on the coast. While you're up there, check out the historic West Shelter observation point built by the Civilian Conservation Corps in 1933. There's a good campsite here, too.

Just south of Cape Perpetua, look for Cook's Chasm, a rock formation that spouts water when the waves churn around it; the parking

*Previous spread: RV driving along the Sonoma-Mendocino coastal route Above, from left: the giant redwoods of Lady Bird Johnson Grove; a true American icon – the Golden Gate Bridge*

© Matteo Colombo / Getty Images

Oregon coast. You'll also get a good look at the tallest lighthouse in Oregon, Yaquina Head Lighthouse (not to be confused with Yaquina Bay Lighthouse, 3 miles/5km south). At the cutting-edge Oregon Coast Aquarium (541867-3474; www.aquarium. org), seals and sea otters are cute as can be, and the jellyfish room is a near psychedelic experience.

## 14. Depoe Bay

Though edged by modern timeshare condominiums, Depoe Bay still retains some original coastal charm. It lays claim to having the 'world's smallest navigable harbor' and being the 'world's whalewatching capital.'

## 15. Lincoln City

The sprawling modern beach resort of Lincoln City serves as the region's principal commercial center. In addition to gas and groceries, the town does offer a unique enticement to stop: from mid-October to late May volunteers hide brightly coloured glass floats – which have been hand-blown by local artisans – along the beaches, making a memorable souvenir for the resourceful and diligent vacationer.

## 16. Tillamook

Not all coastal towns are built on seafood and sand. Tillamook has an entirely dfferent claim to fame: cheese. Thousands stop annually at the Tillamook Cheese Factory (800-542-7290; www.tillamookcheese.com) for free samples and a picture-window view of the massive cheese-making factory floor.

## 17. Manzanita

One of the more laidback beach resorts on Oregon's coast is the hamlet of Manzanita –

lot here offers endless views (and no signs forbidding overnight stays). This entire area was once a series of volcanic intrusions that resisted the pummelling of the Pacific long enough to rise as oceanside peaks and promontories. Acres of tide pools are home to starfish, sea anemones and sea lions.

## 13. Newport

Don your marine-biologist cap and head to Yaquina Head Outstanding Natural Area (541-574-3100), a spit of land that protrudes nearly a mile into the ocean. This headland is home to some of the best touch pools on the

much smaller and less hyped than Cannon Beach. You can relax on the white-sand beaches, or, if you're feeling more ambitious, hike on nearby Neahkahnie Mountain, where high cliffs rise dramatically above the Pacific's pounding waves. It's a 3.8-mile (6km) climb to the top, but the views are worth it: on a clear day, you can see 50 miles (80km) out to sea.

## 18. Cannon Beach

Cannon Beach is one of the most popular towns on the Oregon coast. The wide sandy beach stretches for miles, and you'll find great photo opportunities and tidepooling possibilities at glorious Haystack Rock, the third-tallest sea stack in the world. For the area's best coastal hiking, head to Ecola State Park (503-436-2844; www. oregonstateparks.org).

## 19. Seaside

Oregon's busiest resort town delivers exactly what you'd expect from a town called Seaside, which is wholesome, Coney Island-esque fun. The 2-mile (3.2km) boardwalk – known as 'the Prom' – is a kaleidoscope of seaside kitsch, with surrey rentals, video arcades, fudge, elephant ears, caramel apples, saltwater taffy and more.

Check your tide table and head to the beach; Gearhart is famous for its razor clamming at low tide. All you need are boots, a shovel or a clam gun, a cut-resistant glove, a license (available in Gearhart) and a bucket for your catch. Watch your fingers – the name razor clam is well earned. Boiling up a batch will likely result in the most memorable meal of your trip. For information on where, when and how to clam, visit the Oregon Department of Fish & Wildlife website; it's a maze of a site, so just Google 'ODFW clamming.'

## 20. Fort Stevens State Park

Thousands of vessels have been lost in the Graveyard of the Pacific, from warships to barges to freighters. A few are occasionally visible at low tide, but the easiest one to spot is the Peter Iredale, resting at Fort Stevens State Park. The ship was driven onto the shore by rough seas on October 25, 1906, and the wreckage has sat embedded in the sand ever since. Today, kids have made a jungle gym out of the rusted skeleton and families picnic and build sandcastles on the nearby sand at low tide. (No lives were lost in the wreck, so don't let the thought of ghostly sailors dampen your fun.)

## 21. Astoria

Astoria sits at the mouth of the Columbia River, where you'll find some of the Pacific's most treacherous waters, thanks to river currents rushing out where ocean tide is trying to get in. The town has a long seafaring history and has seen its old harbour attract fancy hotels and restaurants in recent years. The Columbia River Maritime Museum (503-3252323; www.crmm. org) sits right on the edge of the Columbia River, offering a look at everything from old boats to washed-up maritime mementos. A Coast Guard exhibit – featuring a rescue boat plying dramatic, fake waves – makes you really appreciate the danger of their job.

## 22. Oysterville & Nahcotta

The charm of these old communities – the only ones on the bay side of Washington's Long Beach Peninsula – derives not just from their history but also from the absence of the beachfront towns' carnival atmosphere. Tiny Oysterville stands largely unchanged since the oyster boom of the 1870s.

*Right: Oregon's Cannon Beach, one of endless coastal attractions to break your journey for along Hwy 101*

# Index

# Index

**The Vanlife Companion**
August 2018
Published by Lonely Planet Global Limited
CRN 554153
www.lonelyplanet.com
10 9 8 7 6 5 4

Printed in Singapore
ISBN 978 1 78701 8488
© Lonely Planet 2018
© photographers as indicated 2018

**Managing Director, Publishing** Piers Pickard
**Associate Publisher & Commissioning Editor** Robin Barton
**Written and compiled by** Ed Bartlett and Becky Ohlsen
**Editors** Nick Mee, Yolanda Zappaterra, Christina Webb, Nora Rawn
**Art Directors** Daniel Di Paolo, Katharine Van Itallie
**Print Production** Nigel Longuet

Lonely Planet Office

Ireland
Digital Depot, Roe Lane (off Thomas St),
Digital Hub, Dublin 8,
D08 TCV4

**STAY IN TOUCH** lonelyplanet.com/contact

COVER IMAGE ©Justin Foulkes / Lonely Planet
BACK COVER IMAGES: ©Courtesy of Ben and Mande Tucker, ©Courtesy of Mzark Finke and Jolie King,
©Courtesy of Mirte van Dijk, ©Courtesy of Eric McCutcheon and Fanny Rice, ©Courtesy of Zach Both

Paper in this book is certified against the
Forest Stewardship Council™ standards.
FSC™ promotes environmentally responsible,
socially beneficial and economically viable
management of the world's forests.